Beginning To Read
the Fathers

Boniface Ramsey, O.P.

PAULIST PRESS
New York/Mahwah

Library of Congress
Catalog Card Number: 84-62564

ISBN: 0-8091-2691-5

Published by Paulist Press
997 Macarthur Boulevard
Mahwah, N.J. 07430

Printed and bound in the United States of America

Contents

iii

for
Luke Armour
Luke Truhan
and
Dominic Whedbee

Preface

Beginning To Read the Fathers arose out of an invitation extended to me by the monks of the Abbey of Gethsemani in Kentucky to give them some conferences in the summer of 1977 on the Fathers of the Church. These conferences, reworked into essay form, have become the nucleus of the present volume, which expands considerably on the original talks.

Certainly not every aspect of the Fathers' concerns has been treated here, nor does each chapter exhaust the theme to which that chapter is devoted. Far, far more could be said about God and Christ, about the human condition, about martyrdom and monasticism than appears in the chapters treating of those things. By the same token, I have concentrated on patristic literature written before the Council of Chalcedon (451), since it was then that the Fathers were most characteristically themselves and that nearly all of the greatest of them lived, without, I hope, having utterly neglected the succeeding period. Comprehensiveness, then, is not the aim of this book; it is rather simply to give readers in as unpretentious a way as possible a taste of the great writers and preachers of the ancient Church, so that they may continue to read them on their own with some confidence if they have a mind to. For those who are drawn to the further investigation of problems that this book can only hint at, the select bibliography that appears in the closing pages should provide a start.

I must confess that, in pursuing this project, I am seeking to pass on an intense love for the Fathers that I acquired while studying patrology under Johannes Quasten at The Catholic University of America, and that has endured and deepened

1

through the years in the course of my own reading and teaching. To this love there is added a sense of urgency, for anyone who is familiar with the history of the Christian Church realizes full well that needed renewal has come to the Church only when it has reappropriated for itself the legacy of the Fathers. Unfortunately, however, the Fathers continue to be little known, despite what has appeared to be a resurgence of interest in them. It is not enough simply to make allusions to Augustine, Origen and others in theology, liturgy, ancient history and Church history courses and elsewhere, where none were made before; that cannot satisfy, although it may whet one's appetite for more. If this book, which is no substitute for reading patristic texts themselves intelligently in their entirety, can serve as a stimulus for doing just that, it will have achieved its purpose.

Unless otherwise noted, all of the translations included here have been newly made. I owe a vast debt of gratitude to Larz Pearson, who translated the greater part of the Greek. For the translation of scriptural passages I have used the Revised Standard Version of the Bible as a model. Thanks are due to Edward O'Neill, O.P., who read the essays through in an earlier redaction, and particularly to John Allard, O.P., who not only read them in their present form but corrected the proofs too in my absence. Dr. Francine Cardman and Nicholas Ingham, O.P. kindly read the original conferences. It goes without saying that I am myself responsible for any defects that the present work may contain. The chapter on the human condition appeared in the December 1981 issue of *Spirituality Today* in abbreviated form, and it is reprinted here with the editor's permission.

It was Luke Armour, O.C.S.O., of the Abbey of Gethsemani, who thought of all of this in the first place; I am grateful to him for many things, and this is but one of them. The present book is rightly offered and humbly dedicated to him and to two other dear friends at Saint Joseph's Abbey in Spencer, Massachusetts.

Boniface Ramsey, O.P.

The Dominican House of Studies
Washington, D.C.
Easter 1984

I

Beginning To Read the Fathers

The Fathers of the Church have traditionally been a formidable lot—distant in time, in style of thought and in manner of expressing that thought, a phalanx of austere old gentlemen with beards and books. The impression of the formidable is only increased when one casts one's eye over the four hundred or so volumes of J.-P. Migne's *Patrology*, more than a hundred thousand pages of Greek and Latin, in which the writings of most of the Fathers are kept as safe as if they were under lock and key.

The Fathers have always been prominent in the life of the Church, and they have constantly been invoked for every sort of thing. But they have suffered from their prominence; they are famous but not well known. Like so many famous people, they are cited and alluded to, but few go to the effort of exploring their thought. The purpose of this short collection of essays is to serve both as an introduction to the writers of the ancient Church and as a stimulus to the reader to continue in them on his own, to become more familiar with them. There are deep joys to be gotten from reading, for example, Origen, Athanasius, Gregory of Nyssa and Augustine, who are writers very frequently mentioned in these pages. And they are not esoteric joys: they are universal, accessible to all of us. They are the joys of reading lofty hearts expressing themselves on lofty themes, and of reading very human hearts expressing themselves in human ways. Many of the things that a professor of English literature might say in introducing his students to Shakespeare or Milton a patrologist could say in introducing his students to Jerome or John Chrysostom. But the Fathers offer something besides the great literature that only lofty and human hearts can

3

produce. Because of who they are, they have something more specific than that to give us. Who are they then, and what can they offer us?

Who Are the Fathers?

Four criteria are traditionally mentioned for determining who a Father is. The first of these is antiquity, and indeed the very term "Father" (whence come the terms "patristic," "patristics," "patrology" and "patrologist," all related to the study of the Fathers) suggests a certain venerable quality associated with age. The era of the Fathers begins sometime in the first century—at the latest by around the year 96, when the so-called *First Letter of Clement* was written, but perhaps as early as 50 or 60 or 70, when the anonymous work known as the *Didache* may have been composed. It concludes in the East with the death of John Damascene around the year 750, although for the West different cut-off points are given: the death of Gregory the Great in 604, that of Isidore of Seville in 636 and that of the Venerable Bede in 735. In fact, however, much of the spirit of the Fathers, their understanding of God and of life, continues well into the Middle Ages in the West. Saint Bernard of Clairvaux, for example, an important figure of the twelfth century, has been called "the last of the Fathers," and others even later than he could perhaps qualify for that title. In the East, one could claim, the patristic spirit has never disappeared. This criterion, then, like the others, is thus somewhat arbitrary, as anyone knows who has tried to assess where one age of history ends and another begins.

A second criterion is that of holiness of life, and here the arbitrariness is still more evident. By the standards with which we measure holiness today, a number of the best known Fathers would in all probability be disqualified. Tertullian displays a very unpleasant fanatical and even cruel streak, Jerome had a notoriously nasty and unforgiving temperament, Theophilus of Alexandria was an opportunist of the worst sort, and Cyril of Alexandria persecuted his enemies relentlessly. If we defined holiness more in what could be considered Old Testament terms we might more closely approach the Fathers' own understanding of it. One is reminded particularly of the words of Psalm 149:6, about the people of Israel who had "the high praises of God in their throats and two-edged swords in their hands." That is to say, the Fathers were often characterized by a zeal, sometimes a terrible zeal, for the things of the Lord. But such a zeal is very frequently combined with less laudable aspects—unwillingness to compromise, self-righteousness, rigidity, manipulativeness, irascibility and the like. At the same time, however, the Fathers knew how to be tender. The very Jerome who in his mean-spiritedness excoriated his ex-friend Rufinus even in death was also capable of saying how in his own sinfulness he would lie at Jesus' feet and bathe them with his tears and wipe them with his hair.[1] For Jerome and all the others, God and Christ were intensely real persons with whom it was possible to experience a profound relationship. We can catch a small glimpse of this in the many instances where the Fathers refer to Jesus not simply as "Jesus" but as "my Jesus," a phrase that betrays a wonderful sense of intimacy.

Orthodox teaching is the third criterion that is usually given. This implies two things. First of all it means that a Father must have left something behind, however small, that could be called a teaching (all that remains of the second-century Papias, for example, is thirteen fragments, some of which are only a few lines long); or at least that a Father must have left a reputation behind, since the writings of some Fathers have disappeared and only their names survive (such is the case with the second-century Miltiades and Apollinarius of Hierapolis, both of whom are mentioned in Eusebius' *Ecclesiastical History*).

The second implication in this regard is that the teaching, or the reputation for teaching, must have been orthodox. Here again, though, we are confronted with a certain arbitrariness, since some of the opinions of the patristic era would not always be accepted as orthodox according to the stricter standards of more recent times. Famous examples of these are the doctrine that the Son and the Spirit are somehow subordinate to the Father, which is to be found in numerous writings of the second and third centuries, and Origen's notion of the *apokatastasis*, which was the belief that all creation, even the devil, would ultimately be saved. The subordinationism of the earliest centuries was something that the Church eventually outgrew as theological concepts and language developed. The *apokatastasis*, on the other hand, was an idea that was never generally accepted. In both of these instances, nonetheless, we see theologians sincerely struggling to penetrate certain truths of the faith. Subordinationism was an attempt to understand the threeness of the Godhead, whereas the *apokatastasis* expressed Origen's elaboration of the scriptural datum in Psalm 110:1 and 1 Corinthians 15:25 that in the end Christ would reign and all his enemies, presumably even the devil, would be subject to him.[2] In neither case was there ever anything less than a desire to be orthodox and to attain to the truth. Even Augustine, whose intentions were unquestionable and whose theology was to become a touchstone of orthodoxy, would take positions with which the Church could not, in later years, be in accord.

Sometimes, then, the Fathers speak and write in a way that would eventually be seen as unorthodox. But this is not the only difficulty with respect to the criterion of orthodoxy. The other great one is that we look in vain in many of the Fathers for references to things that many Christians might believe in today. We do not find, for instance, some teachings on Mary or on the papacy that were developed in medieval and modern times. This poses an ecumenical problem: Roman Catholics would say that such teachings represent a natural development and are at least not contrary to the mind of the Fathers, but most people in the Reformation tradition would say that they are rather a kind of deviation.

The upshot as far as the criterion of orthodoxy is concerned is that it must be used with discretion. What we can affirm with confidence is that the Fathers agree among themselves and with us on what can be called the rudiments of a Christian confession—belief in a triune God; in a Christ who is at once divine and human and who exercises a salvific role with respect to the human race; in the inerrancy of the Scriptures; in the fallen condition of the human race and its need for and its possibility of redemption; in certain saving signs, chief among them baptism and the Eucharist; in the Church, among whose members loving unity must be preserved; and in the value of prayer and asceticism. Belief in these things, which the Fathers unanimously proclaimed, even if they proclaimed them in different ways, continues to be the distinguishing mark of Christianity to this day.

The fourth and final traditional criterion is ecclesiastical approval. This quite simply means that a Father is considered to be such by the Church at large. The most obvious sign of this approval is the designation "saint," which is attributed to a large number of the Fathers. Conspicuously lacking this title are some of the greatest writers of the early Church, in particular Tertullian and Origen, and this corresponds to the ambivalent regard in which the Church holds them. Thus it would seem that there are degrees of approval.

Their Diversity and Their Unity

From what has been said up to this point it should already be clear that the Fathers are not a particularly homogeneous group of persons. This is something that deserves to be stressed because there is a great temptation to gloss over differences among individuals and collectivities when speaking of virtually any historical era; it is too easy to imagine that, because they lived at the same time, everyone thought and spoke the same way. The generalizations that result destroy the beauty of history and trivialize it. The danger of treating the Fathers in such a manner is particularly great in the Church, which has tended to do this for apologetic purposes.

But for the very reason that the patristic era lasted nearly seven hundred years, from sometime in the first century to the middle of the eighth, there were bound to be differences of emphasis and concern. The Church of the earliest Fathers expressed itself largely in apologetic writing, defending itself and its teachings against pagan and Jewish attack and rumor. Much of the fourth century was preoccupied with the mystery of the Trinity and the relations of the divine persons to one another, whereas the end of the fourth and most of the fifth century were concerned with the person of Christ. From then on the integration of the barbarians into Christian civilization was a significant issue in the West, while Christological disputes continued to dominate in the East.

Within these seven hundred years or so there are hundreds who qualify as Fathers, some of whom left only one small work behind, while from others scores of treatises, sermons and letters have come down to us. They range in talent from men like Origen and Jerome and Augustine, all of whom changed the course of Christian thought in some way or another, to persons like Arnobius of Sicca and Zeno of Verona, who would not be missed if their works were lost, but who in any event provide some small insight into the ways of the early Church. They are, variously, scintillating, tedious, sober, vulgar, profound and superficial, compassionate and prejudiced (they are notorious for being anti-Jewish), and often a single Father, because he is human, will manifest each one of these qualities.

In addition to the differences generated by this vast expanse of time and number of personalities involved, there are geographical and cultural differences as well. There were writers virtually everywhere that Christianity spread—from England in the West to Persia in the East, from Germany in the North to Ethiopia in the South. Within these huge confines Latin, Greek, Syriac, Coptic, Arabic and still other languages were spoken and written. But even within one language area there were cultural distinctions. Thus, for example, the Latin-speaking North Africans, with their rigor and passion, cannot be mistaken for the more concise writers of Rome and most of the rest of Italy, who also spoke Latin. And among those who spoke and wrote in Greek there were Byzantines, Cappadocians, Antiochenes and Alexandrians, each with their own theological thrust. Differences in language and culture gave rise to differences in expression, making it possible to say the same thing in a more narrowly theological way or in a strikingly poetic way, and sometimes, unfortunately, making it possible for two parties to misunderstand and suspect one another. These differences also gave rise, no less importantly, to differences in forms of praying and celebrating the liturgy.

The realization of this great divergency in time, personality, space, language and culture ought to dispel any notion that the Fathers were a kind of monolithic group with a monolithic way of thinking. Monolithic thought, indeed, is a phenomenon of more recent vintage in the Church, and it is almost exclusively (it could be argued) a phenomenon of the Western Catholic Church. It has been traced variously to the consolidation of a large segment of Europe under Charlemagne at the beginning of the ninth century, to the Gregorian Reform of the eleventh century, to the movement behind the suppression of Abelard in the twelfth century, to the Council of Trent and the Counter-Reformation in the sixteenth and seventeenth centuries, and to the First Vatican Council in the nineteenth century. Perhaps, on the other hand, the ecclesiastical monolith is nothing more than a myth. It is at any rate not patristic.

While it may be true that the Fathers were often intolerant in a number of respects, the breadth and generosity of spirit of which they could be capable, and which in fact most characterizes the early Church, is well expressed in a passage from a letter of Augustine. Writing to a certain Januarius, who had evidently been disturbed by different ecclesiastical customs in the course of some journey of his and who had questioned Augustine about these, he replies:

> In the first place, the chief thing that I want you to hold on to is that our Lord Jesus Christ, as he himself says in the gospel, has laid upon us an easy yoke and a light burden. Hence he bound the society of his new people by sacraments that are few in number, very easy to observe and very rich in significance, such as baptism consecrated in the name of the Trinity, communion in his own body and blood, and whatever else is commended in the canonical scriptures, with the exception of those things that we read of in the five books of Moses and that imposed a burden on the servitude of the people of old because of the state of their hearts and the prophetic times. Those things that are not in Scripture, however, but which we hold as traditions, which in fact are observed throughout the world, we understand to have been commended or commanded either by the apostles themselves or by plenary councils, whose authority in the Church is most useful. Examples of these are the Lord's suffering, resurrection and ascension into heaven and the Holy Spirit's descent from heaven, which are solemnly celebrated each year, and

whatever else that is similar and that happens to be observed by the universal Church wherever it exists.

But there are other things that vary according to locale and region, such as that some people fast on Saturday while others do not; that some people daily communicate the Lord's body and blood while others receive it only on certain days; that in some places there is no day when the Eucharist is not offered, although in others it is only offered on Saturday and Sunday, and in still others only on Sunday. Whatever else there may be in this category, all such things are a matter of freedom, and there is no better practice for the serious and prudent Christian to follow with regard to them than to act in the way he sees the Church acting wherever he happens to be. For whatever is not contrary to the faith or to good morals ought to be considered as indifferent and should be observed for the sake of fellowship with those among whom one is living.[3]

In similar fashion the Church historian Socrates, writing toward the middle of the fifth century, some forty years or so after Augustine wrote his letter to Januarius, devotes a long and highly interesting chapter of his *Ecclesiastical History* to the different customs that were observed in the different churches of his day—ranging from fasting to clerical celibacy to the celebration of Easter. This diversity he commends, while pointing out that it existed in apostolic times as well.[4]

What all this means, of course, is that one cannot make easy generalizations about the early Church, and the important implication is that one cannot make easy generalizations about the Church's tradition. Just because Ignatius of Antioch, to take one famous example, emphasizes the role of the bishop in the early second-century churches of Antioch and Asia Minor does not mean that anyone else felt the same way about the bishop at that time, or even that bishops existed in other churches at such an early period. Likewise, Justin Martyr's description of the austere Roman liturgy in the middle of the second century would hardly prepare one for the elaborate celebrations that took place in sixth-century Constantinople, even though in essentials they would be identical. Neither is Origen's anthropology like Augustine's, nor does Theodore of Mopsuestia interpret Scripture exactly as Ambrose does. One could give numerous instances along these lines. To know one Father or one period of time, then, is not to know the Fathers as a whole.

Yet, in the face of this diversity, besides sharing a faith that was one in its essentials, even if expressed in different ways, there are several other aspects that the Fathers have in common and that, to some extent, set them apart from writers of other ages. The first such aspect is the quality of their commitment to divine things, or, better, to what we today might call theology; this is of a piece with the zeal that was spoken of previously under the heading of the criterion of holiness. Their involvement in this regard is passionate, and they could certainly not be characterized as detached observers of the theological scene. Indeed, nearly everyone in the ancient world was passionately concerned about such things, for God—or the gods—was an ever-present reality, as were angels and demons. Nearly everyone was convinced that the unseen world with which theology dealt was in fact a more real world, and one more profitable to know about, than the visible one. God—or the gods—had a role to play in human affairs, and his role was the overriding one. Theological matters were the subject of discussion then much as politics or sports are now. Gregory of Nyssa has an amusing passage in one of his treatises written at the height of the Arian controversy toward the end of the fourth century, in which he describes how ordinary people could get caught up in what would appear to be the most speculative questions. When you approach the money changer, he writes, he philosophizes with you about the nature of the Begotten and the Unbegotten; the baker tells you that the Father is greater than the Son, when what you really want to know about is the price of bread; and the man who draws your bath is of the opinion that the Son is not to be numbered among beings.[5] Knowing that such was the case, one can understand why the struggle between Arians and orthodox over the place of Christ in the Trinity so troubled and exhausted the Mediterranean world of the fourth century and, in general, why religion has claimed as many lives as it has. Only to us moderns are religious issues recondite and obscure.

It must be admitted that this great involvement in theology was at least to some degree the result of a love of intellectual discussion and disputation, which was very much a part of ancient Mediterranean culture. But it was also to a large extent the result of a deep preoccupation with salvation, and it is this preoccupation, however implicit, that provides patristic literature with its principle of unity and its most all-embracing theme. What place is there for me in the divine economy, the divine plan? What do I have to do to be saved?—questions such as these lie at the bottom of virtually every patristic writing. The place of the Holy Spirit, the nature of Christ, the celebration of the liturgy: each of these had a bearing on my salvation and consequently could not be regarded as a merely speculative matter. This was especially true with respect to the mystery of Christ, as we shall see in a later chapter. We could suggest that, precisely when salvation became a less overriding factor, then theology became more removed from daily life.

Inasmuch as theology was something of passionate interest to the Fathers, it was thus something to be experienced or felt as well as something to be known in an intellectual way. Hence what the Fathers write appeals to the heart as well as to the mind. This is quite understandable in the light of the rhetorical background of so many of them. The rhetorical training characteristic of education in the Roman Empire during most of the patristic era gave the Fathers formidable tools of persuasion. They were accomplished preachers and were expected to be such by their hearers, the vast majority of whom were of course not intellectuals. In this capacity they were well aware that it was not enough simply to speak the truth; they knew that the truth had to be spoken—or written—in an eloquent and convincing manner, that it had to persuade the will. Augustine was particularly aware of this, as he demonstrates in his great treatise on the interpretation of Scripture, *On Christian Doctrine*.[6] But all the other Fathers knew it too.

It is this quality of approaching theological truth as something to be experienced that gives patristic writing its peculiar power and that even transforms it into literature. It is a writing that is, for the most part, vigorous and compelling. Here it should be said too that it is a writing that is free from jargon, at least if by jargon we mean a technical language intended to be understood by initiates or experts. The Fathers did in fact use a technical language, some of whose terms have come down to us—words like *homoousios* and *persona* and *physis*. These words are theological jargon today, but they were the common currency of the fourth and fifth centuries, and nearly everybody knew what they meant. The Fathers spoke and wrote in order to be understood not merely by other theologians but by ordinary educated people, and since most of them preached regularly (the greatest of them, Origen and Augustine, preached several times a week) they knew how to express themselves in a comprehensible way. In them we might say that the pastoral aspect of theology triumphed over the professional.

Of course, just because the Fathers spoke and wrote plainly in their own day does not mean that we in our day can understand them without difficulty. Whoever has read them realizes that he is confronting a different mode of thought and expression. In particular, two things are characteristic in this respect. The first might be called, quite simply, longwindedness. What most Fathers take five pages to say could easily be said in one by a modern writer, without much of a sense of compression. Partly this is the result of transferring a rhetorical style to paper without making the adaptations that a modern reader would expect. Partly this is because conciseness was not a value in antiquity. And partly this is a function of the fact that the notion of a logical and unified progression from one point to another in an argument or exposition was relatively foreign to the Fathers and to the thought of their time. The Fathers did not always, or even often, rigorously pursue an idea to its conclusion; they were more inclined, when something interesting came up in the course of an argument, to devote themselves to that interesting thing and only after that, if ever, to return to the original argument. That is to say, they were frequently digressive, much as we thing of garrulous persons as being digressive. This is by no means to say that they were illogical; it is to say, rather, that their logic was their own.

Gregory the Great, writing in the evening of the patristic era, speaks quite openly of this style when he discusses how a preacher should treat the Scriptures.

The preacher of the sacred word should imitate the manner
of a river. For if a river, as it flows through its channel, comes
upon valleys along its banks, it immediately flows with full
force into them, and when it has filled them up it at once
returns to its course. This is exactly the way the preacher of
the divine word should be—so that when he is discussing
something, if perhaps he finds an occasion near at hand to
be edifying, he should as it were force the streams of the
tongue to the neighboring valley and, when he has filled up
the plain with his instruction, he may return to the course of
his main topic.[7]

It was exactly as Gregory described the ideal preacher, with his
readiness to get off the topic and into side issues, that the Fathers
wrote and spoke.

The second characteristic of patristic writing that frequently
presents a difficulty to the modern reader is the extensive use of
imagery and symbolism, which itself often contributes to the
longwindedness just mentioned. Thus, for example, in his beautiful treatise *On the Unity of the Catholic Church*, written in the
middle of the third century, Cyprian heaps up images in order
to illustrate the mystery of the Church's unity: the Church is a
sun with many rays, a tree with many branches, a spring with
many streams, a mother prolific in offspring, a faithful wife; it is
reminiscent of Noah's ark, Christ's seamless garment and the
paschal lamb, to name but a few things.[8] In Cyprian's case this
imagery tends not only to elaborate but even to enhance his
exposition, but this is not always so. Sometimes it can confuse
and obscure, which is the case with a famous image used by
Ignatius of Antioch, who seeks to describe Christian life in terms
of constructing a building:

[You are] like stones of the Father's temple, having been
made ready for the building of God the Father and carried
up to the heights by the engine of Jesus Christ, which is the
cross, using the Holy Spirit as a rope. And faith is your windlass, and love is the road leading up to God.[9]

What has happened here, as so often happens, is that the image,
which is ultimately only a vehicle for conveying meaning rather

than an end in itself, has to some degree taken on a life of its own, which then conflicts with the truth that the image is supposed to illuminate. When Ignatius speaks of rope and windlass and attaches to them the concepts of Holy Spirit and faith, we can see that the image as such has gotten the upper hand.

A further aspect that the Fathers share among themselves is their absorption in Scripture, which very frequently serves as the source of their imagery. But a discussion of the Fathers' approach to Scripture must wait until the following chapter.

Finally, the Fathers all have a deep reverence for authority and tradition and, with that, for antiquity. This too, along with so much else, they share with the rest of the ancient world. The antiquity of a thing was of itself sufficient to command attention and respect, and what had been said in the past was by that very token somehow canonized. From the specifically Christian point of view, of course, this made sense because Christianity was a religion founded upon events recorded in the Old and New Testaments that were part of history and hence "old." Tradition was the expression of contact with those events, a contact which brought salvation, and it consisted most simply in the representation of those events by word or action. The representation in terms of action was liturgical; in particular there were baptism and the Eucharist, both of which united the believer with Christ in his death, burial and resurrection. The representation in terms of word was, of course, the teaching about the events in question, not only about Christ but about the whole Old Testament as well, which foreshadowed Christ.

In the course of the centuries it was inevitable that this repeated representation in action and word should have grown more elaborate, a process that is usually referred to as the development of doctrine (at least as far as the word is concerned, although by extension it applies to the liturgy too). It might just as aptly, however, be called the development of tradition. This was a process, in any event, that we may safely say most of the Fathers were either unaware of or whose existence they would have conceded only with a great deal of qualification. When Basil, for instance, speaks about certain customs that were observed in the latter half of the fourth century but were not found in Scripture—the sign of the cross, prayer in the direction of the East, threefold immersion at baptism and other similar things—he feels obliged to say that these have been handed down by the apostles themselves, but in a hidden manner.[10] They are as old as the Scriptures, therefore, and as authoritative as if they were scriptural; there is no question here that they might have developed since scriptural times. Hence it is interesting that, toward the middle of the fifth century, Vincent of Lérins should have admitted to a development of tradition and worked out a theory in which he compares such a development to the growth of the human body.[11] Yet he does this in the context of warning against innovation.

The innovation that the Fathers did pursue, then, was largely unconscious. Their intention was to pass on to another generation what they themselves had received, and it was in the course of this act of passing on the tradition that the tradition slowly developed. It is rare indeed when a Father proposes something that he knows to be new, as Origen does occasionally and with a certain tentativeness in his great treatise *On First Principles*. The ideal was rather to cleave completely to the past, and hardly a greater compliment could be given a person than to say that he had done precisely that. It is in those terms that Basil writes to the people of Neocaesarea to praise their bishop Musonius, who had just died:

A man has died who surpassed all his contemporaries in every human good at once. He was a pillar of his homeland, an ornament of the churches, a pillar and support of the truth, a bastion of faith in Christ, the protector of his friends, unyielding to his enemies, a guardian of the ancestral laws, an enemy of innovation, manifesting in himself the primitive form of the Church. He fashioned the church that was committed to him according to the ancient model, as if to a kind of sacred image, so that those who lived with him seem to have lived with those who shone like lights two hundred years ago and more. Thus that man put forth nothing of his own nor anything of recent invention, but, as in the blessing of Moses, he knew how to bring out from the depths of his heart, namely from the good treasures there, old store and old things before new ones.[12]

It is not to be wondered at that with such a mentality the Fathers tended as a rule to accept and reflect upon things as they were rather than to question why they should have been such. That is to say, they presupposed the fundamental rightness of the order of things as they saw and understood it. More specifically, they assumed the rightness of the political and social world in which they lived. While decrying certain flagrantly immoral practices, they accepted the Roman Empire with its structures, and they countenanced slavery, torture and the derogation of women, among other things. They might have wished the mitigation of some things, but most of them could hardly have imagined their abolition.

What Can They Teach Us?

Thus far we have spoken of the Fathers in themselves, in their diversity and in the qualities that they have in common. We might speak of them now with respect to their relationship to us. What do they have to offer us?

Most obviously, perhaps, the Fathers offer us a unique and privileged look at the ancient Church. Granted that this is not the Church of the apostolic era, it is nonetheless the Church that emerged fresh from that era and that first developed what might be called the apostolic tradition. It was in the patristic era that the Church took recognizable shape, and it is to that time, consequently, that we must return if we want to ask why the Church is the way it is and not some other way. The Fathers were the first to face the full spectrum of problems and objections that Christianity was bound to encounter and that it continues to encounter, and they provided responses that are classic, if not canonized. God as one and three, Christ as human and divine, the Church as spotless and sinful, the coherence of Scripture, the moral obligations of the Christian—these are issues that the Fathers first addressed and that are still debated.

To be familiar with history gives one, in general, a broad perspective on human affairs and helps make it possible for one to separate the transitory from the enduring. For what is perennial in human nature is perennial in history, and we can recognize ourselves already in the ancient Sumerians and Egyptians and, indeed, even in cave art. To be familiar with the history of the Church makes a person able to do something that it has always been difficult for Christians to do, namely to distinguish accidentals from essentials. The possibility of making such a distinction, which is perhaps more significant in Christianity than in any other religion, is at the heart of Christian thought, and the failure to make it has led to schism and other traumas in ecclesial life. It is especially true that familiarity with the Fathers offers this possibility, for we may reasonably say that the essential elements of any movement or idea must have been at least inchoately present at their beginnings. That this is so in the case of the Fathers is recognized by every main-line Christian Church—Roman Catholic, Orthodox, Anglican and Reformation.

To know the Fathers, then, is to grasp the essentials of Christianity or, in other words, to be educated in the *sensus catholicus*, in the sense of what is truly Christian.[13] There is no easy way to gain this education, for the Fathers are many and diverse, as it has been the burden of much of this chapter to show. It is the very experience of unity in diversity, however, that highlights what is central in Christian doctrine and what is peripheral. Very few things are binding, Augustine suggests in his letter to Januarius, cited earlier, and there is liberty with respect to the rest. When the Fathers agree among themselves as to what is central or essential, then it would seem that the Christian of today must either agree himself or have extremely cogent reasons for disagreeing. Some such unanimously agreed upon patristic teachings have been mentioned earlier in this chapter under the heading of the criterion of orthodoxy, and to these the vast majority of Christians of today would certainly assent. Would they assent as well to the notion of the superiority of virginity to marriage, or to that of the double meaning of Scripture, which the Fathers also agreed on? It would have to be said that, if modern Christians could not agree, they at least could not dismiss such notions out of hand. Ideally, perhaps, they would seek to understand why the Fathers said what they did and try to see where the truth lies in it for us today.

In addition to an education in essentials, reading the Fathers also provides an experience in uniting heart and mind in theology. The Fathers' zeal and passionate concern have already been alluded to. That they evidence this in the most open way sets them apart from the Scholastic theologians who came upon the scene in the twelfth century, the prince of whom was Thomas Aquinas. In these latter the appeal to reason is foremost, and the unadorned truth is felt to be sufficiently compelling. Although the greatest Scholastics were themselves blameless in this regard, the emphasis on the appeal to reason eventually opened up to theological rationalism, the rigorous deduction of truths from premises, an intellectual affair not necessarily grounded in the experience of God or in a compelling interest about salvation. In this situation it became possible for the theologian to be an immoral person or even, paradoxically, an atheist: one might simply concede the existence of God for the sake of argument, and from that certain theological conclusions would follow; or one might study theology—*other* people's ideas of God—just as one would pursue any other discipline. In any event, one need not be affectively involved with God.[14]

The patristic conception of the theologian stands in profound contrast to the rationalistic conception. Gregory Nazianzen speaks for all the Fathers when, in his *First Theological Oration*, he places the theological task in the context of the divine mystery. In the face of this mystery in fact the best response is silence. But those who do dare, as it were, to speak about God must "have been very carefully proven and made great progress in contemplation, and first of all have purified both body and soul from the filth of vices, or be in the process of purification."[15] Shortly thereafter he complains about those who seem to be skilled in talking about God but who practice none of the virtues and pursue no form of asceticism.[16] It is obvious that, for Gregory, the theologian is supposed to be a person of high sanctity.

Theology as a work of holiness is a typically patristic idea, then. Typically patristic also is the idea that theology is approached as a whole, rather than subdivided into what would later be the branches of Christology, ecclesiology, moral theology, and so forth. The Fathers were synthesizers and generalists, whereas modern theology is for the most part analytic and specializing. It is hard to read a patristic writing of virtually any kind and not get a sense of something broader than the immediate issue, whatever that may have been. The entire Christian mystery almost always seems to make its presence felt in some fashion. This is a result, in part, of the Fathers' intensity of purpose, which favored the constant reiteration of basic truths. It is also partly a result of there having been a great dominant theme, that of salvation or the divine economy, which gathered other mysteries about it. Consequently, reading the Fathers offers an experience of theological integrity and a grasp of the whole.

Both the moral and the theological integrity that characterize the Fathers, to which must be added their profoundly scriptural thrust, suggest that the Fathers are uniquely suited to be "spiritual writers." The Church has recognized this quality by including patristic homilies and treatises in the liturgy of the hours, and the Fathers have traditionally constituted a large part of the monastic program of *lectio divina,* or spiritual reading.

By way of conclusion it would be well to speak about how to read the Fathers. Here we have to begin by recalling some of the things that make the Fathers foreign to us—their distance in time, their style, their culture, even their mood. In the face of this foreignness the first requirement is openness on the part of the reader, an openness that we might be expected to have when approaching Homer or Dante for the first time. For, despite their foreignness, which is admittedly considerable, the Fathers are human beings like ourselves, confronting the same problems with some of the same emotions. They spoke and wrote precisely with the intention of communicating to others, not to be obscure, and hence there is the real possibility of our meeting them.

This meeting, however, must obviously be on their terms. There are some things that we cannot expect from them, and if we are disappointed with them it will probably have been due in great part to our own inability to "get into" another way of thinking and expressing oneself.

Yet, of course, openness or sympathy is not sufficient. One cannot simply pick up something written in another era and begin reading in the hope of understanding. Ordinarily the reader should have some background about the person of the Father, the purpose of the writing and the historical setting. Frequently there will be something about this in an introductory essay accompanying the work. The notes with which most translations are supplied are also important and should be consulted.

An appendix to the present book contains a list of patristic works, with a brief description of each, which could serve as the basis of a program of reading in the Fathers.

II

Scripture

To understand how the Fathers approached Scripture is probably the most indispensable means to understanding them in general. Patristic writings are often saturated with biblical quotations and allusions. A vast amount of the Fathers' productivity was given over to biblical commentaries, especially on Genesis, the prophets and the Gospels. At the very least we may say that, even when the Fathers were not commenting directly on Scripture, they considered themselves to be motivated by what the Scriptures said.

We cannot deny that the early Church was subject to many influences: the works of Pythagorean, Neoplatonic and Stoic philosophers made a profound impression on the minds of most of the Fathers, even if in an unconscious and indirect way. This influence has been noted since at least the late nineteenth century and often decried as the "Hellenization" of Christianity—the replacement of a biblical world view and theology by a Greek one.[1] Yet, despite this undoubted influence, whether for better or for worse, the Bible was nonetheless the great textbook of the ancient Church and, to the extent that the Fathers made use of Greek philosophy, they made use of it precisely in order to understand their own sacred writings. Moreover, whether they are to be judged as consistent in this or not, they saw the Bible as the rule against which all philosophy and all human thought were to be measured.

Indeed, some of the earliest Christians seemed unwilling to concede an independent existence to the elements of Greek philosophy that they recognized as good. They felt, instead, that such elements must have come ultimately from the Scriptures or from scriptural personages. Thus Justin writes in the middle of the second century that Plato's doctrine of creation as well as a kind of inchoate notion of the Trinity was borrowed from the beginning of Genesis.[2] Even Augustine had been of the opinion that Plato had met Jeremiah in the course of a journey into Egypt, whence he took away with him many of the prophet's views,[3] although he later retracted this for chronological reasons.[4]

Linked with the untenable idea that the Greeks owed the better aspects of their philosophy to some kind of contact with the Scriptures was another idea: that Moses was more ancient than any of the Greeks, and that the latest prophets were at least as ancient as the earliest Greek philosophers and legislators. Writing for pagan readers at the end of the second century, Tertullian expresses this position:

> Their high antiquity, therefore, gives great authority to these writings. Among you also it is a kind of religion to demand belief because of age. The work of a single prophet, in whom may be seen the upgathered riches of the whole Jewish mystery (which has become ours as well), is far older than all the substances and all the materials, the origins, the classes and the contents of your ancient literature; older also than most nations, famous cities of the histories and collections of annals; older, finally, than the very forms of letters, which are the indicators and guards of things, than (I do not think that we are yet exaggerating) your very gods, the temples and oracles and sacred rites. If you have perchance heard of a certain Moses, he is of the same age as the Argive Inachus. He precedes Danaus, who is the most ancient among you, by nearly four hundred years (just seven less than that); he antedates the overthrow of Priam by about a thousand years. I can even say that he is five hundred years earlier than Homer, and I follow others in that opinion. The other prophets, too, the most recent of them, even if they come after Moses, are seen to be as early as your first sages and legislators and historians.[5]

In this passage the Fathers' veneration for antiquity comes to the fore quite clearly. Yet there is also an element of defensiveness here, for if Moses is not earlier than everyone else, then what he wrote is necessarily less authoritative than Homer or the others. There is a defensiveness as well with respect to Christianity's relatively recent appearance on the world scene, which was a point against it in pagan reckoning; if Christianity could claim such ancient writings for its own, then, so much the better.

In addition to being the most ancient of books, the Bible was also, in the mind of the Fathers, the most universal of books. We can see this, for example, in Basil of Caesarea's nine sermons on the opening lines of Genesis, the *Hexaemeron*, where he finds teachings on all aspects of creation. Jerome's prologue to his *Commentary on Isaiah* has some extravagant words on what is contained in that prophet. Besides proclaiming the birth, death and resurrection of the Savior, it instructs the reader in physics, ethics and logic. "Whatever there is in the Sacred Scriptures, whatever the human tongue can speak and the understanding of mortals can accept is contained in this volume."[6] The same kind of thinking occurs in Origen, who discovers in the three books attributed to Solomon—Proverbs, Ecclesiastes and the Song of Songs—the three branches of Greek learning—moral, natural and inspective—which in any event the Greeks had borrowed from Solomon.[7]

It is Augustine who, more than anyone else, canonizes this idea in his great work *On Christian Doctrine*. To him it is plain that all learning of any enduring value can be reduced to the Scriptures. This is coupled with the notion that learning from other sources, namely pagan writings, presents dangers to the Christian soul. If one is to study the pagans at all, one should do so exclusively for the sake of understanding the Bible better. Thus, for instance, it is helpful to be familiar with works on natural history or numerology when the Scriptures allude to an animal or a number whose deeper significance one cannot readily grasp. Otherwise, however, one would do best not to stray too far from the Scriptures,

> for whatever a person may have learned elsewhere, if it is harmful, it is condemned there [in the Bible]; if it is useful, it is found there. And even if someone has found everything taught usefully elsewhere, he may there find much more

abundantly things that exist nowhere else at all, but that are only learned in the marvelous depth and marvelous simplicity of those writings.[8]

With this concept of universality there was a corresponding scriptural mysticism. The writings that contained all knowledge were also an infinite spiritual treasure. The fourth-century Syrian Ephrem states this most beautifully in his *Commentary on the Diatessaron* when he compares the Scriptures to a spring that a thirsty person can drink from without ever either exhausting the spring or quenching his thirst.[9]

The Two "Senses" of Scripture

By far the most significant aspect of the patristic approach to the Bible, however, is the Fathers' firm belief that Scripture had two senses or two levels of meaning, which we may simply call here the literal and the spiritual. This was an article of faith for the entire early Church, and all the Fathers held it, although they applied the principle of two senses in different ways and to greater or lesser degrees. Origen sets down this doctrine in uncompromising terms at the beginning of his treatise *On First Principles.* After laying out the Church's position on the Father, Son and Spirit, on the human soul, free will, the demons and the creation of the world, he declares:

> Then [we believe] that the Scriptures were composed by the Spirit of God and that they have not only a meaning that is manifest but also another that is hidden as far as most people are concerned. For what has been described are the forms of certain sacraments and the images of divine things. About this the universal Church is in accord, that the whole law is spiritual. What the law is full of, however, is not known to all but only to those to whom it is given by the grace of the Holy Spirit in a word of wisdom and knowledge.[10]

The teaching is elaborated by Jerome in an unfortunately typical anti-Jewish way. Commenting on the deeper meaning of Leviticus 11:3 ("Any animal that is cloven-footed and ruminates is clean"), he says in a homily:

> The Jew is single-hoofed, and therefore he is unclean. The Manichean is single-hoofed, and therefore he is unclean. And since he is single-hoofed he does not chew what he eats, and what has once gone into his stomach he does not bring up again and chew and make fine, so that what had been coarse would return to the stomach fine. This is indeed a matter of divine mystery. The Jew is single-hoofed, for he believes in only one Testament and does not ruminate: he only reads the letter and thinks over nothing, nor does he seek anything deeper. The Christian, however, is cloven-hoofed and ruminates. That is, he believes in both Testaments, and he often ponders each Testament, and whatever lies hidden in the letter he brings forth in the spirit.[11]

This passage is important for linking together two related issues that will be discussed, namely belief in a spiritual sense and acceptance of two Testaments (the Jews, of course, accepted only the Old and the Manicheans only the New). Although Jerome was wrong in saying that the Jews did not recognize two senses of Scripture, as we shall see shortly, the point is clear: it was Christian practice to seek beneath the letter for the deeper spiritual meaning of the sacred writings.

That Christians should have read deeper, mystical meanings into the letter of the Bible was the result of a number of conditions. First among these, perhaps, was the fact that ancient peoples, as well as the Church, believed at least implicitly that the world in which they lived was composed of two levels, that of the seen and that of the unseen. Indeed, we may well say that even today most people hold for this in some way or another. Of these two levels the seen was considerably the less important, and to have known only the seen would have been to be blinded to the aspect of reality that counted. To the pagan, the woods, fields and streams, the town and the home were populated with gods, demons, nymphs and sprites. To the Christian, these spirits were replaced by demons and angels and by the all-pervading presence of God himself. All of visible creation was thus charged full of the mystery of the invisible. When Plato developed his doctrine of ideas, of which the material images were mere shadows, we may say that at least to some extent he was reflecting this common conception in a more philosophical way. The notion is carried over into Christian literature perhaps most strikingly in Augustine's *City of God*, whose theme is ultimately that real history is the hidden story of souls on their way to God, rather than the story of the rise and fall of empires and nations; the latter is only a kind of foil to the former.

Within this ambience, although not necessarily related to it in direct fashion, pagans and Jews were in search of a deeper meaning to their sacred literature. Already some centuries before the Christian era pagan philosophers had begun to reinterpret the myths of the gods, which they had come to realize were unworthy of divine beings when taken according to the letter. In so doing they actually restored much of their original meaning. Thus the stories of incest, murder and the like associated with the gods began to be understood as allegories of natural phenomena rather than as referring to real deeds. That Jupiter committed incest with his mother Ceres, for example, was to be seen as an allegory of the rain (symbolized by Jupiter) falling on the earth (symbolized by Ceres) and rendering it fertile. The early fourth-century Christian apologist Arnobius of Sicca attacks the pagans for this and asks how they knew that such myths were not to be taken literally.[12] He goes on to suggest that the pagan reinterpreters have reversed a traditional process: whereas in the past it had been the custom to cover up shameful deeds with allegorical language, now the pagans were saying that innocent things were to be understood as hidden beneath a veil of shameful language.[13]

While pagan recourse to hidden meanings in the divine myths probably had relatively little influence on Christians, its Jewish counterpart was quite influential. Rabbinical allegorization of the Old Testament had existed for some time before the coming of Christ.[14] Paul himself spoke of a deeper meaning in the Exodus and subsequent events in 1 Corinthians 10:1–5, and he did the same with regard to Sarah and Hagar in Galatians 4:22–27, when he spoke of the two women as an allegory of the two covenants. It was Philo of Alexandria, however, a contemporary of Paul, who was the greatest of the Jewish allegorizers.

His numerous works, particularly on Genesis, influenced Clement of Alexandria and Origen and, through the latter, Ambrose and many Western Fathers.

Consequently there was both an atmosphere that was favorable to looking beneath the surface of things and a precedent for doing so in sacred literature, whether pagan or Jewish. In this atmosphere and with this precedent the early Church was able to approach the Old and New Testaments.

Indeed, the Old Testament cried out for a deeper reading. Almost from the start of the Christian era this Testament had been a stumbling block for many. In the middle of the second century a certain Marcion shocked the Christian community by asserting that the God of the Old Testament could not be identified with the God of the New, who was the Father of Jesus. The Old Testament God, the Creator, was bellicose and arbitrary, the author of evils, whereas Jesus' Father was a God of love.[15] The Manicheans, who arose a century later, said much the same things, as we know primarily from Augustine's attacks on them. In addition they maintained that the old laws and customs were laughable or barbarous and could have no meaning whatsoever for anyone who professed belief in the Gospel.[16] Understood literally, the Fathers themselves acknowledged, the Old Testament was very often a scandalous document that glorified cruelty and promoted a morality that could no longer be countenanced.

In a passage in his *Confessions* Augustine expresses the relief that he felt when he found out that the Old Testament had a message that lay beneath the surface of the letter. This he discovered on hearing Ambrose preach at Milan, when he himself was not yet baptized.

> I rejoiced that the ancient Scriptures of the law and the prophets were set before me now to be read not in the way whereby previously they appeared absurd, when I used to insist that it was as such that your saints understood them, when in fact it was not thus that they understood them. I listened gladly to Ambrose when he would often say in his sermons, earnestly commending it as a rule: "The letter kills, but the spirit gives life." For, once the mystic veil had been drawn aside, he would disclose in spiritual fashion things that seemed perverse when taken literally.[17]

It would not be too much to suggest that the belief in a spiritual meaning preserved the Old Testament for the Church.

Given both the atmosphere of the age and the need to make sense out of the Old Testament in particular, then, the early Christians could hardly have avoided understanding the Scriptures in spiritual terms. Yet there is a further reason for what we may certainly see as a rampant recourse to the spiritual sense among the Fathers. It is an interest in and a love of the obscure, the *recherché*; it is a delight in words and in literary games that will test the reader's intellectual prowess.[18] We can find this idea expressed in both Origen and Augustine, who speak for many others. In the *Contra Celsum* Origen writes that "the Word so desires that there be wise persons among believers that, for the sake of exercising the hearers' intelligence, he hides certain things under enigmas and wraps others up in obscure sayings; some things are in parables and others in problems."[19] And Augustine remarks that truths appear much more attractive—he cannot explain to himself precisely why this is so—in elaborate figures than in plain language. Such figures stimulate the appetite, and when their hidden meaning is uncovered the pleasure is all the greater.[20] Numbers in the Old and New Testaments especially lent themselves to the pursuit of the most fantastic interpretations along this line. We need only glance through the various patristic texts that treat of the dimensions of Noah's ark and the number of animals and human beings that were saved in it. The length to which a numerical interpretation could go, however, is epitomized in Augustine's famous exegesis of John 21:11, which narrates the apostles' catch of one hundred and fifty-three fish. We can almost picture Augustine's own delight as he expounds on this number at considerable length in one of his homilies: in it he discovers the Ten Commandments, the Holy Spirit, the number of the saints, and God both three and one.[21]

Interpretations Beyond the Literal

These were the conditions, then, that made it possible for Christians to seek beyond the literal sense of the Scriptures. The ramifications of the spiritual, however, demand some explanation, since it is susceptible of several qualifications.

In the first place a distinction must be drawn between the typological and the allegorical senses, although this distinction was not made by many of the Fathers. (Types were often spoken of in allegorical terms. When Paul, for example, says in Galatians 4:24 that Hagar and Sarah stand for two covenants, he uses the word "allegory," although in fact Hagar and Sarah are types and not allegories of the two covenants.) A type may be understood to be a fact from the Old Testament that was taken by the Fathers to have a true historical significance but that was also capable of a further and deeper meaning. Numerous Old Testament personages and events were thus seen as types of Christ, the Church and the sacraments. Isaac on his way to be sacrificed by Abraham, for instance, was a type of Christ, as was the paschal lamb and Jonah in the belly of the sea monster; the Israelite people were a type of the Church, and the crossing of the Red Sea and the manna were types of baptism and the Eucharist respectively. In none of this typology was the historicity of the archetype ever questioned. On the contrary, the historical fact was often a sacred reality in itself, although its sacredness was overshadowed by that of the reality which was prefigured. In addition to the historical emphasis of typology, it was governed by a certain tradition that determined the bounds within which it could be employed. This meant that given Old Testament personages or events were universally recognized as types, and no one would confer a meaning on them that would conflict with the typological; if another meaning were conferred, it was understood to be secondary. The flood, for instance, was a type of baptism, and only secondarily could it be taken for something else.

In allegory, on the other hand, history was generally either denied or, for the sake of the deeper sense, ignored. In the first case, for example, Origen denies completely the existence of an earthly paradise, saying that the Genesis narrative is intended exclusively to point to certain mysteries.[22] As an instance of the second case, Augustine, undoubtedly alluding to Origen, says that paradise is to be understood literally as well as allegorically, but he suggests a number of different allegorical possibilities that effectively do away with the significance of the historical paradise.[23] More important than this, however, is that allegory held to no tradition but for all practical purposes seems to have operated freely within the relatively broad limits set by orthodox belief. It was largely the work of imagination, and the imagination of one Father could well be at variance with that of another. Depending on the point he wished to make, in fact, the same Father could at different times allegorize the same passage in different ways. The dangers here were obvious even to the Fathers who used allegory extensively, and Jerome, for one, complains about the heretics who with their allegorizations are able to substantiate their own perverse teachings. The orthodox way, he suggests, is to tread the narrow path between an over-literalism on one side and an over-allegorization on the other.[24]

The allegorical, furthermore, was able to be broken down into two or three subdivisions. For Origen, in addition to the literal sense, which corresponded to the human body by reason of its externality, there was a moral or ascetical sense that corresponded to the soul and also a spiritual or mystical sense that corresponded to the human spirit.[25] Ambrose speaks of three senses besides the literal—the natural, the moral and the mystical or rational. The natural deals with natural ethics, while the moral touches upon the Christian ethical teachings of a given scriptural passage. Finally, the mystical or rational probes most deeply into the meaning of the Scriptures; the mystical sense, writes Ambrose, fills the soul with love of the heavenly word, establishes a union between the soul and divine reason and reveals wonderful mysteries.[26] Augustine also mentions three senses in addition to the literal or what he calls the historical sense—the aetiological, the analogical and the allegorical. The aetiological gives the cause for why something is done, the analogical demonstrates the unity between the Old and New Testaments, and the allegorical teaches the deeper meaning of things that are not to be taken literally.[27] Cassian, Augustine's contemporary, finds three senses as well besides the literal or historical—the tropological, the allegorical and the anagogical. The tropological is the moral sense, "pertaining to the improvement of life and practical instruction." The allegorical (which we might rather call the sacramental or the typological) uncovers mysteries of the new covenant that are hidden in historical events, while the anagogical rises "from spiritual mysteries to certain more sublime and more sacred secrets of heaven." The city of Jerusalem is a good example of something that may be understood according to four senses: "Historically it is the city of the Jews; allegorically it is the Church of Christ; anagogically it is that heavenly city of God which is the mother of us all; tropologically it is the human soul, which frequently under this title is either blamed or praised by the Lord."[28] It was due to Cassian's influence that the medieval writers interpreted Scripture in fourfold fashion.

As complex and as arbitrary with respect to designation as the spiritual sense of Scripture may have been, the literal too lent itself to a certain complexity and arbitrariness of designation. Here we may distinguish between the historical and the intended meanings of Scripture. The historical meaning was simply the understanding of the historical fact precisely as historical. Depending on the scriptural passage and the Father interpreting it, such a fact might or might not also be subject to a spiritual interpretation. Augustine suggests that, for example, the account in Galatians 1:18 of Paul going up to Jerusalem to see Peter is not really capable of being understood in a spiritual way, whereas the narrative of Abraham's two sons, begotten by Hagar and Sarah, is capable of being so understood, as Galatians 4:22–27 shows.[29]

The intended meaning, on the other hand, might not be couched in historical language or appear to have much historical foundation, although it is actually the true meaning of the letter. Augustine is the most important representative of this position, and when he proposes to give a literal commentary on the first three chapters of Genesis, what he is really setting out to do is to "support according to the correctness of the letter what the person who wrote is saying."[30] That is, Moses, the supposed author of Genesis, does not intend to speak strictly historically when he says that creation occurred in six days, or when he says any number of other things. His intent, rather, is to convey something more profound—about the Trinity, about the nature of creation, about the angels and about the human condition; to uncover this is to uncover the real literal meaning of Genesis. It is obvious that here the difference between literal and spiritual, as those terms are ordinarily used, begins to blur considerably.

For the most part, however, the Fathers simply occupied themselves with two senses, the literal and the spiritual, without making further distinctions. Taken most broadly, the patristic approach to these senses may be resolved into three schools— one that gives overwhelming weight to the spiritual sense, often to the detriment of the literal; one that holds a more or less middle position; and one that gives overwhelming weight to the literal sense, often to the detriment of the spiritual, although without denying the existence of the spiritual.

The most significant and influential representative of the first school is Origen, who in his treatise *On First Principles* says that all of Scripture has a spiritual sense, but it is not all to be taken literally.[31] The middle position is occupied by someone like Augustine, who has an appreciation of both letter and spirit even though he is capable of very elaborate allegory, or by Cassian, who is also at home in both senses.

The Antiochenes in the East and the Pelagians in the West are the most important representatives of the third school. Pelagian exegesis, an example of which we shall see shortly, was frequently moralizing and could well make do with a more literal understanding of the biblical text. As for the Antiochenes, the great exegetes of the fourth and fifth centuries like Theodore of Mopsuestia and Diodore of Tarsus rejected an allegorical interpretation of Scripture and stressed the literal or historical without at the same time denying a spiritual sense. As a rule, however, they were very sparing in their use of this sense, and they were convinced that it could only be found in close conjunction with the historical. The spiritual meaning, which they called *theoria* (insight), existed in such a way as not to destroy the historical, and thus it was very similar to typology.[32] Diodore explains the Antiochene position in his *Commentary on the Psalms:*

> Our exegesis [of the Psalms] will be historical and strictly literal. We shall not rule out a higher meaning or *theoria*, for history is not opposed to *theoria*; on the contrary, it is the

basis and substructure of higher insights. But one must beware lest *theoria* appear to do away with the subject: this would no longer be *theoria* but allegory, for where it is necessary to search out another sense alongside the text there is no longer *theoria* but allegory. In fact the Apostle by no means did away with history [presumably in Galatians 4:22–27] by introducing *theoria* and calling this *theoria* allegory. He was not ignorant of the terminology, but he wished to teach us that it is necessary to understand even the term "allegory," if it is determined by the context, according to the rules of *theoria*, without doing any damage to history. But the innovators in Holy Scripture, who think themselves so intelligent, whether because they are incapable of historical exegesis or after they have intentionally traduced it, introduced allegory, not according to the Apostle's concept but according to their own vain opinion, thus forcing the reader to understand things as the same that are completely foreign to one another. For example, instead of "abyss" they understand "demons"; instead of "serpent" they understand "the devil"; and so forth.

Diodore goes on to say that he can in fact accept, for example, Cain and Abel as symbols of the Synagogue and the Church respectively, and the paschal lamb as a symbol of Christ, for in so doing he at once maintains the historical and finds a higher sense.[33]

As an instance of the three schools' approach to Scripture we may take three different interpretations of Matthew 19:16ff and its parallels, the story of the rich young man who came up to Jesus and asked what he had to do to gain eternal life, and who went away sad when heard that in order to be perfect he would have to embrace poverty.

In this case the overwhelmingly spiritual position is held by Augustine, who demonstrates here his talent for allegorizing. The point of his interpretation, reiterated in a number of writings and sermons, is to show how the difficult demand to be poor could be in accord with the divine mercy, for Matthew 19:24 ("It is easier for a camel to go through the eye of a needle than for one who is rich to enter the kingdom of God") seems unequivocally to shut the rich out from heaven. For Augustine, the rich person compared to a camel is really a proud person, since in the end it is pride and not wealth of itself that is sinful. To that extent Augustine's interpretation is along the classic lines laid down by Clement of Alexandria at the end of the second century, which we shall soon see. In his interpretation of the camel and the eye of the needle, however, Augustine reaches a new level of spiritualizing. The camel, being a beast of burden, is an image of Christ humbling himself by becoming a man. The needle signifies the sorrows borne in suffering, as it may be used to prick and cause pain, and the needle's eye is the acute anguish involved in suffering. "Through the eye of the needle, then, the camel [Christ] has already entered. Let the rich not despair: they shall enter in safety into the kingdom of heaven."[34] Thus Augustine transforms riches into pride and a camel into Christ so that the rich who are humble may enter heaven, and by so doing he preserves the mercy of God in Christ without eliminating the difficulty of the demand to practice what then becomes in fact the heroic virtue of humility.

In Clement of Alexandria's late second-century treatise *Who Is the Rich Man That Shall be Saved?* we have an instance of the middle position. As with Augustine, Clement's concern is to reconcile a hard demand with the divine mercy. Unlike Augustine, however, Clement does not resort to elaborate allegory in order to do this; in fact, to all intents he ignores the verse on the camel and the eye of the needle, so rich in allegorical possibilities, in the course of his interpretation. Convinced that "the Savior teaches nothing in merely human fashion but instructs his disciples with divine and mystic wisdom," he is sure that this passage about the rich young man conceals a hidden meaning.[35] For him this meaning is simply that, in the Gospel, riches are equivalent to the desire for riches; they are not to be understood in a material way. Therefore the rich person who will not be saved is one who is obsessed with the idea of wealth, whether he be materially rich or poor.[36]

In the treatise *On Riches*, written in the fifth century by either Pelagius or his disciple Fastidius, we find an entirely different tack taken with regard to Matthew 19:16ff. Here is an example of the overwhelmingly literal position. The author first attacks the allegorizers who weaken Jesus' demand that the rich must sell all that they possess. They would say that riches really mean sins (like pride) and that thus the rich must get rid of their sins; or that the riches of the young man in the narrative symbolize the outmoded precepts of the old law, which he must no longer observe; or that the rich young man himself is a symbol of the Jews but not of the Christians.[37] Later in the treatise the author argues against those who allegorize the verse about the camel and the eye of the needle.[38] His final words on the narrative in question and the various spiritual approaches to it are a classic critique of certain arbitrary elements in spiritual exegesis:

> But why do those who are accustomed to treat almost everything in the Old Testament allegorically or mystically and to interpret what is in the New literally as precepts or deeds that actually took place, so that what was done in the Old prefigured the truth of the New, forget their custom or change it and put it in reverse only when it comes to the question of wealth? Then, in order to defend wealth, they understand the things that were done under the law in a literal way and without any mystical imagery. The evangelical precepts, on the other hand, once all their literalness and historical truth have been done away with, they try to cover over with an allegorical veil, as if here alone the New Testament was a figure of the Old, although it is acknowledged that in everything the Old is an image of the New. For they want to understand the wealth of Abraham and David and Solomon and the others in a literal manner. But when something is read in the Gospel about the contempt of riches they are at pains to corrupt it by a metaphorical treatment— although it is better, as I have said, to allegorize the commandments of the law than those of grace.[39]

The ordinary method of commentators on the Scriptures was first to set down the literal or historical meaning, which they did with relative brevity, and then move on to what was for them the far more important task of expounding the spiritual sense. This was the case even with Origen and others who leaned heavily on the allegorical. Origen himself was the foremost biblical scholar of antiquity and by no means ignored the literal meaning, when he thought that one existed, although he considered it inferior to the spiritual. Nearly all would have agreed with the fourth-century Didymus the Blind, who was influenced by Origen, that "in fact it is impossible to understand the spiritual or elevated thought without the shadow, which is the letter, or without the preliminary propaedeutic sciences."[40] This concern for the letter and for actual history, the "shadow" as it were of the deeper spiritual reality, is particularly evident in someone like Jerome, who had studied Hebrew, just as Origen had. Yet he clearly sees the literal in terms of a point of departure for the spiritual. Examples of this abound in his commentaries on the prophets. We may take as typical his exegesis of Isaiah 3:7 ("On that day he will speak out, saying: I am not a healer, and in my house there is neither bread nor clothing; do not make me leader of the people"). Jerome begins by listing variant readings in the passage from three Greek editions of the Old Testament as well as from the original Hebrew text, and then he proceeds to the literal commentary:

> But the person who has been chosen as leader will speak. And as the people had desired to have him as prince whom they see to be richer than themselves, so the one who has been chosen, reflecting on his poverty and weakness, bears witness that he is unworthy of the honor offered him and cannot heal vices; that is to say, he who can hardly attend to his own needs cannot cure the sick, give food to the hungry and clothe the naked.

With this the spiritual interpretation, which has already been hinted at in the last few words, is given at greater length:

> Therefore let us not concur immediately in the judgment of the multitude, but when we have been chosen to lead we shall know our real worth and shall be humbled under the mighty hand of God, for God, who resists the proud, gives grace to the humble. How many there are who promise others food and clothing and do not have bread and clothing because they themselves are hungry and naked, and do not have spiritual food and do not keep Christ's tunic whole! Full of wounds, they boast that they are healers. They do not observe what Moses says: Send someone else. Nor do they

keep the other commandment: Do not seek to become a judge, lest perhaps you be unable to remove iniquities. Jesus alone heals all sicknesses and infirmities. About him it stands written: He heals the brokenhearted and binds up their wounds.[41]

After having pursued certain scientific preliminaries by noting the textual variations, then, Jerome turns to a literal commentary, which is little more than a paraphrasing of the scriptural passage. Finally there comes the spiritual interpretation, which is moral and, in its culmination, Christological. The pattern of treatment here is in many respects paradigmatic.

Exegesis, in Context and out of Context

How was a reader to know whether a given passage was to be taken literally or spiritually? Several of the Fathers mention principles that govern their exegesis in this regard. For Origen the rule is, simply put, that a passage may be understood literally when it is reasonable and not unworthy of God.[42] Any passage, as has already been pointed out, may be understood spiritually. Augustine's rule in this respect is basically the same. For him, however, the determining factor is love, and whatever can be understood as promoting love of God and neighbor when taken literally need not be approached spiritually.[43] Cassian remarks that a passage is to be understood spiritually if, when taken literally, it would do harm to a person's interior life. He gives the example of some monks who obeyed to the letter Christ's injunction in Matthew 10:38 to take up one's cross and follow him, and who by carrying wooden crosses on their shoulders became objects of ridicule.[44]

Both Origen and Augustine, the two most influential interpreters of the Scriptures in the early Church, agree on a still more fundamental exegetical principle—namely that Christ is the deepest meaning of the Old and New Testaments. "Among the texts of the law," Origen writes, "one can find a great number that are related to Christ in typological or enigmatic fashion."[45] In Augustine's words: "Not for any other reason were all the things written before the Lord's coming which we read in the Sacred Scriptures than that his coming might be commended and the future Church prefigured, that is, the people of God in every nation, which is his body."[46] Jean Daniélou speaks for all the Fathers when he remarks in his book on Origen that

> essentially there are only two meanings in Scripture, the literal and the Christological. But the Christological meaning can in turn be subdivided into as many sections as there are aspects in Christ himself. Christ may be considered either as an historical person manifested in the events recorded in the Gospels, or as living a hidden life in the "sacraments" of the Church which is his body, or as appearing at the *parousia* at the end of the world and reigning in glory.[47]

A further peculiarity of patristic scriptural interpretation, in addition to the belief in a spiritual sense, is the Fathers' habit of dealing with biblical passages out of context. This occurs frequently, despite Augustine's demand that a passage of Scripture should be treated in relation to its larger setting.[48] This is in large part the result of the early Church's conviction that any scriptural text, no matter how humble it appeared, was a repository of wisdom and grace inasmuch as it was no less inspired by the Spirit than any other text. We can see this, for instance, in John Chrysostom's first homily *On the Statues*, where he announces that he will preach on an admittedly unprepossessing verse, 1 Timothy 5:23 ("No longer drink only water, but use a little wine for the sake of your stomach and your frequent ailments").

> If even this brief and simple word, which seems to have nothing valuable for the multitude, can be seen to offer wealth to us and an exalted philosophy, how much more will those that immediately display their abundance fill the attentive with boundless treasures! Therefore we ought not to pass over those passages of the Scriptures that seem simple, for these too are from the grace of the Spirit, and the spirit's grace is never small and insignificant, but great and wonderful and worthy of bestowing magnificent gifts.[49]

If it was true that every verse of Scripture contained so much, it would be possible to treat every verse as an independent unit. It could well be treated in context, but just as well out of context.

And if a passage could be taken out of context it could as easily be transferred to another context. The justification for this was the absolute unity of Scripture, which is well expressed by Jerome in one of his homilies: "All of Holy Scripture is bound together, and it has been united by one Spirit. It is like a single chain, one link attached to another, and when you have taken one, another hangs from it."[50] Hence the very frequent custom of bringing passages together that had no relationship to one another apart from the chance use of the same word. There is a notable example of this in Origen's *Commentary on the Song of Songs*. In the process of interpreting Song of Songs 2:15 ("Catch us the foxes, the little foxes, that spoil the vineyards, for our vineyards are in blossom") he goes through every other passage in the Bible that makes the least mention of foxes and brings each of them to bear somehow on the verse in question.[51] The result of such an approach is frequently to make a commentary on the Scriptures look like an exercise in the use of a stream-of-consciousness technique.

It must be clear that the interpretation of Scripture in the early Church was an affair that offered almost innumerable possibilities and variations. The notion that a deeper meaning could exist in so many cases and the process of discovering that meaning, to say nothing of the meaning itself, must often seem arbitrary and even bizarre to modern readers who are familiar with modern methods of exegesis. Ancient exegesis would seem to have to be relegated to the realm of pure curiosity, without any contemporary significance at all. In this regard, however, several things can be said.

The first is that modern biblical scholarship, with its good and bad aspects alike, has not come from nowhere but has in fact been built upon the labors of the Fathers, particularly of men like Origen and Jerome. We are not alone in trying to understand the deepest truth of the Scriptures; the Fathers too were led by the same zeal and followed what were for them acceptable methods to get at that truth. We may be confident that they did indeed attain to that truth, which is the second thing that must be said. To suggest that only Christians of the nineteenth and twentieth centuries have been and are capable of understanding the Bible is to deny the Bible's universality—that it is addressed to all people of all times, not only to the learned of a particular time—and consequently to reduce Christianity to a kind of modern gnosticism. The truth that the Fathers discovered is perhaps not recognizable as such in many or even most of its particulars, that is, in the interpretation of individual words or passages. In their understanding of the whole, however, they are in manifest possession of the truth. For the Christian, after all, the Bible is ultimately about nothing else than Christ and the Church and the instruments of salvation, and it may be justly said that whoever reads the Scriptures only as history or even as a work of high ethical quality has not understood their real meaning. Their real meaning is a hidden one.

Finally, it should be noted that, however the results of patristic exegesis may be looked at by modern eyes, it was for the Fathers a labor that could only be entered upon in a spirit of prayer and with an upright heart. Like every other aspect of patristic theology, then, it was a work that engaged both mind and heart. As Athanasius writes at the end of his treatise *On the Incarnation of the Word:*

> In addition to study and real knowledge of the Scriptures, integrity of life, purity of soul and Christlike virtue are required. . . . Whoever wishes to understand the mind of the sacred writers must first cleanse and purify himself by holiness of life and imitate the saints themselves by behavior similar to theirs.[52]

Coming from minds and hearts thus shaped, the Fathers' interpretation of Scripture cannot in the end be completely without value.

III

God

In order to see how the Fathers approached the mystery of the Godhead, it is necessary to be aware of some of the misconceptions about God that they were obliged to face. One of the first of these misconceptions to make an appearance has already been alluded to in the previous chapter; it held that there were two Gods, one the wicked but just Creator of the universe, the God of the Old Testament, and the other the merciful Father of Christ, the God of the New. At the basis of this heresy was an attempt to understand and explain the existence of evil. Tertullian, writing about the beginning of the third century, shows how Marcion, the supposed author of the heresy, came to think in this way:

> While [Marcion was] brooding over the question of evil and where it comes from (as many do nowadays, and especially heretics), his perception became clouded by the very enormity of his curiosity. It was thus that he lighted upon the words where the Creator declares: I am he who creates evil. Since he was already convinced from other arguments that are satisfactory to every perverted mind that he is the author of evil, so he now understood the Creator to be that evil tree which brings forth evil fruit, namely evil things, and then he presumed that there should be another God, after the analogy of the good tree bringing forth good fruit. Consequently, since he found that Christ had, as it were, a different disposition than the Creator, one of simplicity and pure benevolence, it was easy for him to argue that in Christ a new and theretofore unknown divinity had been revealed.[1]

42

Tertullian then proceeds to demolish all of Marcion's arguments. But despite Tertullian's effectiveness, Marcion had simply struck upon a perennial problem, which was to recur most notably shortly thereafter in the form of Manicheanism. How was one to explain the coexistence of good and evil in the universe, and how was the apparent difference between the God of the Old Testament and that of the New to be reconciled? These thoughts never ceased to nag at the minds of reflective persons and made Marcion's solution a plausible one. To this day it is plausible to many. The great psychologist Carl G. Jung, to give one significant example, plays a variation on Marcion's theme and speaks in terms of God's "shadow" side, his "dark" side, which acts in an incomprehensible, arbitrary and sometimes cruel manner.[2]

The keystone of Tertullian's attack against Marcion was his emphasis on the divine unity and the logical impossibility of the existence of two Gods. But the attempt to preserve the unity of God led in turn to other aberrations, at least among some of the earliest theologians. One of these was modalism, also known as Sabellianism, which maintained that the three Persons of the Trinity were actually only one Being assuming three different roles, or hiding behind three different masks. According to Tertullian, a certain Praxeas held this view, teaching that "the Father himself came down into the virgin, was himself born of her, himself suffered, himself, in a word, being Jesus Christ."[3] Hence the derisive and more descriptive name for the heresy, partripassianism, meaning that it was the Father who had suffered and died.

A second significant attempt to preserve the divine unity, while at the same time holding to a trinity of Persons, was subordinationism. This could exist among undoubted heretics, such as the Arians, whose teachings convulsed most of the fourth century. Some of them believed that the Son and the Spirit were ultimately only creatures, even though they were exalted creatures, and others held that they were divine, but in an inferior sense. Subordinationism could also be found among some otherwise orthodox early Fathers, who were struggling to hold the different aspects of the mystery together without altogether succeeding, and evidently without realizing what the implications of their formulations might be. Thus the second-century Justin Martyr could speak of the Son and the Spirit as God, but as occupying the second and third places after the Father, who is "the unchanging and eternal God, the begetter of all things."[4]

In brief, these were the most important of the unorthodox ways of understanding the mystery of God's oneness and threeness. Always they were marked by the tendency to emphasize one aspect of the mystery at the expense of another, as is the case with all heresies. Gregory of Nyssa speaks of the Church's balancing of the trinity on the one hand and the unity on the other, keeping the two truths in tension, as the mean between Judaism and polytheism, which avoids the errors of each. For the Jews, in their zeal for the unity, deny the Son and the Spirit, while the Greeks have a plurality of gods.

> From the Jewish thought-system we should hold fast to the unity of the [divine] nature, while from the Greek thought-system we should retain only the distinction of *hypostaseis* [persons]. In this way, the irreligious tenets on each side find in each other a corresponding remedy: for the fact of number in the Trinity is a remedy for those who misconstrue the unity, while the assertion of the unity is a remedy for those who squander themselves in polytheism.[5]

Despite the excesses of the unorthodox, which are often nevertheless understandable, there was scope within orthodoxy for fruitful speculation on the mystery of the Godhead. Some of this speculation was later to be rejected because it was imprecise. One such imprecision was Justin's notion of Son and Spirit occupying second and third places. Other speculation was fundamentally orthodox but not sufficiently rich, so to speak. This was the case with the late second- and early third-century concept of the imminent and emitted Word—the Word, or Second Person, being enclosed in the bosom of the Father and only being uttered or expressed before the act of creation.[6] Likewise, some of the terminology that this speculation employed was eventually abandoned because it was subsequently taken up by the unorthodox and thus seemed inappropriate to express catholic truth.

A particularly beautiful concept that is found in the letters of Ignatius of Antioch at the beginning of the second century and was later dropped because some gnostic groups made use of it is that of God as silence.[7] The idea appears in three places in Ignatius and is mentioned only briefly. Here it is most clear: "There is one God, who manifested himself through Jesus Christ, his Son, who is his Word, coming forth from silence, who in all things was pleasing to the one who sent him."[8] In the light of other texts[9] we can infer that Ignatius understood the Father to be somehow silence itself—silence that produces, from its infinite depth, a Word, the Son. Hence silence seems to be for Ignatius what essence (or *ousia*) would be for later Fathers, namely the real that cannot be further defined, the very ground of reality. "Silence" best expressed who the Father was, just as "Word" best expressed the Son. This idea of silence, which is only suggested in Ignatius, would appear later on in modified form. It was crucial in much gnostic thought, and it shows up, for instance, in the so-called *Excerpts from Theodotus*, second-century gnostic fragments collected by Clement of Alexandria.[10] Thus the notion virtually disappeared from orthodox Christianity.

A related concept, which never caused any subsequent embarrassment to the orthodox, was that of the divine ineffability. For all their emphasis on the silence at the heart of the divine, the gnostics were never really theologians of the ineffable: on the contrary, with their endless probings into heavenly mysteries and their far-fetched speculations they were all too eager to reduce the divine to human terms. "Silence" itself was for them, unlike for Ignatius, a delimiting term that gave a kind of handle to the divinity and even provided a certain power over it.[11] It is precisely this tendency to delimit that Justin, the first theologian among the Fathers to lay stress on the divine ineffability, sets out to combat. "There is no one," he remarks, "who can give a name to the ineffable God, and if anyone dares to say that there is one, he suffers from an incurable madness."[12] And in another place he writes:

> Anyone who might be able to impose a name on God would have to be more primordial than God himself. Father, God, Creator, Lord, Master—these are not precisely proper names; the basis for their application to God lies in his gifts and

works. . . . The style of address "God" is not a proper name, but rather is a sort of judgment that lies at the core of the human being about a state of affairs that has no other explanation ready to hand.[13]

It was characteristic of heretics to seek to delve into the Godhead and to explain its mysteries. The fourth-century Eunomians, a branch of the Arians, were, like the gnostics, guilty of this. Gregory Nazianzen condemns their brashness in his *Theological Orations*, reproaching them for rendering the divine mystery banal by their constant talking about it, even in the most inappropriate places.[14] They went so far as to say that it was possible for the human mind to conceive of God's very essence. Gregory counters by noting that, while we are able to know some of the divine qualities (incorporeality, for example), we cannot know the subject in which those qualities inhere.[15] This is due fundamentally to human dullness of comprehension rather than to a desire on God's part to be incomprehensible.[16] Indeed, human beings can hardly grasp the wonders of creation, never mind the wonders of the divine being.[17]

Divine ineffability, divine incomprehensibility: it is typical of the Fathers to have emphasized this aspect of God, central to their thought and, of course, very much in the tradition that they had inherited from Judaism. With respect to those whose questions about the divine smacked of curiosity—what was God doing before he created the world? and how does the Father bring forth the Son?—Irenaeus would write: "We should not be ashamed to leave to God difficulties too great for us."[18] In his commentary on the Apostles' Creed, written at the beginning of the fifth century, Rufinus cautions his readers specifically about their approach to the mystery of the eternal generation of the Son: "I do not want you to discuss or to involve yourself out of curiosity in this deep mystery, for fear that, while prying too persistently into the splendor of inaccessible light, you may lose that little glimpse that has been conceded to mortals as a divine gift."[19] In heaven itself, some Fathers said, there would still be a kind of veil. Augustine voices this opinion when we writes that even there we would never be able to comprehend God fully: "When will you be able to say: This is God? Not even when you see him, for what you shall see is ineffable. The Apostle says that he was caught up into the third heaven and heard ineffable words. If the words are ineffable, what is he whose words they are!"[20] Gregory Nazianzen on the other hand, with his belief that human obtuseness was responsible for the divine obscurity, suggests somewhat more optimistically that human beings will be capable of grasping God's nature and essence in the next life.[21]

All in all, patristic theology, with rare exception, is not so much concerned with the unfathomable inner essence and operation of the Godhead as it is, to use Justin's words, with "his gifts and works," the divine initiative toward humankind that was known as the "economy." We need only look at the earliest creeds to see the reflection of this. There the bulk of the confession of faith is devoted to the Son in his role as Redeemer, while the other Persons are given only the merest mention: the Father appears simply as Father and sometimes also as Creator, while the reference to the Spirit is often equally austere, nothing more than "I believe in the Holy Spirit." Even in the course of explaining the Creed to those about to be baptized, Cyril of Jerusalem says that a bare minimum of knowledge of the Trinity is enough: "For our salvation it is sufficient to know that there is a Father and a Son and a Holy Spirit."[22]

Knowing the Father in the Word and Cosmos

Although the credal mention of the Father may have been nothing more than a few words, yet the realization was that the Father was already mysteriously known in his Word, generated from eternity in the depths of the Godhead in an act too lofty to comprehend. In a magnificent formulation Athanasius writes of him that

> he is the good offspring of the one who is good, his true Son, the power and wisdom and reason of the Father. He is not this by participation nor by any derivation of these properties that would be extrinsic to himself, as is the case with those who participate in him and whom he makes wise and powerful and rational. No, in and of himself he is properly the

wisdom, reason and power of the Father—light, truth, righteousness, virtue itself, the express image and splendor and likeness of the Father. In a word, he is the consummate fruit of the Father, the sole Son and changeless image of the Father.[23]

As Athanasius writes elsewhere, the knowledge of the Father in the Word is the distinguishing mark of humankind, and it is absolutely necessary for human happiness:

> Now how could it possibly be to creatures' advantage to be ignorant of their Creator? How could they be rational apart from recognizing the Word of the Father in whom they have come into being? Were their knowledge limited to what is of this world, they would be indistinguishable from brutes. What purpose would there be to God's creating them unless he had willed that they should know him? Against such an eventuality, God in his goodness makes them share in his image, our Lord Jesus Christ, and fashions them after his own image and likeness. In this way, graced with a knowledge of the image, through that image they might have a knowledge of the Father and in a knowledge of their Creator might lead a happy and blessed life.[24]

In both these passages Athanasius alludes to human beings' share in the Word, which was the means by which they would attain to that knowledge of the Father which was their destiny. This share in the Word was the rational nature, the possession of which made the human being the image of God or, as some would prefer to say, the image of the image, since the Word himself was the perfect image.[25] "Christ the first-born of God . . . is the reason of which every race partakes," Justin Martyr writes, and he adds that, even before Christ came, those who lived according to this reason had the right to be called Christians.[26]

The incarnation of the Word was intended to reveal the Father all the more clearly. "Through the Word itself, made visible and tangible," Irenaeus says in a famous passage, "the Father was manifested, though not all alike believed in him. But all saw the Father in the Son, for the Father is the invisible of the Son, and the Son is the visible of the Father."[27]

If the Father could be known in the Word, who was his image, he could also be known in the universe that he had created through that Word. As Irenaeus writes in the same place: "Through creation the Word reveals God the Creator, and through the world the Lord who made the world, and through the handiwork the artificer."[28]

But the inner coherence of the universe, in turn, was understood to reveal the Word. While the mere fact of creation's existence manifested the Father who was the source of being, its marvelous order bore witness to a divine reason who was the Word. Such at least is a theme frequent in the Greek Fathers. Clement of Alexandria speaks of this Word as a symphonist who

> structured the universe into a melody and tuned the discordant sound of the elements into an ordered harmony, a harmony that would prevail through the whole. The ocean he made free-flowing but restrained from invading the earth. Earth, which had previously been swept along, he fixed in place with the ocean as its boundary. Fire's frenzy he moderated with air, just as one would mix the Dorian mode with the Lydian. The bitter chill of the air he softened with the embrace of fire. The dissonance of the universe he mixed into a harmony. This deathless song [the Word], the mainstay and harmony of the universe, stretching from the center to the extremities and thence to the center, has harmonized the whole in accord with that plan of the Father that was the object of the psalmist's admiration.[29]

More than a century later Athanasius develops this idea at some length in his treatise *Against the Pagans*. He says that, had the universe not been created through the Word (thus imagining an impossible situation), it would have been in danger of dissolving again into that nothingness out of which it had been made. But, as it is, all creation partakes in the Word, and for this reason it abides in being. Yet even more wonderful than that it should abide in being is the fact that it does so harmoniously. Here Clement's musical imagery reappears:

> If a musician were to tune a lyre and with virtuosity harmonize high and low notes and the middle tones with the oth-

ers, he would produce a single melodic line. In like manner, the whole universe is like a lyre in the hands of the Wisdom of God. He combines creatures of the air with those of the earth, the celestial with those of the air. He compounds the whole of its parts and directs it by his decree and will. The world and its unified arrangement is his masterpiece of beauty and harmony. Yet all the while Wisdom remains unchanged in the presence of the Father; into whatever he moves he brings design in accord with the Father's plan. The truly baffling feature of his divinity is that by one and the same decree he directs all things simultaneously, continuously and collectively: both the straight and the curved, what lies above and between and beneath, the wet and the cold and the warm, things that we can see and things that we cannot. Each is ordered in a way appropriate to its own distinctive nature. Thus, simultaneously and by his decree, he directs the straight as straight and the curved as curved. Things intermediate he moves in just that way. The warmth has warmth, the dry aridity. The whole ensemble is present to him and is enlivened and structured according to the constitution of each. By his activity a marvelous and truly divine harmony is achieved.[30]

The Spirit and the Trinity

In his treatise *On First Principles* Origen writes that, while the activity of the Father and the Son has to do with creation, and so is extended not only to saints and sinners but also to dumb animals and even to lifeless things, yet that of the Spirit is confined to the saints alone.[31] That sanctification is the Spirit's special activity is found in virtually all the Fathers. Frequently associated with the idea of the restoration of the image of God in humanity, it is in turn connected with the revelation of the image of God, the Word, so that as the Son manifests the Father the Spirit manifests the Son. After a person has been purified of his sins and the image of God in him has been restored, Basil says, "he [the Spirit], like the sun overwhelming a purified eye, will show you in himself the image of the invisible [the Word], and in the blessed contemplation of the image you will behold the ineffable beauty of the archetype [the Father]."[32]

In his function as sanctifier the Spirit was also associated with the mystery of the Church. The first Creed that we possess in its entirety, cited by Hippolytus at the beginning of the third century, links the two by speaking of "the Holy Spirit in the holy Church."[33] Among some heretical groups, and notably in Montanism, an enthusiastic sect that flourished in Asia Minor in the second and third centuries, his role overshadowed that of Christ. For them, the Church of the Spirit had superseded the Church of the New Testament, the Church of which Christ was head. This was an idea that returned to haunt Christianity in the Middle Ages with Joachim of Flora, among others, and never fully disappeared. For the orthodox, though, the Spirit was the source of every gift in the Church. "Where the Church is," Irenaeus writes, "there is the Spirit of God, and where the Spirit of God is, there is the Church and every grace."[34] This is most likely what Hippolytus means by "the Holy Spirit in the holy Church." The Church is simply the place of the Spirit.

But the exact status of the Spirit, his relation to the Father and the Son, his particular functions and even his very existence were always more difficult to grasp than those of the other two Persons. This was perhaps because, to some extent at least, the process of sanctification that was appropriated to him was of its nature a hidden and mysterious thing. His name itself was no help in identifying more precisely who he was, since Father and Son were spirit as well as he. A still further difficulty in this regard was the fact that the Scriptures, in particular the Old Testament, did not speak clearly of him. Gregory Nazianzen takes advantage of this to suggest a development of doctrine.

The Old Testament announced the Father openly and the Son more obscurely. The New made the Son manifest and alluded to the divinity of the Spirit. Now the Spirit is in our midst and he declares himself to us more openly. For it was not safe, when the Father's divinity had not yet been confessed, for the Son to be announced openly; nor, when the Son's divinity had not yet been admitted, to impose the Holy Spirit as a kind of heavier burden, if one may speak in such a fashion, lest some of us might, as if weighed down with too much food and with eyes weakened by the sun's rays, be unable to grasp even what lay within our powers.[35]

The most consistent argument in favor of the Spirit's divinity, at least among the Eastern Fathers, was that which relied upon the baptismal formula, according to which a person was baptized in the Trinity and hence of course in the Spirit as well. If only God could save a person and, more specifically, render him divine (as the Easterners liked to say), then the Spirit into which a person was baptized was necessarily divine.[36] Even the heretics who denied the Spirit's divinity performed baptism with this formula and could hardly fail to see the logic of the orthodox position. It was not, however, until the Council of Constantinople in 381 that the Spirit took his undisputed place in the Trinity, equally to be worshiped and glorified with the Father and the Son.

Among the Western Fathers not long after the Council of Constantinople a fateful development was occurring with respect to speculation about the Spirit's relationship to Father and Son. This relationship was generally characterized in the East in the later fourth century as a proceeding forth from the Father through the Son. Gregory of Nyssa expresses it thus in his treatise *That There Are Not Three Gods:* "We believe that one is the cause [the Father] but that the other [the Son] is from the cause. And concerning him who is from the cause we make another distinction. For one is immediately from the first cause, and another [the Spirit] is through that which is immediately from the first cause."[37] In Ambrose and more especially in Augustine, however, we see the idea that the Spirit proceeds immediately from both Father and Son as from a single cause or source.[38] This was a concept that the Eastern Church would eventually find itself unable to tolerate, the rejection of which became the touchstone of orthodoxy in the East. But the history of that would bring us beyond the scope of the patristic period.[39]

Now, although certain activities were ordinarily assigned to particular Persons, the Fathers were anxious not to give the impression that the Persons acted independently of one another. Thus, for example, it was not the Spirit alone who sanctified, although this function was appropriated or attributed to him; he did it, rather, in conjunction with the Father and the Son. "Nothing in the Trinity can be called greater or less," Origen explains, after having written about the place of the Holy Spirit, "for there is but one fount of divinity, who upholds all that he has made by his Word and Reason, and who sanctifies by the Spirit of his mouth all that is worthy of sanctification."[40] That the unity of the Godhead proceeded from the Father as from a source has already been alluded to; it was a typically Greek idea. Cyril of Jerusalem expands on this, showing a concern for the proper use of prepositions that would manifest this one source of divinity: "The Father *through* the Son *with* the Holy Spirit bestows all gifts. The gifts of the Father are not one thing, those of the Son another and those of the Holy Spirit something else. For there is one salvation, one power, one faith. There is one God, the Father; one Lord, his only-begotten Son; one Holy Spirit, the Paraclete."[41]

If the Easterners tended to find the basis for divine unity in the Father, who is seen as the source of Godhead without being at the same time more divine than the other two Persons,[42] Augustine, who influenced all subsequent Western thought, emphasized the divine essence as the basis of that unity.[43] Consequently he insists that everything that is said with respect to the divine essence must be posited of each of the three Persons, but not in such a way that what is so posited is understood to exist in the plural rather than in the singular. "Thus the Father is great, the Son is great, the Holy Spirit is great; yet there are not three greats but one great."[44] The difference between the Persons is, as others had concluded before Augustine, a matter of their relationship to one another.[45] The result of Augustine's emphasis on the divine essence as the unifying factor, with the accompanying insistence on the absolutely equal participation of each Person in that essence, was a tendency in the West for the Persons to lose the particular characteristics that tradition had attributed to them and even to "disappear" as Persons before the one Godhead. This seems to have been especially the case with the Spirit.

But there are other sources for our knowledge of how the Fathers approached the mystery of the divine apart from works that deal expressly with the notion of God. The Fathers also occasionally let certain underlying conceptions, or preconceptions, appear that must be taken into consideration as well.

Without at least some small acquaintance with these we cannot understand a good deal of early Christian thought, into which hidden streams frequently flowed. One of these that is characteristic can be mentioned, and then contrasted briefly with its counterparts: it is the notion of the dreadful God of judgment, which seems to have been peculiar to North Africa. We find it at the beginning of the third century in Tertullian, in whom we might have expected it, since he is customarily somber and even grim.[46] But we see it in Cyprian too, when he speaks of God's awful revenge against Christians who had betrayed their faith in the persecution of Decius in the middle of the third century,[47] and there are traces of it in Augustine toward the beginning of the fifth century. The pre-Christian Carthaginians practiced human sacrifice on a wide scale, and it would seem that there was something in the North African temperament that demanded an exigent deity, since in North Africa more Christians were martyred, and the cult of martyrs flourished more extensively, than anywhere else in the ancient Church. When the Empire became Christian and the opportunity for martyrdom ceased, the horrors of the Donatist schism in North Africa took its place, with an extremist wing of the Donatists—the so-called Circumcellions—committing either murder or, as often happened, suicide. None of this might have occurred if the North African Christians, like their pagan ancestors, had not conceived of God, at least to some degree, in very harsh terms. It was perhaps not the predominant aspect of their idea of God, for they could speak of him as loving and merciful too, but it was *an* aspect. Even Augustine, as has been suggested, may not have remained uninfluenced by this unconscious stereotype. His opinion on the unhappy fate of infants who die unbaptized earned him a scathing reproach from his Pelagian opponent, Julian of Eclanum, who accused him of portraying God as a criminal and turning him into a being even more perverse than the pagan gods who used to be worshiped in those parts.[48]

This view seems hardly to have existed elsewhere. The God of the Greek Fathers was often merciful to a fault, and divine punishment was held to be therapeutic rather than vengeful. Why this was so must probably be sought, once again, in the temperament of the people. It corresponded also to a more optimistic theology that laid greater stress on freedom of will than the West did, and which permitted the Greeks to approach God on a level where they were surer of themselves than Westerners were. In other parts of the West, too, although emphasis was laid on God's justice, it was simply not the same thing as in North Africa. Peter Chrysologus, a northern Italian, could write toward the middle of the fifth century about a human being's incapability of standing before the divine presence and of God's transcendent holiness: "Who is free [of sin] in the presence of God? Who is not a liar in God's eyes? Who can exult before the terror of the supernal majesty? The archangels tremble, the angels quake, the powers are terrified, the elders of heaven cast themselves upon their faces, the elements flee, the rocks dissolve, the mountains flow away, the earth shakes. . . ."[49] Yet there is no hint of divine vindictiveness here.

If there were some flaws in the Fathers' conception of God, if they emphasized one aspect over another, it was because they, like we, tended sometimes to project their own feelings and needs onto the divinity, even as the more ignorant tended to think of God in terms of a human body—an idea that had to be constantly combatted in the early Church.[50] Here, touching upon a theme that has recurred, we can turn to Augustine for a final word. "Hardly anything can be found that is worthy to be said of God," he writes. "And most things that we are obliged to say about him, which people measure rather in human terms, are barely understood even by a few spiritual persons. . . ." And he goes on to show how easily scriptural terms are misunderstood when used of God:

> It is easily seen that regret [for instance] does not occur in God as it is spoken of in human beings. But it is not easily seen that even mercy, such as the human person experiences it, is not divine. . . . Thus when he [God] regrets something he is not changed, but he brings about a change. When he is angry he is not moved, but he does justice. When he is merciful he does not sorrow, but he sets free [those who are sorrowing]. And when he burns with love he is not aflame, but he inflames [others]. . . . He is ineffable.[51]

IV

The Human Condition

The Fathers agreed on the blissful state of the first parents in paradise before the fall, but they held somewhat different opinions on the exact nature of that state and, by consequence, what the fall from it consisted in. A glimpse at these opinions gives some notion of how they looked at the human condition in general, for they always regarded the first parents in paradise as models of what human life should be like, while they saw the circumstances involved in the fall as constituting the archetypal pattern of human sinfulness.

A number of the earliest Greek Fathers pictured Adam and Eve as children. Irenaeus, certainly the greatest theological genius of the second century, is the best example of this. He speaks of the first parents as little ones whose

> thoughts were innocent and childlike, and they had no conception or imagination of the sort that is engendered in the soul by evil, through concupiscence, and by lust. . . . They were in their integrity, preserving their natural state, for what had been breathed into their frame was the spirit of life.

And, as a rightly disposed sexuality was invariably a criterion for the paradisal state, he adds: "For this reason they were not ashamed as they kissed each other and embraced with the innocence of childhood."[1] Because they were children, however, they were not yet perfect, but it was intended that they should grow into perfection, and so pass from simplicity and guilelessness to wisdom and maturity. In this they were to provide a model for all who were to follow them. For only the one who is uncreated is perfect, and he is God. But the human person had first to be created, and having been created to make progress, and having made progress to come to adulthood, and having come to adulthood to increase, and having increased to grow strong, and having grown strong to be glorified, and having been glorified to see his Lord.[2]

In Irenaeus' view it was a childish lack of discretion, making Adam easily misled by the devil, as well as disobedience, which was responsible for the fall.[3]

Clement of Alexandria has an interesting variation on this. "In paradise the first man was free as a child at play," Clement writes,

> for he was a child of God. But when he succumbed to pleasure (for the snake that crawls upon its belly is to be taken as a symbol of pleasure, earthly vice, which is naturally inclined to material things) and wandered, led by lust alone, then, by dint of his disobedience, the child became an adult. Heedless of the Father's voice, he was ashamed to be in God's company—so great is the force of pleasure. Once free because of his simplicity, the human person becomes enslaved because of sinfulness.[4]

The differences in the points of view are interesting. In Irenaeus Adam's innocence was naive and a liability, and it was intended that he should mature. For Clement, on the other hand, this innocence was freedom, and Adam's sudden growth into adulthood was the result of his descent into the slavery of sin. Clement, too, speaks of disobedience in the form of pleasure as the cause of the fall, but there is no mention of pleasure in Irenaeus.

Athanasius, writing more than a century after Clement, chooses to emphasize something else in his discussion of paradise. Adam, he says, "had his mind fixed on God in a freedom unhindered by shame," and he associated with the angels "in that contemplation of things perceived by the mind which he enjoyed in the place where he was."[5] This is echoed in Cyril of Alexandria still a century after that: according to him, Adam's mind was "ever intent upon the visions of divine reality."[6] For

Athanasius the fall was prompted by self-centeredness. Here he
extends what occurred in paradise to the whole human family:

> Once human beings diverted their attention from heavenly
> concerns, then they began to devote attention to themselves
> . . . with the result that at that moment they fell into bodily
> yearning and, to their shame, realized their nakedness—not
> so much that they were stripped of clothing as of the contem-
> plation of the things of God. For they had transferred their
> attention to what was contrary to the things of God. As soon
> as they stopped attending to what is one and true (that is, to
> God) and stopped longing for him, all that was left for them
> was to launch themselves upon variety and upon the neces-
> sarily fragmentary desires of the body.[7]

Ultimately the fall into self-centeredness is a fall into nothingness. Since human beings have been created out of nothingness,
Athanasius writes, when they turn away from the God who is
being itself they turn back to the non-being from which they
have come.[8] The result of this reversion to non-being is the creation and worship of idols, which themselves do not really exist.[9]
    Still another view of the fall is represented by the fifth- and
early sixth-century Syrian monastic writer Philoxenus of Mabbug, for whom the first sin was "the desire of the belly," or gour-
mandise. "The tempter, clever as he was," Philoxenus says,

> saw that this was the most powerful of the passions and that
> it occupied the first place in us. He drew near to it, stirred it
> up and afterward sowed laxity and, after that, desire. And
> that is how the passion of fornication made its appearance as
> well: As soon as they had eaten, the eyes of both were
> opened, and they knew that they were naked. . . . See how
> the beginning of the universal sin and the transgression of
> the first commandment was the desire of the belly; it is
> through that that all the sins and every punishment have
> come upon us.[10]

Some of the Fathers tended not to stress the role of the body
in paradise, and Origen, in one notorious passage, goes so far as
to suggest that Adam and Eve were simply minds contemplating

God, which only took on bodies when they were cast out of paradise. This was, in his view, the deeper meaning of Genesis 3:21, where it is said that God made garments of skin (here human bodies were understood) for Adam and his wife.[11] But these lines from Scripture were more soberly interpreted by other Fathers as symbolizing, for example, that the first parents had lost the innocence associated with nudity and were now covering themselves with deceit and self-deception.[12] Origen's opinion, tempting as it may have been to many (for we must admit that a certain discomfort with the body was rather widespread in the early Church, and indeed in the ancient world at large), was eventually repudiated. The body not only existed, to be sure, but it enjoyed a bliss of its own in paradise. For paradise was itself a physical place—a position that Augustine vehemently defended in *The City of God* against those who could understand it only in allegorical terms.[13] The characteristics of the body there, it was agreed by those who discussed the matter, were integrity, tranquillity and freedom from every irrational movement.

Augustine, whose teaching on the primal state is very extensive, dwells at length on what the human body must have been like in paradise. He is certain that its every member was under the control of the will, enlightened by reason. This was especially true of the generative organs that, in the fallen human condition, act with what appears to be sovereign freedom: "Sometimes they do not act as the mind wills, while sometimes they act against its will."[14] However, human beings lost control over more than their generative organs, although these were the most obviously arbitrary in their movement. In an amusing passage in *The City of God* Augustine points out that some people can wiggle their ears, move their scalp and even their hair and do other things less worthy of mention; all of this they can accomplish at will, thus manifesting to us now what complete control over one's body in paradise must have been like.[15] This disobedience of the body to the higher human faculties was a fitting punishment for Adam's disobedience to God.[16]

In addition to control over his body, Adam possessed dominion over irrational creation, which existed for his enjoyment. This is the reason why, Gregory of Nyssa explains, he was created on the sixth day:

For that great and precious commodity, the human person, had not as yet entered the universe of existing things, for it would not be appropriate for the ruler to make his appearance before the things over which he would rule. But once his dominion had been readied, once the Creator of all things had prepared a sort of royal dwelling place for the would-be king, only then was the ruler proclaimed. This royal dwelling was the earth and the islands and the sea and the sky, arching over all like a roof. Within this palace were stored riches of every kind: all that is in flora and fauna; everything that has sensation and breath and life; and, if one can count material things as riches, then also whatever has the beauty to be prized in human sight—gold, silver, the gems that human beings delight in. And after the Creator had cached away an abundance of these things in the bosom of the earth as if in a royal treasury, he has the human person make his appearance in the world, to contemplate some of these things and to rule over others. In this way, by reason of the enjoyment that he would derive from them he might appreciate his benefactor and, on the basis of the beauty and immensity of the things that he could see, he might track down the ineffable and incomprehensible power of their Creator.[17]

We must turn to Gregory of Nyssa again for a final characteristic of the paradisal state. This was the communion that the first parents had with the angels, and Gregory speaks of it in images dear to the Greek mind. "There was a time when rational creation was a single chorus, intent upon the one leader of the chorus and moving and turning to that harmony of triumph which arose from him and which was according to the commandment." With sin, however, the cosmic harmony was destroyed, and the first parents, who had enjoyed the companionship of the angels, were cast out from their society. In a hostile world their descendants waited for that moment when they would be rejoined with the divine choirs.[18]

The fall, then, was variously the result of disobedience, the lure of pleasure or egoism. Yet a deeper question was that which asked how Adam and Eve had succumbed to sin in the first place, how such a disastrous option might even have been available to them. The human being is inclined to both good and evil,

Melito of Sardis explains in his second-century Easter homily, just as a clod of earth is capable of receiving two different kinds of seed.[19] Methodius of Olympus elaborates on this more than a century later:

> A sort of midpoint between two extremes, the human person is neither absolute righteousness nor utter evil. Rather, he is poised squarely between incorruptibility and corruption, and depending on which of the two he gives the nod and inclines to, he is said to alter his nature in the direction of whichever one wins out. If to corruption he inclines, he then becomes corruptible and mortal; if to incorruptibility, then incorruptible and immortal he becomes. Positioned midway between the tree of life and the tree of the knowledge of good and evil, he is transformed into the essential character of the tree whose fruit he has tasted. In and of himself, a human being is neither of the trees. Only when he consorts and keeps company with corruption does he become corrupt; should he come into contact with the unguent sap of life, however, he will become incorruptible and immortal again.[20]

Augustine's answer to the question is, typically, more aware of the human mystery involved. Because the human person was made from nothing, he says, taking up a theme that Athanasius had employed before him, so he was capable of falling back into nothingness, for he had experienced pride, he had turned away from God and begun to live for himself, which "is not as yet to be nothing, but to approximate to nothing." Thus a secret corruption, arising from the very tenuousness, so to speak, of Adam's creation from nothing, had already preceded the evil act, and pride had prepared the way for the more manifest sin of disobedience. This was an illustration of the principle that all open sin is preceded by a hidden fault.[21] The notion of a fall before the fall is not foreign to other Fathers. It appears in Origen, too,[22] and also in a poem written about the middle of the fourth century by Ephrem. Ephrem says there that, since the devil could not enter paradise, Adam and Eve had to leave it momentarily in order to go out to him. There, having already jeopardized their bliss by this act, they are successfully tempted to the fateful deed.[23]

Life after the Fall

With the fall nearly all Adam's gifts disappeared—his innocence, his contemplative abilities, his control over his body and
over all irrational creation, and his harmony with rational creation. His children shared in this because they were mysteriously
implicated in Adam's history, as Ambrose states most succinctly:
"I fell in Adam, in Adam I was cast out of paradise, I died in
Adam."[24] For his descendants who realized what they had lost,
their whole life could be seen as an attempt to gain back what
had disappeared: it was a pilgrimage of return. And indeed the
image of life as pilgrimage or journey was a popular one in the
early Church. "Refresh yourself and pass on," Augustine says.
"You are journeying; think about to whom you are going."[25] By
far the most famous use of the journey image is in Origen's
twenty-seventh homily on the Book of Numbers. There he
speaks of the forty-two stages of the Israelites' passage from
Egypt to the land of Canaan, described in Numbers 33, as symbolic of the soul's journey to God. The people set out from
Egypt, which represents slavery and the worship of false gods,
and slowly acquire virtue for themselves at their different stopping places.

> When the soul sets out from the Egypt of this life, that it may
> hasten on to the land of promise, it necessarily proceeds by
> way of those stages which have been prepared with the
> Father from the beginning. I believe that the prophet, mind-
> ful of them, said: These things have I remembered, and I
> have poured out my soul, because I am going to the place of
> the wonderful tabernacle, to the house of God. Those are the
> stages, and those the tabernacles, of which he says else-
> where: How lovely are your tabernacles, Lord of hosts! My
> soul yearns and faints in the courts of the Lord. Therefore the
> same prophet also says in another place: Much has my soul
> wayfared. Understand, then, if you are able, what these way-
> farings of the soul are, in which it weeps over itself at length
> with a certain groaning and sorrow. But the understanding
> of these things dims and grows dull until it itself [the soul]
> makes its pilgrim way. Then indeed it shall be thoroughly
> instructed, and it shall indeed understand what was the rea-

son for its wayfaring, when it has entered into its rest, namely into the paradise which is its fatherland. Mystically catching sight of this, the prophet said: Return, my soul, to your rest, for the Lord has dealt bountifully with you. But in the meantime it wayfares and journeys on and goes by stages, and the reason for the use of this has been determined by the divine promises, as also the prophet says somewhere: I afflicted you, and I fed you with manna in the desert, because your fathers did not know, that what is in your heart might be made manifest. These, then, are the stages by which the journey is made from earth to heaven.[26]

The Fathers are full of references to the difficulties of this journey and to the miseries of the present life. This is a theme that Augustine sounds in particular. "What is it to be born other than to enter on a life of toil?"[27] "From the moment that a person has begun to live in this dying body death draws nearer to him. For in the whole course of this life (if in fact it can be called life) its mutability tends toward death. . . . This whole life is nothing but a race toward death, in which no one is allowed to stand still for a little while or to move more slowly."[28] "All this life of ours is a weakness, and a long life is nothing but a prolonged weakness."[29] According to Augustine, mutability is the curse of human existence: human beings are changeable and restless because nothing earthly can satisfy them, and with much change there comes a profound weariness.

Whatever you do, if you persevere in it you grow weary. If you were worn out by walking and continued to walk you would grow weary from that and die. So as not to grow weary from walking you rest yourself by sitting down. If you stay seated you die. A heavy sleep was oppressing you; you must stay awake lest you die. [Yet] you would die in staying awake unless you returned to sleep again. . . . Whatever you do is dangerous.[30]

This is to say nothing of sin, however, which was at the root of the hard human condition and continually making itself felt. Even if there may be some debate in contemporary theology as to what we mean when we speak of original sin, the Fathers' constant teaching on the absolute necessity of baptism, which was implicit in the practice of infant baptism and which reached a culmination in Augustine, leaves no doubt about their own perceptions. There was, moreover, an inclination to sin even after the saving washing, but this was differently emphasized in East and West. Only a Greek Father like Clement of Alexandria could have devoted a treatise to spiritual perfection in which the implication is that a life without sin is possible at least for a few in this world. The "gnostic," or perfect Christian, Clement writes, has gained mastery over himself and is never tempted, except by divine permission, and then only for the benefit of others.[31] His whole life is one of prayer and communion with God; he "lives in the spirit with those who are like him in the choirs of the holy ones, even though he is still detained on the earth."[32] Later Greek Fathers re-echo this idea, even if in other words. There is no denial of the reality of sin: in the pursuit of the spiritual life it is the greatest obstacle to be overcome, to be sure, and Clement's gnostic, for example, had to strive to set himself free from desire, for only the Lord was free from desire to begin with.[33] This is what the ascetic life, with all its pain and struggle, was about. But the possibility of overcoming the obstacle of sin existed, and once this had been accomplished the spiritual person found himself constantly growing in perfection. Such a person's present state of sanctity, Gregory of Nyssa maintains, "even if it seems to be great and exalted, is the beginning of something still greater and more exalted. . . . The greater and superior good always holds the attention of those who participate in it and does not allow them to look at the past. In those who are enjoying what is more excellent, the memory of what is inferior is wiped out."[34] For Gregory the very mutability of the human person, which is so painful a realization for Augustine and for others as well, indicates the possibility of perfection. Precisely because a being can change it can advance ever more closely to God.[35] Finally, from Anthony of Egypt we learn that perfection, or the virtuous life, although it requries the daily practice of asceticism, is in principle the simplest thing possible. It flows from human nature. "When you hear about virtue do not be afraid of it or treat it as a foreign word. For it is not distant from us. No, the thing is within us, and its accomplishment is easy if we only have the will for it."[36]

This typically Eastern view found no great counterpart in the West, particularly after Augustine's time. Whatever the reasons for the difference between Greeks and Latins may have been, it is certain that the Latin attitude toward human perfectibility was not so optimistic. Here we turn again to Augustine, for whom the question of the possibility of human sinlessness had been raised by the Pelagians, who held that Christians were capable of living sinless lives. Augustine deals with this in a number of places, and in one treatise he admits the possibility of a person's being without sin, "for if we denied the possibility we derogate both from the free will of the one who by his will desires it and from the power and mercy of God who by his help brings it about."[37] But it is another question as to whether anyone in fact can be found without sin. Augustine concludes from the Scriptures that no one, not even a day-old infant, is sinless, while the saints themselves must pray daily: "Forgive us our trespasses." This is the result not only of scriptural exegesis but also of observation. Augustine's pessimism becomes particularly clear in his answer to the question as to why people fall into sin when they have been given the possibility of not sinning: "Because they are unwilling. But if I am asked why they are unwilling . . . I might briefly say this much: they are unwilling to do what is right either because what is right is unknown to them or because it is unpleasant to them."[38] From this he goes on to speak of grace, and from there to predestination—all radicated in the mystery of God himself. Augustine, whose *Confessions* reveal a preoccupation with his own sinfulness, would simply not have accepted the gnostic sanctity of Clement of Alexandria or, indeed, any spiritual teaching that would imply that one could ever rise so high as to leave his sins in the dust below; certainly he would not have understood the self-confident "willing it" of Anthony of Egypt.

We would be missing, finally, a very important aspect of early Christian anthropology if we failed to take into account the influence attributed to demons in human life. This too was a result of the fall. So great was the demonic influence felt to be that Origen devotes a chapter of his work *On First Principles* to "how the devil and the opposing powers are, according to the Scriptures, at war with the human race." He expends much of his effort, however, on putting the demons' role into perspective. Some simple Christians think, Origen says, that the demons' powers are so overwhelming that they drive people into sin, and that if there were no demons there would be no sin. But this is not the case; sin arises from within, and the demons take advantage of our sinfulness and aggravate it, although they do in fact introduce some evil thoughts into our hearts as well.[39] In any event, we are not alone in the fight against the evil powers, since there are good spirits too who come to our aid. Here Origen recalls a passage from the second-century *Shepherd* of Hermas,[40] which speaks of two angels in the human person, one of righteousness and one of wickedness, each competing for his soul.[41]

It is in monastic and more especially in desert literature that we find the consciousness of the demonic influence raised to its highest pitch. Athanasius' *Life of Anthony* is virtually a treatise on demonology, and in it we are struck constantly by the conviction that the demons are ubiquitous and inescapable: "There is a great multitude in the air around us, and they are not far from us."[42] For chapter on chapter Anthony speaks of their powers of transformation, deception, vision, and their ability to confuse and terrify the souls of the unwary.

The fact that the most important theologians, men of the caliber of Origen and Athanasius and Augustine, spend pages on the demons indicates that belief in their power was not restricted to the superstitious or to unschooled monks; it was simply a datum of early Christianity that was accepted by all.

The Soul as the Image of God

These, then, were the liabilities of the human condition, which were radicated within the human person and in the unseen powers without. And sin, which was at the heart of all this, touched men and women not only as individuals but in society as well. The Fathers harped on avarice in particular, which cut the classes of society off from one another and caused the wealthy to forget that "the earth was made in common for all, rich and poor alike."[43] Melito of Sardis draws up a catalogue of social sin when he speaks of the fall and of the legacy that Adam bestowed on his descendants:

> Father lifted sword against son, and son laid hands on his father and impiously struck the breasts that nursed him, and brother killed brother, and guest and host acted unjustly toward one another, and friend murdered friend, and man slew man with tyrannous hand. Everyone on earth, therefore, became either a manslayer or a parricide or an infanticide or a fratricide.[44]

Nonetheless the Fathers' understanding of human life on earth was not unrelievedly bleak. Even Augustine, for all his undoubted pessimism, could write at length toward the end of *The City of God* on the blessings of human existence, after he had retailed its miseries. Among these blessings were the begetting of children, the mind's powers of invention and discovery, the beauty and utility of the human body, to say nothing of the remarkable qualities of irrational creation.[45] Augustine too writes most nobly of the joys of friendship and of the pleasure that a group of friends could take in one another's company.[46] It was a commonplace to list the divine gifts to humankind,[47] but of these gifts the supreme benefit, as Basil calls it, was that the human person was created in the image and likeness of God.[48]

Some of the Fathers, Clement of Alexandria and Origen, for example, make a distinction between image and likeness. The image of God is what is received at birth, while his likeness is something achieved by the effort of a lifetime. "The human person was given the dignity of the image in his first creation," Origen writes, "but the perfection of likeness is reserved for the consummation."[49] Gregory of Nyssa has a variation on this in which image and likeness appear as two aspects of the same reality. For him image is a static concept, and likeness is dynamic: "Likeness is the acquisition or progressive realization of the image; it is a striving for assimilation, a modeling of self according to the exigencies of the image, which God has deposited in us like some preliminary sketch."[50] A final instance of the different meanings attached to each term is from Filastrius, a fourth-century bishop of Brescia. He distinguishes between the two by saying that the image is simply the human soul, common to all—pagans, Jews, heretics and Christians alike—while the likeness has to do with faith and good works and is something in which only holy persons and Christians share.[51] Other Fathers, however, make no distinction whatsoever between the two words, and Cyril of Alexandria says rather bluntly that, if there is a difference, no one has been able to prove it to him.[52]

Whether speaking in terms of image and likeness or of image alone (we shall use the latter for the sake of convenience), the Fathers were almost unanimous in saying that it was in the soul that a resemblance to God was to be found. (But this view is nuanced considerably by the second-century Syrian Tatian, who, in contrast to others, held that it was not the soul pure and simple but rather the soul that was the temple of the Holy Spirit that was the image of God. Anything else was what Tatian called "mere humanity"—totally unlike God, and only differentiated from animality by the fact that humans could speak articulately and animals could not.[53]) Some of the Fathers would also try to take the body into account in a secondary sort of way, mentioning, for instance, the upright posture and the concomitant ability to gaze heavenward as imaging the divine, but this was never an important theme.[54] The body of itself could not, in any event, be the image of God. "Is flesh the image of God?" Ambrose asks, as if in disbelief. "Therefore there is earth in God, for the flesh is earth. Therefore God is bodily. Therefore, as flesh, he is frail and subject to the passions."[55] Rather it was in the soul's faculties of reason, freedom of choice and dominion, primarily, that the image was said to exist.

Reason was, for the Fathers, not what we usually mean it to be, namely a detached ability to think, which can easily descend into rationalism. It included not only thought but intuition, which is the reasoning of the heart, as well as understanding, judgment and an aptitude for the good. It was a participation in the Word of God himself, who was, as Justin Martyr expressed in the middle of the second century and as we have noted in the previous chapter, "the reason of which every race partakes."[56] This reason, in which perhaps most Fathers found the divine image, made human beings "partakers of the power of his

[God's] own Word, possessing, so to speak, a kind of reflection of his Word," as Athanasius says.[57] And, because for the Fathers reason was a participation in the Word, it possessed, unlike our "reason," a supernatural connotation: to be reasonable was to act in a graced way, to be open to the whole realm of the supernatural. Its exercise could never be considered a merely "natural" act.

A second characteristic of the soul as image of God was free will, which was stressed by other Fathers. This was often understood to be simply a part of reason—"the free movement of the rational soul."[58] More explicitly, as Gregory of Nyssa writes with respect to Adam,

> the human person was the image and likeness of that power which rules over all existing things. This is why he also possessed mastery over himself, as a likeness to him who exercises universal sovereignty. In no sense was he the slave of any external necessity. No, he made up his own mind about what was right, and by his own free will chose as he pleased, with the result that, to this very moment, the disaster he chose dominates the human race.[59]

The idea of free will is emphasized more among the Greeks than among the Latins, who tended often to think in terms of what hindered its exercise. And the notion of the human person, which we met earlier in Methodius of Olympus, as perfectly balanced between good and evil, capable of choosing the one or the other with equal facility, would have been quite unfamiliar to a Westerner before Augustine, and unthinkable after him. Then those who, like Cassian, did not always affirm the clear predominance of grace and the divine initiative over free will found themselves under suspicion.[60]

It was among the Antiochene Fathers that the idea of dominion over irrational creation as constituting an aspect of the image of the divine met with the most acceptance, although it was not unknown elsewhere. Diodore of Tarsus asks: "How, then, is a human being the image of God? By way of dominion, by way of authority."[61] John Chrysostom poses the same question: "What is this 'to our image and likeness'? He [God] speaks of an image of sovereignty, and just as no one is superior to God in heaven, so let no one be superior to the human being on earth."[62] Like reason and free will, dominion too existed only in a flawed state. This explained the human's fear of wild beasts. Nevertheless there were exceptional persons in whom this lordship not only over domestic but even over wild animals had at least been temporarily restored. There are examples of this aplenty in the lives of the monks of the desert, many of whom, we are told, possessed not only the power to command animals of all sorts but even experienced a remarkable sympathy with them.[63]

It was Augustine who, more than anyone else, plumbed the depths of what the divine image in the human person meant. His insight, which does not fall precisely into any of the above categories, was that the faculties of the soul—memory, understanding and will, or love—mirrored the three Persons of the Trinity. This is indeed the supreme moment in patristic speculation on the image of God in human creation. The inner memory of the mind by which it remembers itself and is present to itself is analogous to the Father; the inner understanding by which it understands itself and in a way expresses itself is analogous to the Son; and the inner will by which it loves itself, thus binding together memory and understanding, is analogous to the Spirit. These three faculties, always together, and having always been together since they began to be at all, whether we were aware of them or not, Augustine writes—"if we discern this, we discern a trinity; this is not God himself, to be sure, but it is already an image of God."[64]

Depending on how they conceived of the divine image in other respects, the Fathers held either that it could be obliterated on account of sin, or that sin would only obscure it. In the former case, of course, it was a question of a complete recovery. The possibility of a total obliteration of the image was the view of a minority, however. In the latter case, though, it was a matter of restoration, often spoken of in terms of the refurbishing of a work of art that had been overlaid with filth.[65] And to the extent that the image of God was obliterated or obscured in a person, to that extent one might say that he bore in himself the image of the devil, as Ambrose, for example, suggests.[66]

Creature at once of splendor and of tragedy, the human being was, in the words of Gregory Nazianzen, "small and great, humble and exalted, mortal and immortal, earthly and heavenly, having some things in common with the lower world and others with God, sharing some things with the flesh and others with the spirit." He continues by remarking that that restoration of the image of which we stood in need could only have come about through Christ's incarnation.[67] The human condition, then, demanded the coming of Christ, and we cannot continue to speak of that condition apart from the mystery of the incarnation.

V

Christ

There is an interesting passage in Tertullian's treatise *On the Resurrection of the Flesh* that speaks of the creation of the first parents with reference to the foreseen incarnation of Christ:

> Now a great thing was taking place when this matter [human flesh] was being constructed. It is honored as often as it feels the hands of God, as often as it is touched and pulled and drawn out and fashioned. Think of God as totally occupied with and given over to this—with hand, perception, labor, counsel, wisdom, providence and, above all, with love itself, which produced its features. For although it was clay that was being molded, it was Christ who was in mind as the one who was to become man, because the Word was to be both clay and flesh, just as the earth was at that time. For thus had the Father spoken to the Son: Let us make man according to our own image and likeness. And God made man. What he fashioned, therefore, he made to the image of God, that is, to the image of Christ.[1]

These words, which echo something that was written by Irenaeus more than a generation earlier,[2] at least suggest that the incarnation would have occurred even if the first parents had not sinned. Adam and Eve, created in innocence, were fashioned according to the form of the Christ who was to have come as a consequence of their creation rather than as a consequence of the transgression of the commandment that in fact took place.

The more common view, however, restricts itself to a narrower reading of the scriptural data. According to this view, the Word was made flesh precisely because of human sinfulness, and in the context of this view there is no speculation as to whether the incarnation would have happened had the transgression not been committed. As Athanasius speaks of this in his great treatise on the incarnation, there was a certain inevitability, given the sin of the first parents, about the Word taking upon himself the human condition. On the one hand, God's plan would have been destroyed if he had permitted the dissolution of the humanity that he had created, although this would have been the just punishment of the primordial sin. It would have been unseemly for such a dissolution to have transpired, as this would have appeared to convict the Creator of powerlessness in the face of sin. On the other hand, however, it was necessary that God be consistent with the law that he himself had established, namely that death and dissolution were to be the punishment for sin. Mere repentance could not satisfy the demands of that law, nor could repentance save human beings from the corruption of sin that had touched them at the core of their existence. This being the case, only the Word, who had brought humankind out of nothing in the first place, could call it back from death and annihilation. By the same token, only the Word, by taking on mortal flesh, could suffer on behalf of his creation and so fulfill the divine law that required punishment for the transgression.[3]

> Thus, therefore, taking from our own [bodies] one that was similar, because all were subject to the corruption of death, he surrendered it to death on behalf of all, giving it over to the Father. He did this with loving-kindness so that, when all had died in him, the law of corruption that had affected human beings might be abolished, and when its power had been exhausted in the Lord's body it should thenceforth have no more occasion against other human beings like him. And having brought human beings back from corruption, he returned them incorrupt once again and called them back from death to life by the body that he had taken to himself and by the grace of the resurrection—making death disappear from them like straw before fire.[4]

Sin, then, was the reason for the incarnation of the Word. This is the point made so succinctly and powerfully by the unknown late fourth- or fifth-century composer of the *Exsultet*, when he speaks paradoxically of the original sin as the "happy fault, which merited such and so great a redeemer." It is in this light that virtually all of ancient Christology must be understood—that Christ's coming and what he accomplished in the flesh were for the sake of saving human beings from the consequences of sin.

Orthodox and Unorthodox Christologies

The demands imposed by the mystery of salvation or redemption gave urgency to the task of understanding how it was that Christ was uniquely fitted to be the Savior. That Christ was indeed the Savior was a fact challenged, it would seem, not even by the unorthodox. The difference between them and orthodox Christians consisted rather in how each group saw him as capable of effecting salvation, and this was in turn rooted in their respective views concerning his constitution. That is to say, how, if at all, was Christ both God and man?

It would seem that there are six classic unorthodox responses to this question. The first of these, and perhaps the most ancient, is docetism. The gist of this view was that Christ only appeared to have a body and hence that he only appeared to be human. Ignatius of Antioch refers to docetists at the beginning of the second century as "atheists" who say that Christ's suffering was a mere semblance.[5] A second such heresy was adoptionism, also very ancient, which asserted that Christ was not the natural Son of God but rather a man who had been adopted by him, this act of adoption usually said to have taken place at Jesus' baptism in the Jordan. Third, there was Arianism, which has already been mentioned several times in these pages. The Arian position was fundamentally that Christ was a creature, although a creature somehow divine; in this it resembled adoptionism. Apollinarianism, a late fourth-century heresy named after Apollinaris of Laodicea, who was a fervent opponent of Arianism, held that Christ was both human and divine, but with the Word itself taking the place of Christ's human soul or mind. The reason for this was so that Christ would be without the mutability and tendency to sin that Apollinaris associated with the human mind or soul, as he explained in a letter to a synod of bishops: "The Word himself has become flesh without having taken on the human mind, a mind changeable and enslaved to filthy thoughts, but existing as a divine mind, unchangeable and heavenly."[6] Then there was Nestorianism, so called after an early fifth-century bishop of Constantinople, which effectively separated Christ's humanity and divinity into two distinct persons by tending to deny anything other than a merely moral union between them. Finally there was monophysitism, taken from the Greek term for one nature, which spoke of Christ's humanity, although real, as a property absorbed by his divinity—"like the sea receiving a drop of honey, for as soon as the drop has been mixed with the water of the sea it vanishes."[7]

Two things are common to these otherwise relatively disparate conceptions of Christ. The first is something that may in fact be observed of any heterodox tendency, namely the willingness to push a single aspect of a given mystery to its logical extreme, with the result that other aspects lose their rightful place or disappear entirely. This is evident in the six ways of thinking about Christ that have just been cited. In each of them either Christ's humanity or divinity, or the unity or duality of his make-up, has been overemphasized. The upshot of this process is a kind of rationalization of the mystery in question, which then empties it of its content. The Fathers, by and large, tried to hold onto all the facets of a given mystery, although they themselves did not always succeed entirely. Perhaps, indeed, it is impossible to succeed entirely, mystery being what it is. It seems evident that, on the whole, ancient orthodox thought was somewhat more at home, so to say, with Christ's divinity than with his humanity. Maybe this is due exclusively to the fact that Arian and other attacks on his divinity forced orthodox thought to stress this aspect of his constitution, Arianism having been regarded as far more dangerous than, for example, monophysitism. Maybe, on the other hand, this stress on the divinity of Christ also represented a deep-seated instinct about how best to understand Christ; it undoubtedly reflected certain demands of popular piety. It definitely comes as a shock, in any event, to read in Tertullian's treatise *On the Flesh of Christ* about specific aspects of Christ's humanity, particularly his birth.[8] His graphic language does not strike us as typical of the Fathers.

Yet in a number of places we can see an admirable balance established between Christ's humanity and divinity. This is the case, for instance, with the great confession of faith that was subscribed to at the Council of Chalcedon in 451. This represents a high point in ancient Christology, and it replies to each of the heresies already mentioned in at least an implicit manner.

> Therefore, following the holy Fathers, we all with one voice teach that our Lord Jesus Christ is one and the same Son, the same perfect in divinity, the same perfect in humanity, truly God and truly man, the same consisting of a reasonable soul and a body, consubstantial with the Father according to divinity, the same consubstantial with us according to humanity, like us in all things except sin; begotten of the Father before the ages according to divinity, but the same for us in the last days, born for us and for our salvation from the Virgin Mary, the God-bearer, according to humanity; one and the same Christ, Son, Lord, only-begotten, in two natures, without confusion, without change, without division, without separation, the distinction of natures being in no way abolished because of the union, but rather the characteristic property of each nature being preserved, and concurring in one person and one subsistence, not as if Christ were parted or divided into two persons, but one and the same Son and only-begotten God, Word, Lord, Jesus Christ, just as the prophets of old spoke concerning him, and our Lord Jesus Christ instructed us, and the creed of the Fathers has handed down to us.

The second common point has already been suggested. It is that the heresies that have been catalogued were, at least in part, assertions about how Christ could save the human race. Overemphasis on the divinity to the detriment of the humanity (as in the case of docetism, Apollinarianism and monophysitism) indicated a presupposition that it was precisely God who could save, and that the presence of humanity in Christ, to whatever degree, could be an intrusion and even a drawback in this respect. Overemphasis on the humanity to the detriment of the divinity (as in the case of adoptionism, Arianism and, effectively, Nestorianism) indicated, by the same token, a presupposition that the divinity detracted from Christ's solidarity with us and thus reduced or nullified his power to save.[9]

The orthodox insisted upon both a complete humanity and a complete divinity because they saw this as the only way to preserve the very values that the heterodox themselves wanted to preserve. It was necessary that Christ be human and share in every aspect of human nature except sin because, as Gregory Nazianzen explains in a justly celebrated formula directed against the Apollinarians, "that which has not been assumed [by Christ] has not been healed, but what is united to the divinity is also saved. If only half of Adam fell, then let what is assumed be half also. But if the whole Adam fell, he must be united to the whole of him who was begotten, and so be saved as a whole."[10] If Christ's humanity is simply an appearance, Ignatius suggests in one of his letters, then human life has no real meaning.[11] Likewise it was necessary that the Savior be divine because, as Athanasius writes in his work on the incarnation, "being Word of the Father, and over all things, it followed that he alone was able to re-create everything, to suffer on behalf of all and to intercede for all with the Father."[12]

It is Cyril of Alexandria, in the first third of the fifth century, who is the great theologian of the union of the two aspects, human and divine, in Christ. Cyril's contemporary Nestorius had separated them for the very purpose of maintaining each in an unconfused way, so that in his humanity Christ would be solid with us and able to help us in our struggle, while in his divinity he would be untouched by that struggle. In his writings against Nestorius Cyril shows the dangers that beset the possibility of salvation if such a separation is posited. For human nature alone, he insists, cannot abolish death or preserve from destruction. It must form a unit with the Word for it to have any saving efficacy.[13]

One of the themes that have been sounded in the previous few lines, namely the solidarity of the divine Word with humanity for the sake of salvation, is important throughout patristic thought. It is the theme that Irenaeus in particular pursues toward the end of the second century in his theology of recapitulation, or *anakephalaiosis*. For Irenaeus, drawing on the insight of Paul in Romans 5:14, Jesus is the new Adam. As the old Adam did, so too the new Adam sums up the entire human race in himself:

> Christ Jesus our Lord came in fulfillment of the divine economy and he recapitulates all things in himself. In everything the human being is the handiwork of God; thus he has recapitulated the human being in himself: he was invisible and became visible, incomprehensible and became comprehensible, incapable of suffering and became subject to suffering, the Word and became a man, recapitulating all things in himself.[14]

Elsewhere Irenaeus explains that the genealogy in Luke, which stretches back from Jesus to Adam, is intended to demonstrate that "he has recapitulated in himself all the dispersed nations that descended from Adam, and all tongues and generations, as well as Adam himself."[15] More than that, Jesus passed through each stage of life, from infancy to old age, in order to sanctify and save it:

> He came to save all through himself—all, that is, who through him are reborn to God: infants, children, boys, youths and old people. Therefore he passed through each age, becoming an infant for infants, sanctifying infancy; a child among children, sanctifying those of this age and, at the same time, setting an example of filial affection, of righteousness and obedience; a young man among the young, becoming an example to them and sanctifying them to the Lord. So also he was an old man among the old, that he might be a perfect teacher in all things, not merely with regard to revelation of the truth but also with regard to this age, sanctifying the old and becoming an example to them as well. And thus he came even to death, that he might be the first-born among the dead, having pre-eminence in all things, the prince of life, the first of all and the one who goes before all.[16]

Implicit in this theology of solidarity, which Irenaeus of all the Fathers expresses most strikingly, is the notion of a certain dynamism associated with the person of Christ. For Irenaeus, for example, it is sufficient for Christ to have taken upon himself a particular aspect of the human condition for that aspect to be redeemed. The logical conclusion of this view was that all that Jesus accomplished, no matter how apparently insignificant, had salvific effects. "Everything that Jesus does," writes Jerome in explaining why Mark 11:7 found it necessary to record that Jesus rode on an ass, "is a sacrament. He is our salvation. For if the apostle tells us: Whether you eat or drink or whatever else you do, do all things in the name of the Lord—are not these much more our sacraments, when the Savior walks or sits or eats or sleeps?"[17] This dynamism even extended to his clothing, as Hilary says in commenting on the story of the healing of the woman with the flow of blood in Matthew 9:20-22: "The power abiding in his body added a health-giving quality to perishable things, and a divine efficacy even went as far as the fringes of his garments. For God was not divisible and able to be contained, as if he could be shut up in a body."[18] Finally, a very oft-cited instance of the power that radiated from Christ is associated with his baptism in the Jordan. Jesus' mere contact with the Jordan was sufficient to cleanse it and, along with it, all the waters of the earth, so as to make them suitable in turn for cleansing those who would be baptized. This is an idea that appeared already at the beginning of the second century in Ignatius of Antioch[19] and that was canonized by frequent use.

Nowhere is Christ's dynamism more evident, however, than in his suffering, death and resurrection. In his *Great Catechism* Gregory of Nyssa explains that, in order for him to have saved humanity, Christ's life had to have been bounded by the same two extremities that constitute boundaries for each human life—a beginning and an end. In words reminiscent of Irenaeus he writes: "The power amending our nature had to reach to both points. It had to touch the beginning and extend to the end, covering all that lies between."[20] So Christ had not only to be born but to die as well, and against those who object that the transcendent nature should never have experienced death he continues:

> Having in mind to share in our human condition, he had to undergo all that is characteristic of human existence. Human life is bounded at either end. Passing through only one of these boundaries would have left his purpose only partially achieved, for he would not have attained the other boundary. Yet it is possible that a person well-schooled in our faith might claim, on better grounds, that his birth was not a cause of his dying but rather that he accepted birth in order to experience death. The possessor of unending life could not have accepted bodily birth out of a need for life, but to summon us from death to life. No part of our humanity was without need of being delivered from death. For this reason, as one would lay a hand upon someone who was asleep, he stooped down to our lifeless body. So close did he come to death that he was touched by it himself and through his own body provided human nature with the principle of the resurrection, by his power raising the whole of humanity together with him. From no source other than the lump of our humanity did there derive the flesh that was to receive God and that was exalted together with the divine through the resurrection. Look to our own bodies: the activity of one of our senses is perceived throughout the whole body that is united to it. In the same way, inasmuch as our human nature constitutes a sort of unitary living body, the resurrection of one single part passes into the whole. The continuity and unity of our nature permits the part to communicate with the whole. What aspect of our religious doctrine is outside the realm of probability if he who stands upright stoops down to raise up the fallen or the slumbering?[21]

At this second boundary or extremity of Christ's life the cross has immense significance. It is both ineluctable fact and symbol so rich that its meaning could hardly be exhausted. Athanasius devotes considerable effort to explaining why crucifixion was the most appropriate manner for Christ to have died, rather than, for example, a death from sickness or beheading. Christ chose this most ignominious of executions to show that he was truly the Lord of life and equal to any suffering that death could devise. It was thus that he bore the curse for our sake, which Deuteronomy 21:23 had prophesied of him when it called accursed anyone who hung upon a tree. With his arms stretched out Jesus embraced both Jews and Gentiles, uniting both to himself; and, thrust aloft into the atmosphere, he purified the air of the demons who made that element their inhabitation.[22]

For an anonymous Greek homilist of the third century the cross is a kind of cosmic tree, which supplants the old tree of Eden. The image is so remarkable that it bears being reproduced in its entirety.

> This tree is my everlasting salvation. It is my food, a shared banquet. Its roots and the spread of its branches are my own roots and extension. In its shade, as in a breeze, I luxuriate and am cared for. Its shade I take for my resting place; in my flight from oppressive heat it is a source of refreshing dew for me. Its blossoms are my own, my utter delight its fruits, saved from the beginning for my harvest. Food for my hunger and well-spring for my thirst, it is also a covering for my nakedness, with the spirit of life as its leaves. Far from me henceforth the fig leaves! Fearful of God, I find it a place of safety; when unsteady, a source of stability. In the face of a struggle I look to it as a prize; in victory, my trophy. It is the narrow path, the restricted road. It is Jacob's ladder, the passage of angels, at whose summit the Lord is affixed. This tree, the plant of immortality, rears from earth to reach as high as heaven, fixing the Lord between heaven and earth. It is the foundation and stabilizer of the universe, undergirding the world that we inhabit. It is the binding force of the world and holds together all the varieties that human life encompasses. It is riveted into a unity by the invisible bonds of the Spirit, so that its connection with God can never be severed. Brushing heaven with its uppermost branches, it remains fixed in the earth and, between the two points, its huge hands completely enfold the stirring of the air. As a single whole it penetrates all things and all places.[23]

To such a degree does the cross participate in the work of salvation that one could almost understand this passage to be speaking of Christ himself. And indeed the cross primarily symbolizes Christ—both the suffering God-man, of course, and the

Word who sustains the universe. "Hail to you, O cross, you who hold the cosmos together as far as its outermost boundaries!" as another anonymous early Greek author depicts the apostle Andrew greeting the cross that was to be his own instrument of execution.[24]

It goes without saying that all of this is in keeping with the cross' form, which is archetypal. Justin Martyr, earliest of the Fathers to discuss its symbolism at any length (along with the unknown author of the so-called *Epistle of Barnabas*), poses the question to the readers of his first *Apology:* "Observe all the things that exist in the world and see whether they could be used or go on existing without this figure [of the cross]." He continues by demonstrating that the shape of the cross is ubiquitous and indispensable: it constitutes the essential design of masts and plows, of the human body and even the human face.[25]

The mystery of the cross also offered the opportunity to speak of Christ in terms at once more human and more heroic. Thus for the late fourth- and early fifth-century Maximus of Turin, as for a number of other Fathers, Jesus nailed to the cross may be compared to Ulysses tied to the mast of his ship to avoid being allured by the Sirens' song. Since Jesus has successfully avoided shipwreck by this means, passing through the world unscathed by its cruel delights, it is possible for the whole human race to do the same.[26]

Our Dynamic Union with Christ

So it is that the Word united himself to humankind for its salvation by an act that culminated in his crucifixion. But this represents only one part of the mystery of Christ and of salvation. The other part is that humankind should in its turn be united to him, and particularly to his death and resurrection. This union with Christ or conformation to him is accomplished first of all in a sacramental way in baptism. Fellowship with Christ in his suffering, death and resurrection is in fact the primary effect of baptism, according to Cyril of Jerusalem, and not simply remission of sins or the grace of adoption as children of God.[27] The theme is a commonplace. "Be crucified yourself through your baptism," John Chrysostom says in a homily, " . . . for baptism is a cross and a death."[28] And he goes on to give the familiar citations from the Scriptures that support this statement, concluding by pointing out that baptism is of course not only a death and burial but a resurrection as well: "Only wait a little while and you shall see youself sharing in his benefits. For if we have died with him, says blessed Paul, we believe that we shall also live together with him. For in baptism there are both death and resurrection at the same time."[29]

Union with Christ and conformation to him are also effected in the Eucharist. "In the figure of bread his body is given to you," Cyril of Jerusalem tells those who have just been baptized,

> and in the figure of wine his blood is given to you, so that by partaking of the body and blood of Christ you may be one body and one blood with him. For thus also we become bearers of Christ, because his body and blood are distributed throughout our members. Thus, according to the blessed Peter, we become partakers of the divine nature.[30]

There is a passage in a treatise by Fulgentius, sixth-century bishop of Ruspe in North Africa, which is still more explicit in its emphasis on eucharistic conformity to Christ. Fulgentius recalls that the Eucharist is offered to proclaim the Lord's death and that those who partake of it pray that, strengthened by the gift of love that they have received, they might imitate Christ's death and die to sin and live to God.

> Indeed, this participation in the body and blood of the Lord, when we eat the bread and drink the cup, teaches us that we should die to the world and have our life hidden with Christ in God, that we should crucify our flesh with its vices and wicked desires. Thus it happens that all the faithful, who love God and their neighbor, drink of the cup of the Lord's love even if they do not drink of the cup of his bodily suffering. And when they have become inebriated with it they have put to death their members that are upon the earth and, having clothed themselves with the Lord Jesus Christ, they pay no heed to the desires of the flesh. . . . The gift of love

confers this upon us, that we should in fact be what we celebrate mystically in the sacrifice.[31]

There is an interesting passage from Irenaeus in which he
depicts the cross not only as the support and mainstay of the
universe, which is an image that we have already seen, but as
the universe itself, its four ends representing the four extremes
of the cosmos. Because the Word "in his invisible form pervades
us universally in the whole world, and encompasses both its
length and breadth and height and depth . . . the Son of God was
also crucified in these, imprinted in the form of a cross in the
universe."[32] Thus nature too, as well as human creation, is conformed to the cross. The homilists show that as nature participated in the cross, so it also participated in the resurrection. One
of the anonymous early Greek authors previously cited, reflecting a significant tradition, speaks of the complete sympathy with
which irrational creation followed the course of Christ's agony
and victory: stars fell from heaven, the light of the sun was extin-
guished, the earth's rocks were rent. "As the whole universe
trembled and quaked with fear, and everything was in a state of
agitation, the divine Spirit rose again and the universe was given
life, strengthened and returned to its stability."[33] "All the elements, then, glory in the resurrection of Christ," says Maximus
of Turin to his congregation. "I think that the sun itself is
unusually brighter on this day, for it must be that the sun should
rejoice in the resurrection of the one at whose suffering it had
lamented."[34]

Thus the passion and resurrection of Christ, mysteriously
imprinted upon the face of the universe, transcend space and tra-
verse the boundary from rational to irrational creation. But the
passion in particular also transcends time and stretches back into
history. That it and its effects have a retrospective quality is in
fact one of the deepest meanings of the doctrine of the descent
into hell, which was a teaching especially dear to the Eastern
Church, although certainly not unknown in the West either.
According to one ancient homily of uncertain date, Christ carries
his cross and shows his wounds when he enters hell in order to
free Adam and Eve and their descendants. His cross and wounds
cancel the primordial sin.[35] In a poem by the sixth-century

Romanos the Melodist, the author has the demons cry out in despair as the cross, symbol of the victorious Christ, brings salvation to the men and women of the Old Testament who had been held captive by them:

> Oh, how could we not remember the types of this wood! For they were already shown us long ago, on many occasions, in many forms, in those who were saved and in those who were lost. It was by wood that Noah was saved, but the whole world perished unbelieving. Moses, grasping his staff like a scepter, was glorified by it, but Egypt drowned, having fallen into plagues by it as if into deep waters. What it has just accomplished, the cross already showed us long ago in figure. How then can we not weep! Adam is returning to paradise.[36]

The Fathers, beginning with the so-called Pseudo-Barnabas sometime in the first decades of the second century,[37] found the Old Testament filled with images of the cross and types of the suffering Christ—tokens of this retrospection.

And the passion stretched forward into the future, in baptism, in the Eucharist, and in suffering too. In fact all suffering in whatever age was drawn up into Christ's suffering and made his own in mysterious fashion. "From the beginning of the world Christ suffers in all his own," writes the late fourth-century Paulinus of Nola, "for he is the beginning and the end, who is veiled in the law and revealed in the Gospel, a Lord ever wonderful and suffering and triumphant in his saints." He continues by taking up a theme that is very familiar in the ancient Church:

> In Abel he was killed by his brother, in Noah he was mocked by his son, in Abraham he left his homeland, in Isaac he was sacrificed, in Jacob he was a servant, in Joseph he was sold, in Moses he was exposed and made to flee, in the prophets he was stoned and lacerated, in his apostles he was cast about on land and sea, and on the many different crosses of the blessed martyrs he was often killed. So too now he also bears our weaknesses and our sickness, for he is the man who has always been set in the snare for us and who knows how to bear the weakness that we cannot and know not how

to endure without him. He, I say, now also carries about the world for us and in us, that he may destroy it by bearing it, and may perfect strength in weakness.[38]

Perhaps the most striking and prevalent characteristic of this dynamic understanding of Christ, which finds a kind of culmination in his suffering and death, is that of transformation. The Fathers refer innumerable times to the incarnation in terms of 2 Corinthians 8:9: "For you know the grace of our Lord Jesus Christ, that though he was rich, yet for your sake he became poor, so that by his poverty you might become rich." If in some cases he had to be exactly like those whom he was sent to save, nonetheless in others he had to be unlike them. Thus, as Augustine says, he had to be born of a woman because we fell through the woman Eve, and he had to be a human being who could die because we are that as well. On the other hand, however, he had to be a model of humility because we fell through pride, and he had to be foolish because we had been beguiled through the wisdom of the serpent.[39] He took on the opposite of everything that was naturally desirable in the human condition, then, in order to transform our ills into their opposites. Augustine follows this line of thinking again in some remarkable lines in one of his sermons. Commenting on Isaiah 53:2 ("He had no form or comeliness that we should look at him, and no beauty that we should desire him"), he tells his congregation:

> The deformity of Christ forms you. For if he had not wished to be deformed you would not have received back the form that you lost. Therefore he hung deformed upon the cross, but his deformity was our beauty. So let us in this life hold onto the deformed Christ. What is this deformed Christ? Far be it from me to glory, except in the cross of our Lord Jesus Christ. This is the deformity of Christ.[40]

In similar fashion Ambrose, explaining that the name Maria means bitterness, writes: "Thus the Lord came into the bitterness of human frailty [namely into Mary's womb], so that the bitterness of this condition might be tempered and sweetened by the delightfulness and grace of the heavenly Word."[41] Elsewhere in

Ambrose the theme is alluded to in a way typical of many Fathers:

> Jesus is worn out by journeying in order to refresh the weary. He seeks for something to drink, he who will provide a spiritual drink for the thirsty. He hungers, he who will give a saving food to the hungry. He dies, he who will live. He is buried, he who will rise from the dead. He hangs upon the dread wood, he who will strengthen those in dread.[42]

The conception is well known in the East too, and Gregory Nazianzen concludes one of his *Theological Orations* with dozens of such antitheses, which include virtually every aspect of Christ's life.[43]

It seems natural that this Christ-dynamism, so to say, of the early Church should have developed a Christ-mysticism whose highest expression was martyrdom, the supreme conformation to Christ. We need only read some of the earliest narratives of the martyrs to see how closely they followed Christ not only in his suffering but in his glory as well. The classic example of this is the mid-second-century *Martyrdom of Polycarp*, in which Polycarp's suffering and death are pictured as a remarkable reduplication of Christ's own passion. By the same token, to the extent that this dynamism was not present, we have some reason to believe that the impetus for martyrdom was missing too. The fourth-century bishop Filastrius of Brescia, for instance, notes that some of the docetists—who held, as we have seen, that Christ had no human body at all but only the semblance of one, and who also said that Simon of Cyrene was actually crucified in his place by a sort of cruel divine ruse—taught that no one should undergo martyrdom for the name of Christ. They would tell those who were thinking of submitting to the authorities: "You do not know what you are doing, for Christ did not suffer, nor was he crucified. How are you able, then, to confess the crucified one when he was not crucified?"[44]

The Birth of Christ and the Role of Mary

In a passage that was cited earlier, Gregory of Nyssa remarked that Christ's birth was not the cause of his dying but rather that he accepted birth for the sake of the death that was to come. Gregory's thrust is borne out in patristic thought in general: the birth of Christ occupies a relatively secondary place in the consciousness of the ancient Church. Indeed, there seems to have been no liturgical celebration of the nativity until sometime in the fourth century, when it arose presumably in the context of the Christological controversy that Arianism had sparked. (Easter, on the other hand, was certainly observed in the second half of the second century, and most likely even much earlier than that.) In this context it was the mystery or deeper meaning of the incarnation that counted; a tender dwelling on the infancy or childhood of Christ, while not completely unknown, was not really in the Fathers' style.

A sermon of Gregory Nazianzen on the celebration of the birth of Christ, for instance, offers the preacher an opportunity to talk about the divine nature, creation and the fall. With the exception of the very first phrases and some words toward the end, which mention a few elements of the traditional Christmas narrative, one almost has the impression that this is an Easter homily, so frequent are paschal allusions.[45] The Christmas sermons of Augustine are shot through with the paradox of the Word become flesh, as in lines such as these: "Before he was made, he was; and because he was all-powerful he was able to be made, while remaining what he was. He made for himself a mother while he was with the Father, and although he was made from a mother, he remained in the Father."[46] For Augustine the feast of Christmas provides an occasion to speak of the union of the human and divine in Christ that was effected for our salvation. The same is true of the sermons preached by Leo the Great in the middle of the fifth century, which are perhaps the most famous of all patristic Christmas homilies.

Understandably it is in connection with the birth of Christ that, as a rule, reflection on his mother Mary occurs. But there are exceptions; one such is the tragic drama attributed to Gregory Nazianzen and entitled *The Passion of Christ*, in which Mary, who sees her son to his death, plays the most prominent role.[47]

One of the earliest and certainly the most renowned of all Marian patristic themes is the Eve-Mary parallel, which is complementary to the Adam-Christ parallel drawn by Paul in

Romans 5:12-21. Its best known exponent is Irenaeus, who relates it squarely to the event of the annunciation: as Eve was deceived by the devil, so Mary heard the truth through an angel; as Eve disobeyed God, so Mary obeyed his word. Thus the human race that had been enslaved because of the virgin Eve is released from slavery because of the Virgin Mary.[48] Syrian writers extend the parallel further by introducing the unusual idea, which would eventually be taken up in medieval imagery, that Mary conceived Jesus through her ear. "By means of the serpent," says Ephrem in a verse homily on the nativity, "the evil one poured out his poison in the ear of Eve; the good one brought low his mercy and entered through Mary's ear: through the gate by which death entered, life also entered, putting death to death."[49]

Mary's virginity, which the Church maintained from the beginning, was an object of veneration and even awe. Ignatius ranks it with Christ's birth and death as one of three mysteries of singular importance.[50] According to Gregory of Nyssa and others who follow him, the birth of Christ may be likened to the phenomenon of the burning bush in Exodus 3:2. Just as the bush burned and yet was not destroyed, so also Mary brought forth her son without damaging her virginity.[51] With the increasing glorification of virginity toward the end of the fourth century, Mary's own virginity becomes paradigmatic, and as a result she begins to develop into a person of some significance in her own right.[52] When she is defined to be the Theotokos or God-bearer at the Council of Ephesus in 431—against the Nestorians, who had denied her this title—the trend continues even more. This seems particularly evident in the writings and sermons of some of the later Eastern Fathers such as John Damascene, who concludes the patristic era. In them it is possible now to find sermons on the birth of Mary and on her assumption, for example, in which the references to Christ are no longer central.

Christ-Symbols and Christ Devotion

In order to round out the early Church's view of Christ in the brief space at our disposal it is necessary to touch upon two areas that might easily be neglected. They are the symbolism of Christ and devotion to Christ.

As early as the beginning of the second century, in the so-called *Epistle to Diognetus*, we can see a list of titles that are to be used with respect to Christ: "nurse, father, teacher, counselor, physician, mind, light, honor, glory, strength, life."[53] Another such catalogue, slightly shorter, is to be found some years later in Justin's *Dialogue with Trypho;* here Christ is called wisdom, day, east, sword, stone, rod, Jacob and Israel.[54] The bulk of the first book of Origen's monumental commentary on the Gospel of John is devoted to the enumeration and explanation of the Christological titles that are scattered throughout the Scriptures,[55] and the conclusion of the second of Gregory Nazianzen's two great discourses on Christ is given over to much the same thing.[56] Finally, by way of example, there is a poem of Damasus of Rome, written in the last third of the fourth century, which is nothing else than a collection of names for Christ:

> Hope, life, health, reason, wisdom, light, judge, gate, giant, king, jewel, prophet, priest, messiah, sabbath, rabbi, spouse, mediator, sprout, pillar, hand, rock, son, Emmanuel, vineyard, shepherd, sheep, peace, root, vine, olive, fountain, wall, lamb, calf, lion, reconciler, word, man, net, stone, house, everything, Christ, Jesus![57]

We would do wrong to dismiss these titles as "mere" metaphors. It seems obvious that they had some profound meaning for the ancient Church, which was accustomed to taking such symbols with the same seriousness that other ages have taken what appears to be more logical discourse. They could form part of the substance of theological treatises as well as of homilies and poetry. Names are not merely arbitrary, having no intrinsic relation to the objects that they indicate; they have a mysterious content, remarks Origen,[58] and Gregory Nazianzen echoes him.[59] With this in mind we shall look somewhat closely at three more or less typical Christological titles, with the intention of drawing from them some of the richness with which they were endowed by the early Christians.

The first of these is "the east." To the ancients the East was sacred on account of the rising sun and hence on account of the light itself. With this title, then, are connected sun, light, day, dawn and similar concepts, and ultimately even life, which is of course inextricably related to the sun, and resurrection, of which the sun rising in the East is one of the most apt symbols. As the East was the place of the sun's birth, its *oriens*, it also suggested the idea of birth. Moreover, in ancient thought, pagan as well as Judaeo-Christian, the East was the site of the earthly paradise, which evokes the concepts of renewal, harmony and repose. The significance of the image may be appreciated still more when it is contrasted with that of the West, which is the region of sunset and thus of the darkness symbolic of evil, death and Satan. The East, its antithesis, must be simply good.

Consequently, when Christ is referred to as "the east," as he is in Justin's *Dialogue with Trypho* and elsewhere, these associations crowd around that reference. Along with perhaps more obvious sentiments, it also evokes a certain longing or nostalgia, for the East, like the paradise that was located there, is a symbol of the desirable but difficult to attain goal of life. Much if not all of this must have come to mind when, in a dramatic gesture in the ancient baptismal rite, the person about to be baptized renounced Satan by turning from West to East. "For the one who renounces the devil turns to Christ," Ambrose says, "and sees him face to face."[60]

A second such title is "physician." With this the associations are perhaps more manifest. The physician is health-bringer and preserver of life and, for that reason, savior as well. The god Asclepios, whose cult enjoyed tremendous popularity at the very beginning of the Christian era, fulfilled both healing and salvific functions, and it seems likely that Christ's own healing powers were emphasized in contrast to his. The title is of course particularly appropriate when sin is understood in terms of disease. Here the remedy that Christ offers is his own life, adapted in its various aspects to our needs, and thus he is "himself the physician, himself the medicine."[61] Or, again, the remedy is the Eucharist, which Ignatius refers to in striking fashion as "the medicine of immortality, the antidote against death."[62] Or, finally, it may be the sentiments that he sends us, some soothing and some painful, but all curative, just as medicines usually are.[63]

"Teacher" will serve as the third example to cast some light on the content of Christological imagery. This was a title especially dear to the theologians of the Alexandrian tradition, who often conceived of the whole course of human life as a period of instruction. Clement of Alexandria, in fact, composed a treatise entitled *Paidagogos* or *The Instructor*, in which Christ appears as the instructor for every detail of human conduct, even including such things as table manners. On an infinitely more exalted level, he is the teacher who reveals the Father, offering to humankind the knowledge without which it cannot be saved. This is how he is depicted, for instance, in Athanasius.[64] The role of teacher-revealer is apropos for Christ, since he is the Word and hence the "articulation" of the Father.

That Christ is teacher implies discipleship, and thus all Christians are students or disciples of Christ, and the Church itself is a kind of school. Augustine, for whom this is a favorite theme, remarks to his congregation that clergy and laity together are disciples: "Under that one teacher we are disciples along with you in this school."[65]

These three Christological images, and others like them, reveal something of Christ that more narrowly doctrinal statements do not, although it is true that such statements in patristic times are themselves hardly ever without imagery. Each image or title, too, opens up a new aspect of Christ's relationship to the humanity that he has come to save—nostalgic, therapeutic and didactic in the case of the three that have been briefly examined. The number and variety of different titles and images that could be applied to Christ are to a great extent the token of his inexhaustibility. To that degree they represent in their own way a truth that Origen alludes to in a number of places, namely that Christ adapts himself to the needs of individuals, and that individuals see him according to those needs.[66]

As far as devotion to Christ is concerned, the use of images like spouse, brother, friend or king tells us something about the direction which such devotion could take. The history of ancient liturgical devotion to Christ has been set forth in a famous book by Josef A. Jungmann;[67] from his study we know of the development that transformed Christ in the liturgy from the presider at a familial table to, by the second half of the fourth century, a king surrounded by courtiers and other subjects. The development is borne out in early Christian art, which is a subject unfortunately outside our purview. There the image of the good shepherd, the most popular portrayal of Christ in the first three centuries, completely gives way by the early fifth century to a royal and unapproachable Christ.

Yet throughout the patristic era there is a depth of feeling for Christ and a sense of intimacy with him that the emphasis on his royalty would not be able to remove. If this does not overwhelm us it is due to the ancient sense of discretion or sobriety in expressing oneself. The Fathers were not often in the habit of disclosing themselves other than in a rhetorical way (Augustine's *Confessions* are a remarkable exception to this). Nonetheless real emotion sometimes comes to the surface. Thus Origen, commenting on Simeon taking the child Jesus in his arms as narrated in Luke 2:28, could use this passage as an occasion to write about his own relationship with Christ. It is marked by profound tenderness:

> For a long time I was not holding Christ, for a long time I was not pressing him in my arms. I was locked up and unable to escape from my chains. These words are to be understood not only of Simeon but of the whole human race. If anyone leaves the world, if anyone goes out from the prison and the house of captives to reign, let him take Jesus in his hands and enclose him in his arms; let him grasp him completely to his breast. Then, exulting, he will be able to go where he desires.[68]

Toward the end of the fourth century, at the very time that the liturgical and artistic transformation of Christ was occurring, a renewed interest in virginity and evangelical poverty was fostering the same sort of intimacy of which Origen speaks. Both of these states were being embraced for the sake of union with Christ. Virginity, for instance, was spoken of erotically in terms of the Song of Songs,[69] and poverty made it possible to possess Christ more closely. "If I were rich," says Paulinus of Nola, "I would stand in need of God, but as a pauper I shall possess Christ."[70] In the words of Jerome, which were to resound through the Middle Ages, to be poor was to follow the naked Christ in one's own nakedness.[71]

There can be little doubt as to the place that Christ occupied in the life of the ancient Church. He was its focus of attention and emotion; he was the "everything" of which Pope Damasus spoke. And he was this, it seems, because he and his cross were the human race's only hope of salvation.

VI

Church and Ministry

The concept of the Church is perhaps less easy to pin down than anything else of comparable importance in early Christianity. Extended reflection on the nature of the Church as such, unlike reflection on the nature of God or Christ, was almost unknown in the East and, with the exception of Cyprian and Augustine, hardly known in the West either. But that is not to say that we have no idea of how the early Christians looked at their Church. If it was not frequently expressed, or rather not frequently expressed at length, that is very possibly because the Church was the mystery most closely bound up with the day-to-day life of the Christian and nearly indistinguishable from that life itself. It was a mystery *to* which one "belonged" and *in* which one was redeemed. Those were the primary givens. A third given, related to the other two, was that of the Church's separation from the rest of the world—a separation, it should be noted, that was often very conscious of itself.

To use three images that the Fathers sometimes employed when describing it, the Church was mother, ark and virgin-bride. It was a mother because through baptism it bore children who looked to it and who formed a community around it; this expressed the notion of "belonging." It was an ark because it carried a weight of passengers saved from the flood of sin; this expressed the notion of redemption. It was a virgin-bride because it was detached from the world and espoused chastely to Christ; this was the image representing its separation. Of course these characteristics are not exclusive to the ancient Church, but they are manifested with particular clarity in the Church when it exists in a diaspora situation. The ancient

95

Church, at least during the first few centuries, was in precisely such a situation, subsisting for the most part in small groups in a world hostile to it, despised as a newcomer, as untraditional, as insignificant, as subversive.

It must have been to some extent because the Fathers felt so deeply about these reproaches, many of which have been preserved for us in the writings of the second- and third-century apologists, that early on they chose to counter them by emphasizing the hidden importance of the Church in relation to the world about it. The early second-century *Epistle to Diognetus* contains a justly renowned passage that shows very clearly the exalted notion of the Church that had been developed within the first hundred years of its existence. "What the soul is to the body," the anonymous author of this work writes,

> that the Christians are in the world. The soul is extended through all the members of the body, and the Christians through the cities of the world. The soul dwells in the body, but is not of the body, and Christians dwell in the world, but they are not of the world. The soul, invisible, is kept shut up in the visible body, and Christians are recognized as such in the world, but their religion remains invisible. The flesh hates the soul and does battle against it, although it has suffered no wrong, because they oppose its pleasures. The soul loves the flesh that hates it, and its members, and Christians love those that hate them. The soul is locked up in the body, but it is the very thing that holds the body together, and Christians are shut up in the world as in a prison, but they are the very ones that hold the world together.[1]

The author concludes by explaining that the Christians occupy this place in the world because to them has been entrusted the mystery of the Word made flesh, the mystery of salvation by which the world will be saved.[2] The idea of the hidden Church as in some sense the soul of the world occurs again in the apologetic literature of the second century. For the sake of the Christians, Aristides of Athens writes at perhaps the same time as the *Epistle to Diognetus* was composed, "the marvelous things that are in the world flow forth to view." More than that, the very fact that the earth is preserved from destruction is the result of the Christians' prayers, for the rest of humanity is blind to the truth and acts like a drunken man, staggering about in ignorance.[3] Justin Martyr says the same thing about the middle of the century: "God restrains himself from causing the confusion and destruction of the whole world . . . on account of the race of Christians, which he knows to be in nature the reason for its preservation."[4]

In one of the visions of the mysterious *Shepherd* of Hermas, dating from the middle of the second century, the Church appears to the visionary in the guise of an elderly lady. When he asks why she is elderly he receives the answer: "Because she was created first of all; therefore she is old. And for her sake the world was created."[5] Here the dependence of the world upon the Church, which is hidden from its view, is even more strongly accented. The theme of the pre-existent Church is taken up again in an anonymous second-century homily, and there it is elaborated:

> Brethren, if we do the will of our Father, God, we shall belong to the first Church, the spiritual one, the one established before the sun and the moon. . . . The Scriptures and the apostles declare that the Church is not of the present age but from the beginning. For it was spiritual, as was also our Lord Jesus, but he was manifested in the last days so that he might save us.[6]

Finally, in his commentary on the Song of Songs, written toward the middle of the third century, Origen speaks briefly about the Church as pre-existent. He refers to it as the bride of Christ and says that

> you must not think that it is called the bride or the Church only from the time of the coming of the Savior in the flesh, but from the beginning of the human race and from the very foundation of the world—indeed, if I may seek the origin of this deep mystery with Paul as my guide, even before the

foundation of the world. For this is what he himself says: . . .
As he chose us in Christ before the foundation of the world.

Origen goes on to say that the Church has existed in the righteous from the beginning of time, and that in fact Christ became a man in order that he might minister to it.[7]

The idea of the Church's pre-existence is apparently not one that was used to defend it against pagan accusations of being an upstart or untraditional. The development of the notion seems rather to have been due to a theological reflection upon it that was allied to the idea of the pre-existence of Christ. In order to answer these accusations, though, something similar appeared in Christian thought, and it is Justin Martyr who introduces it. "The things that we say we have learned from Christ and from the prophets who preceded him," he writes in his great apology, "are the only truths, and more ancient than all the writers who have ever lived."[8] He proceeds later to unfold his famous theory that the great ideas of the pagan thinkers throughout the ages were really borrowed from the Scriptures, which existed before any pagan writings.[9] Consequently, since the Church inherited the Scriptures, it can claim to have inherited every good thing as well that was derived from the Scriptures. Justin is summarized two centuries later by Ambrose, writing of Socrates: "Whatever is admirable in what the philosopher has written belongs to us."[10] Thus the Church claimed for itself a mysterious unity with all people of every age who sought the truth, a unity with the past that its pagan adversaries, proudly conscious of the antiquity of their own cults, had denied it.

The claim of high antiquity also appears occasionally with respect to the Jews. Ambrose, for example, compares the sacraments of the Church with those of the Synagogue (the term "sacrament" was broadly understood in ancient times, and it could include virtually anything that might be construed as a sign of grace), and he finds the former more ancient than the latter. For the bread and wine offered by Melchizedek in the time of Abraham, as recorded in Genesis 14:18-20, are a type of the Eucharist, and Melchizedek himself, introduced without father or mother, is a type of Christ. And of course Melchizedek is older by far than Moses, who is the founder of the Synagogue.[11]

The Church as a Sign of Unity

Unity was the leitmotiv of early Christian thought on the Church, as it has always been. If we return to the threefold image of the Church as mother, ark and virgin-bride, we see it reflected there. Cyprian of Carthage makes use of all three images in his treatise *On the Unity of the Catholic Church*, the first work of its kind, written in the middle of the third century and directed against a schism about which we know comparatively little. The Church, Cyprian writes, is mother of a single family, and to that family it dispenses the nourishment of salvation. "There is one head-spring, one source, one mother who is prolific in her offspring, from generation to generation. We are born of her womb, nourished by her milk, animated by her Spirit."[12] It is the one ark that alone can bear its passengers to safety. "If anyone outside the ark was able to escape, whoever is outside the Church is able to escape as well."[13] (But Augustine is rather more specific about the ark as a symbol of unity. Commenting on Genesis 6:16, that the ark was "finished in a cubit above," he explains that likewise the Church, "the body of Christ gathered into unity, is raised and perfected. . . . At its summit we are all made one. There is no divergence, for Christ is all and in all, finishing us, as it were, in one cubit above in heavenly unity."[14]) Finally, again in Cyprian, the Church is the virgin-bride who lives not for the pleasure of this world but only for Christ. "The bride of Christ cannot be defiled; she is incorrupt and chaste. She knows but one home; in chaste modesty she guards the sanctity of one couch."[15]

Indeed, Cyprian piles image upon image in his search to impress the importance of unity on his readers. The Church, he says, is like the sun, whose rays are many but whose light is one. It is like a tree with many branches but with a single strength surging through one root. It is like a source from which flow many streams, which nevertheless maintain a unity because of their unique beginning. It may be compared to Christ's seamless garment, which was not divided at his death; or to the house in which the Jews ate the paschal lamb, which was not permitted to be eaten outside; or to a dove, which keeps to one cote and which is faithful to its mate.[16]

For the early Christians it is evident that unity was far more a mystique, so to say, than an organizational desideratum. In fact there was a great deal of diversity in the early Church, as has been noted in the first chapter. What unity existed in it, scattered as it was throughout the Roman Empire and even elsewhere, was not in the area of what we might today call discipline, that is, liturgical practice and administrative organization, although by the beginning of the third century the Church everywhere did pretty much conform to one pattern of organization. Augustine's letter to Januarius, which was cited at length in the first chapter,[17] gives an excellent insight into the sometimes confusing liturgical diversity that existed in the first few centuries.

To the early Christians, therefore, the unity of the Church had to do with nothing less than the content of the faith itself, namely, with what had been derived from Scripture and what had been handed down by the apostles or by the fathers assembled in synod. It was to preserve faith's purity that certain churches such as Rome, apostolically founded and universally recognized to have maintained the apostolic tradition, began to assume a greater importance than others. A relationship with the apostles, who according to a late fourth-century tradition were each said to have composed an article of the Apostles' Creed,[18] was considered to guarantee orthodoxy. When questions of discipline did in fact arise, it was because frequently they were understood to touch upon the faith.

But if unity had to do with nothing *less* than faith, yet it had to do with something *more*, if that may be said: it had to do with love. Wherever love is, there is unity. Cyprian quotes Paul in 1 Corinthians 13:8 ("Love never ends"), and he continues:

> It will exist forever in the kingdom, it will endure forever in the union of the brethren among themselves. Disunion cannot attain to the kingdom of heaven, nor can one who has violated the love of Christ by wicked dissension win the reward of Christ, who said: This is my commandment, that you love one another as I have loved you.[19]

This "union of the brethren among themselves" is presented in ideal form in the Acts of the Apostles in two well known pas-

sages, 2:44–47 and 4:32–35. The classic description of the early
Christian community in patristic literature appears in Tertullian's
Apology, where he speaks at some length of the Christians'
mutual concern, particularly for the poor among them. So great
is their love, Tertullian writes, that even the pagans are drawn
to exclaim: "See how they love one another!"[20]

Thus schism, the fracturing of ecclesial unity, is almost
always characterized as a breach of love, and as love is the greatest of the virtues, so schism is the worst of the vices. Invariably
it appears as something horrible, deserving for itself the punishment of Dathan and Abiram, whom the earth swallowed up
because, as Numbers 16:1–35 records, they had rebelled against
Moses.[21] At the root of schism is that pride and self-righteousness which inevitably conspire to set people against one another.
Where do schisms come from? Augustine asks. "When people
say: *We* are righteous. When they say: *We* sanctify the unclean,
we justify the impious, *we* ask, *we* obtain."[22]

The mystery of the Church's unity, however, does not
merely revolve about itself. It mirrors an even more sublime
mystery of unity and is identical with still another one. "God is
one," writes Cyprian, touching upon that more sublime mystery,
"and Christ is one, and his Church is one, and there is one faith
and one people joined together by harmony into the strong unity
of a body."[23] The Church reflects the very unity of God.
Nowhere is this more evident than in the letters of Ignatius of
Antioch. The harmony of the Church, in its people and in its
ministers, is an image of the divine unity converging in the
Father.

> Just as the Lord, then, being one with him, did nothing with-
> out the Father, either by himself or through the apostles, so
> neither must you do anything without the bishop and the
> presbyters. And you must not attempt to convince yourselves
> that anything you do on your own account is right, but there
> must be in common one prayer, one supplication, one mind,
> one hope in love, in flawless joy, that is Jesus Christ, than
> whom nothing is better. Come together, all of you as to one
> temple of God, as to one altar, to one Jesus Christ, who came
> forth from one Father and yet remained with one and
> returned to one.[24]

And similarly: "Do nothing apart from the bishop, preserve your flesh as the temple of God, love unity, flee divisions. Be imitators of Jesus Christ, as he also was of his Father."[25]

The mystery of the Church is identical with the further mystery of the unity of Christ's body, head and members. This Pauline notion occurs in patristic literature already before the end of the first century, in a letter of Clement of Rome to the church at Corinth in which he complains of a schism that has arisen there. "Why do we divide and tear apart the members of Christ," he asks, "and strive against our own body, and fall into such madness that we forget ourselves—that we are members of each other?"[26] The theme is taken up by subsequent Fathers, until in Augustine it typically achieves a new profundity. In his *Expositions on the Psalms*, a vast work that comments on all one hundred and fifty psalms, Augustine sees Christ's body addressing the Psalms to the Father, sometimes in its head, sometimes in its members, with the one never entirely separated from the other. He, more than any other Father, draws out the notion of the identity of head and members which first appears in Paul. With reference to the image of a body that appears in one of the Psalms he writes:

> We must understand [this image to pertain to] our person, the person of our Church, the person of the body of Christ. For Jesus Christ is one man with head and body, the Savior of the body and the members of the body—two in one flesh, and in one voice, and in one experience of suffering, and, when iniquity shall have passed, in one rest. The sufferings of Christ are certainly not in Christ alone, yet the sufferings of Christ are only in Christ. For if you understand Christ to be head and body, the sufferings of Christ are only in Christ. But if you understand Christ to be the head alone, the sufferings of Christ are not in Christ alone. For if the sufferings of Christ are in Christ alone, in the head alone, how does the apostle Paul, that particular member of him, say: That I might fill up what is lacking of the sufferings of Christ in my flesh? If therefore you are among the members of Christ, whoever you are who hear these words, whoever you are who do not hear them (and yet you do hear if you are among the members of Christ): whatever you suffer from those who

are not among the members of Christ had been lacking to the sufferings of Christ. And so what had been lacking is added; you fill up the measure, you do not cause it to overflow. As much as you suffer, that much had to be brought to the whole suffering of Christ, who did suffer in our head and does suffer in his members, that is, in ourselves.[27]

Elsewhere Augustine identifies the body of Christ which is the Church with that which is the Eucharist. This is strikingly expressed in a sermon on the Eucharist to the newly baptized:

> If you wish to understand the body of Christ, listen to the apostle telling the faithful: You are the body of Christ and its members. If therefore you are the body of Christ and its members, it is the sacrament of you yourselves that reposes on the table of the Lord: you receive the sacrament of you yourselves. To that which you are you respond by saying Amen, and in that response you assent to it. Be a member of the body of Christ, so that your Amen might be sincere.[28]

In another sermon he remarks that unity is the special characteristic of the Eucharist, and that the Church seeks to be what it receives. Gathered together in head and members, it is itself a Eucharist.[29] But the Eucharist was frequently taken also to be indicative of the unity both of the head and members of Christ's body, symbolized by the mingling of wine and water in the chalice during the eucharistic liturgy, and of the members among themselves. Regarding the latter Cyprian writes in one of his letters, taking up a popular theme:

> The sacrifices of the Lord themselves declare that Christian unanimity is bound to itself by a firm and inseparable charity. For when the Lord calls bread made from the union of many grains his body, he indicates our people, whom he bore united. And when he calls wine pressed from the clusters of grapes and many small berries and gathered into one his blood, he likewise signifies our flock joined by the mixture of a united multitude.[30]

It was precisely with this in mind, Augustine says, that Christ chose bread and wine for his sacrament.[31]

Yet real unity could not always be presupposed among all those who partook of the sacrament, since it was available to good and bad alike. Therefore, Augustine writes, echoing Paul, "whoever does not dwell in Christ, and in whom Christ does not dwell, without doubt neither eats his body nor drinks his blood, but rather eats and drinks the sacrament . . . to his own judgment."[32] And so the Church, Augustine confesses, using a favorite image of his from the Gospel, is like a threshing floor, on which there are both chaff and grain together, and it is not until the last judgment that the two will be separated. Whoever breaks away in the meantime from the Church because of its evil communicants necessarily breaks away from its good ones as well. The idea that the Church could thus include both good and bad was an extremely important one, and it impressed itself powerfully upon Augustine only after his experiences with a group of North African schismatics who had left the Church because they could not abide communion with those who they felt were tainted. The Donatists, as they were called after one of their early leaders, arose at the end of the time of persecutions, at the beginning of the fourth century. Having broken with the main body of the Church on account of the infidelity of some of its bishops during the persecutions, who they insisted could no longer celebrate valid sacraments by reason of their sinfulness, they eventually found themselves in an untenable position. For of course it is impossible for a group of human beings to be utterly without sin, and toward the beginning of the fifth century the Donatists were themselves divided into different sub-churches, one claiming greater purity than another. It was Augustine's genius, faced with this problem of a sinful Church and the requirements of holiness, to make the significant distinction between the morality or even the faith of the person administering the sacraments and the validity of the sacraments. "There is no profane and polluted water," he writes with respect to baptism, "over which the name of God is invoked, even if it be invoked by profane and polluted persons, for neither the creature itself [the water] nor the name is polluted. But Christ's baptism, consecrated by Gospel words, is holy both when ministered by the polluted and when ministered to the polluted."[33]

Augustine's idea, however, seemed somehow to compromise the theology of the Church that described it as the spotless and virgin bride of Christ, and even today the possibility of sin and righteousness co-existing in the Church is problematic. The Orthodox in particular find Augustine's distinction between the holiness of the minister and the holiness of the sacrament considerably less than satisfying. Yet, at one and the same time, for Augustine and for the Fathers who followed him, the Church could still be that virgin-bride. This was part of its mystery.

Mother, Ark, and Virgin-Bride

Let us return briefly to the three images of the Church as mother, ark and virgin-bride.

The Church is of course most clearly seen as mother in its bringing children to birth through the sacrament of regeneration, and in its feeding them with the eucharistic food. In this regard one might think again of the beautiful phrase of Cyprian: "We are born of her womb, nourished by her milk, animated by her Spirit."[34] In one of his sermons Chrysostom describes the Church as an exultant mother surrounded by her many children on Easter morning after the numerous baptisms celebrated the previous night. "She sees herself," he says, "as a fertile field, lush and green with this spiritual crop."[35] But perhaps the maternity of the Church appears most remarkably in a rite that immediately followed baptism in some places and that is preserved for us in the early third-century *Apostolic Tradition* of Hippolytus. There we are told that, upon partaking of Communion for the first time, the newly baptized not only received the body and blood of Christ but also drank from a cup containing a mixture of milk and honey.[36] The milk and honey, to be sure, had symbolic value of a scriptural kind: it recalled the biblical land flowing with milk and honey, into which those just baptized had entered in mystical fashion. But, as we know from the pagan Greek physician Soranus of Ephesus, it was also a food that was in fact given to infants in the ancient world shortly after their birth.[37] The Church was thus treating the newly baptized literally as a mother would have treated her newly born infant.

To speak of the Church as a mother was not merely an affectionate rhetorical device among the early Christians, although it was undoubtedly that too. More profoundly, the title indicated the very source of the distinctly Christian life, and the use of it corresponded to a deep need to express the reality of what had taken place in the sacrament of rebirth, baptism: Christians were no longer living according to the flesh, such as those born but once of a human mother, but according to the Spirit, born again from on high. In this connection there is an extremely interesting and revealing letter of Augustine written to a young man named Laetus, who had become a monk but whose mother was trying to persuade to abandon his monastic calling. Augustine remainds Laetus of the Gospel words about hating father, mother, wife and children, and one's own life, for the sake of the kingdom, and he tells him very forcefully that his mother can no longer be loved with a simply earthly affection. Besides that, she herself must "not think it more important that she brought you forth from her womb than that she was brought forth *with* you from the womb of the Church."[38] "Mother Church is also the mother of your mother," he writes.

> She conceived you both in Christ, she was in labor with you in the blood of the martyrs, she brought you forth to everlasting light, she nursed and fed you with the milk of faith and, as she prepares stronger food for you, she is taken aback that you are still crying for the food of an infant without teeth. . . . Does she not show you a dearer womb and heavenly breasts?[39]

Laetus must realize that, although he had been born once, he has been born again; the Church is now his true mother, and he must no longer pine for what he has outgrown.

The image of the Church as ark is somewhat more ambiguous than our first use of it would lead one to believe, namely, that as ark it carried a weight of passengers saved from the floods of sin. That is true to the extent that no one outside the ark was ever saved. Yet to be in the ark did not always guarantee salvation either, even though some of the Fathers seem to employ the image with that intent: "Just as Noah's ark preserved unhurt all whom it took up while the world was in shipwreck," Maximus of Turin says, "so the Church of Peter will return safe all whom it embraces as the world is destroyed by fire."[40] According to Augustine, the ark was rather more like the threshing floor that had room on it for grain and chaff together, for it carried both clean and unclean animals, signifying good and bad.[41] On the other hand, that all kinds of animals were included in it indicated that the Church contained all nations.[42] The Fathers found hidden meaning in every detail of the ark, and Jerome, after having given an extensive sampling of its symbolism, writes: "The day would not be long enough for me to explain all the mysteries of the ark and compare them wtih the Church."[43]

But, with the body of Christ, probably the richest and favorite image of the Fathers for the Church was that of the virgin-bride; it was, after all, an image that had been sanctioned by Paul in Ephesians 5:32. It expressed the intimate union that existed between Christ and his Church, which was nowhere more splendidly expounded than in Origen's almost ecstatic commentary on the Song of Songs, the first great work of Christian mysticism. The image of the virgin-bride also provided the opportunity for the development of the vocation of virginity, which sought to live out the mystical possibilities inherent in the image. With all its eschatological overtones, with its implications of keeping vigil until the bridegroom came and longing for union with him, it was the image with the most thrust and the most dynamism. Moreover, it could not help but illuminate the mystery of Christ himself, who had come in the flesh, according to one tradition already mentioned, in order to minister to the Church; or who had, according to another, given birth to it in the supreme moment of his death, when blood and water, symbolizing the two great sacraments of baptism and Eucharist, flowed forth from his side.[44] Emptying himself, Augustine writes, Christ left his Father, for he did not show himself equal to his Father. And he left his mother also, the Synagogue from which he was born after the flesh, and he cleaved to his wife, that is, to the Church.[45] His mission was for her alone.

Yet very frequently connected with this image of virginity was that of maternity, which is well expressed by Ambrose in his treatise *On Virgins:*

Thus the holy Church, unstained by intercourse, but fertile in bearing, is a virgin in chastity and a mother in offspring. As a virgin she bears us, not by a human father but by the Spirit. As a virgin she bears us, not with bodily sufferings but with the rejoicing of the angels. As a virgin she nourishes us, not with the milk of the body but with that of the apostle, with which he fed the tender age of a people that were still infants. What bride has more children than the holy Church, who is a virgin in her sacraments, a mother to her people, of whose fertility the Scriptures themselves bear witness when they say: For many more are the children of the desolate than of her who has a husband? Our Church has no husband, but she has a bridgroom . . . for, without any danger to chastity, she is wedded to the Word of God as if to an eternal bridegroom, barren of injury, pregnant with reason.[46]

These words serve to highlight the fact that, perhaps more than any other mystery save that of Christ himself, the mystery of the Church was at heart a paradox: it was virgin and mother; one, yet dispersed in many places and characterized by a diversity of customs; immaculate, yet with sinful members; created before time began, yet having come into time. It was a mystery that seemed to defy systematic reflection and to invite, instead, the language of mysticism and imagery—language of which the Fathers were most capable practitioners.

Ministries in the Church

If we are to speak adequately of the Church, we must say at least something about its ministries as well. The beginnings of these ministries are highly mysterious, although a tradition that arose relatively soon and that was almost universally accepted would speak in terms of an orderly transition from the apostles to the first bishops, and thenceforth an unbroken chain from bishop to bishop. In fact the Pauline epistles and the *Didache* inform us that there are apostles (who were not the same as the Twelve), prophets and teachers, and the *Didache* in particular indicates that these were itinerants, never remaining long in one place.[47] Of the exact nature of their functions we are in the dark.

Toward the beginning of the second century, however, a pattern similar to the one with which we are presently familiar begins to emerge. Both Clement of Rome, writing about the year 96, and Ignatius of Antioch, fifteen years later, speak of bishops, priests (or presbyters) and deacons, but make no mention of apostles, prophets and teachers. By the beginning of the third century this latter group, for all intents, disappeared from the orthodox Church, although prophecy, as a specific office, may have survived in a few isolated cases. The scheme of bishop, priest and deacon did not suddenly spring up full-blown at the same time everywhere, yet by the year 200, if not earlier, we may be rather certain that it was pretty firmly established throughout the whole Christian community.

From that point on the ancient Church is indisputably the Church of the bishop. He has succeeded to the mantle of apostle, prophet and teacher—not without tension sometimes—and is the undoubted leader of his community. The early third-century *Didascalia apostolorum* refers to the episcopal office in the most exalted terms, and in so doing it is not expressing an unusual sentiment.

> You, O bishops, are today priests to your people, and Levites, ministering to the tabernacle of God, the holy catholic Church, and standing continually before the Lord our God. You are to your people priests and prophets and princes and leaders and kings and mediators before God and his faithful people, and hearers of the word and preachers and proclaimers of it, and knowers of the Scriptures and of the promises of God and witnesses of his will, who bear the sins of all and render an account for all.[48]

The presbyterate and the diaconate, as well as any functions inferior to these, exist in subordination to the bishop, whose authority is quasi-divine. Ignatius bears witness to the roots of this development already in the first decade of the second century:

> Follow the bishop, all of you, as Jesus Christ follows the Father, and the presbytery as if it were the apostles. And reverence the deacons as the commandment of God. Apart from

the bishop let no one do anything pertaining to the Church. Let that be considered a valid Eucharist which is celebrated by the bishop or by a person appointed by him. Let the people be present wherever the bishop appears, just as the catholic Church is wherever Jesus Christ is. Apart from the bishop it is not lawful either to baptize or to celebrate a Eucharist; but whatever he may approve is also pleasing to God, so that whatever you do may be sure and valid.[49]

It was perhaps primarily in the liturgy that the leading role of the bishop could be most clearly discerned. Ordinarily he alone presided at the Eucharist. As he prayed aloud at the altar the presbyters stood silently on either side of him, while the deacons assisted him in such things as the distribution of the consecrated bread and wine or saw to keeping order in the church. From his *cathedra,* his chair, usually situated at the center of the back wall of the sanctuary, flanked by the presbyters' benches, he was accustomed to preach. This was the bishop's most important function and, until about the beginning of the sixth century, it was only infrequently that priests and deacons preached. The anonymous author of the *Didascalia apostolorum* emphasizes the importance of this ministry in somber language: "You have heard how sternly the Word threatens you if you neglect to preach the will of God—you who are in grave danger of damnation if you do not care for your people."[50] Caesarius of Arles, in a sermon given at an episcopal ordination at the beginning of the sixth century, warns the new bishop to beware of being so caught up in secular affairs that he no longer has time for preaching, and he makes a suggestion for arranging his affairs in such a way that preaching is treated as a priority:

Let secular business be taken care of by your children [namely, members of his congregation], so that your soul may be occupied only with those matters through which salvation is offered to everyone. For just as you would commit a crime against religion if you neglected the word of God on account of preoccupation with secular business, so your children would commit a serious sin if they refused to come to the aid of the Church. Let them, therefore, as true and good Christian children of the Church, strive to handle and direct

with justice whatever pertains to the world, and leave concern for doctrine to you alone. . . . Devote yourself to this one
thing, so that fitly and without ceasing you may teach your
children.[51]

The great bishops, who were all accomplished preachers, felt
keenly the responsibility attached to preaching; it was, according
to Augustine, "a great burden, a heavy weight, a difficult
labor."[52] John Chrysostom devotes two sections of his treatise on
the episcopal office to it.[53] Gregory the Great's extremely influential *Book of Pastoral Care*, addressed to bishops, is more a
handbook on preaching than anything else; its chapters are
arranged in antitheses, with useful advice on how best to preach
to rich and poor, ignorant and intelligent, virtuous and vicious.
Elsewhere Gregory refers to the bishops quite simply as the *ordo
praedicatorum*, the order of preachers.[54] Likewise for Gregory, as
for several other Fathers, the right to preach is synonymous with
the right to exercise ruling authority over a congregation.[55]

Preaching was, in a word, the most characteristic function
as well as the most characteristic mode of expression of the bishops of the ancient Church, and hence of the Fathers, who were
nearly all bishops. In a way that little else does, their preaching
manifests their burning desire to be bearers of the message of
salvation and reveals their remarkable grasp of the fact that their
own salvation and that of their audiences are intimately connected. "What do I wish?" Augustine asks his congregation in
one of his sermons.

> What do I desire? What do I want? Why do I speak? Why do
> I sit here? Why do I live, if not for this reason, that together
> we might live with Christ? This is my desire, this my honor,
> my glory, my joy, my possession. But if you will not listen to
> me, and still I am not silent, I shall redeem my own soul. But
> I do not want to be saved without you.[56]

A brief passage at the opening of a sermon by Peter Chrysologus
in the middle of the fifth century expresses a similar concern:
"You are my life, you are my salvation, you are my glory, and
therefore I cannot bear that you should be ignorant of the knowledge that God has imparted to me."[57]

Whence the pre-eminence enjoyed by the bishop's ministry of the word? It was due mostly to the fact that the word itself enjoyed a pre-eminence that it lost toward the end of the patristic period and did not regain (in the West, in any event), except for relatively brief intervals, until the Reformation. The dignity of the Gospel, proclaimed and preached, demanded the services of the Church's most important officer, the bishop. The late and post-patristic periods would make the word, practically speaking, inferior to the Eucharist, which had become a mystery of awesome proportions. It was not thus in the first few centuries. In his thirteenth homily on Exodus Origen discusses the reverence with which the word of God should be heard, and he compares this with the reverence with which the body of Christ should be received. He notes how careful the faithful are lest even a fragment of the eucharistic bread should fall to the ground, and he says that they would consider themselves criminal—and rightly so—if that should happen on account of their own negligence. But, he asks, why is the care exercised toward the Eucharist so disproportionate to the care exercised toward the word? Why do the faithful consider it less sinful to hear the word in slipshod fashion than to let a particle of the Eucharist fall to the ground for the same reason?[58] Here Origen is expressing the attitude of the early Church, which is echoed later by Jerome[59] and Caesarius[60] in almost the same words: Scripture proclaimed and preached was held in as great honor as the sacrament of Christ's body, and both were equally necessary to the life of the Christian. It was right that the bishop should take this ministry with the utmost seriousness.

In addition to celebrating the Eucharist and preaching, the bishop was also entrusted with the ministry of reconciliation, although he could delegate aspects of it to priests and even to deacons. The short prayer for the ordination of bishops in *The Apostolic Tradition* of Hippolytus, the most ancient that we possess, lays particular stress on this part of the episcopal task. It calls on the Father to bestow upon the one being ordained "the ability to forgive sins according to your commandment . . . and to dissolve every bond according to the power that you gave to the apostles."[61] The *Didascalia apostolorum* refers to the bishop as a physician who is to bring healing to the Church: "Do not withhold the medicine of those who are sick in their sins, but cure them in any way possible and restore them whole to the Church, so that you do not incur the word that the Lord spoke: You subdued them with force and derision."[62] Finally, from a liturgical point of view, the bishop was ordinarily the chief minister of baptism, although in this too he would be assisted by other ministers.

But the bishop was not simply a liturgical figure. He was a person with responsibilities in every area of the life of the community. Chrysostom, in explaining to a friend (in an account that is perhaps fictional, but which nonetheless gives a true picture of the situation) why he fled from the episcopacy, enumerates these responsibilities as so many intolerable burdens—the care of widows, who are especially troublesome because given to complaining and ingratitude; solicitude for the poor; hospitality toward strangers; the visitation of the sick; the overseeing of virgins, which is a particularly delicate occupation since "this flock is of a nobler quality than the rest"; the meting out of justice; and finally the occasional tragic necessity of cutting someone off from full communion in the Church. In everything that the bishop does, Chrysostom remarks, he is subject to the most minute scrutiny from people who have plenty of time on their hands.[63]

So excessive were the demands made upon the bishop that he often found that he had too infrequent opportunity to pray for his flock, which was one of his chief duties, and to devote himself to contemplation. Augustine experienced the tension between the active and the contemplative sides of his calling in a particularly poignant way, and he often indicates how much he would prefer to be praying quietly than to have to be taken up with so many different and exhausting matters. But we know that he is referring to himself when, in a sermon on the transfiguration of Christ, he speaks of Peter, who had wanted to set up three tents on Mount Tabor and remain with the transfigured Jesus instead of returning to the drudgery of daily life.

Peter sees this [the glory of the Lord] and says with human wisdom: Lord, it is good for us to be here. He was suffering the annoyance of the crowd, but he had found the solitude of the mountain, where he had Christ, the bread of the soul. Why should he depart from there to return to labors and sorrows, when he had a holy love for God and hence holy dispositions? . . .

Come down, Peter. You wanted to rest on the mountain. Come down, preach the word, be urgent in season and out of season, convince, rebuke and exhort, be unfailing in patience and in teaching. Labor, sweat, suffer torments, so that you might possess what is signified in the shining garments of the Lord—the brilliance and beauty of good work in charity. For we heard it said in praise of charity when the apostle was read: It seeks not its own. It seeks not its own because it gives away what it possesses. . . . This Peter did not yet understand when he wanted to live on the mountain with Christ. The Lord has reserved this for you, Peter, after your death. But now he himself says: Come down, labor on earth, serve on earth, be despised, be crucified on earth. The life came down that he might be slain; the bread came down that he might hunger; the way came down that he might grow weary on the way; the fount came down that he might thirst. And do you refuse to labor? Seek not your own. Have charity, preach the truth. Then you will come to eternity, where you will find security.[64]

The citation from Ignatius of Antioch that appeared somewhat earlier in this essay[65] implies yet another ministry that was exercised by the bishop, one in which he played a role that was as much symbolic as it was practical: he represented in a visible way the unity of the local church. And, in turn, the bishops in harmony among each other, even though separated by great distances, represented the unity of the entire Church.

One body and one spirit, one hope of your calling, one Lord, one faith, one baptism, one God—let us hold firmly to this unity and defend it, especially we bishops who preside in the Church, so that we might also show forth the episcopate itself to be one and undivided. Let no one deceive the brotherhood by lying, let no one corrupt the faith by a wicked perversion of the truth. The episcopacy is one, each part of which possesses the whole. And the Church is one, even though it is widely dispersed.[66]

When the bishops met together in synod—as happened frequently in antiquity, and not merely in major councils such as Nicea, Constantinople, Ephesus and Chalcedon—then the unity of the Church was manifested in a particularly imposing way. This was true even despite the acrimony that often prevailed at such gatherings.

The episcopal ministry, then, was many-faceted, and it made the bishop the most prominent member of his community from a secular as well as from a religious point of view. For this reason he always had to remember that he was ultimately at the disposition of his congregation, one with them before Christ, and not set above them except in service. "We are your servants—your servants, but also servants with you. We are your servants, but we all have one Lord. We are your servants, but in Jesus, as the apostle says: But we are your servants for the sake of Jesus."[67]

In the shadow of the episcopacy, which, apart from its earliest years, appears so clear and well-defined, the presbyteral ministry tends either to disappear or to become confused with that of the bishop. We know of very few of the great Fathers who remained priests throughout their lives and did not eventually become bishops; the most significant in this regard were Tertullian, Origen and Jerome. Jerome himself, like a number of other Fathers, is somewhat at a loss to explain precisely what it is that distinguishes the bishop from the priest. Commenting on the Epistle to Titus he says that in the beginning both presbyters and bishops were the same, although they had different titles. What happened, in his opinion, was that,

> to remove the seedlings of dissensions, the care of everything was handed over to one person [the bishop]. Thus while presbyters realize that they are subject to the one who has been set over them according to the custom of the Church, let bishops be aware that it is rather by reason of custom than by reason of the Lord's disposition that they are superior to presbyters.[68]

In fact, however, the earliest non-scriptural mentions of presbyters indicate that they served as councillors to the bishop.

Ignatius speaks of the bishop presiding in the place of God, while "The presbyters are to act as the council of the apostles."[69] The *Didascalia apostolorum* says the same thing: "They should be venerated as apostles and councillors of the bishop, and as the crown of the Church, for they are the council and the moderating body of the Church."[70] The ordination prayer for presbyters in *The Apostolic Tradition* speaks only of this aspect of their office, and links them with the elders who assisted Moses in governing the people of Israel.[71]

Yet this is not to say that presbyters did nothing but act as councillors. The letter of Polycarp to the Church at Philippi, written toward the beginning of the second century, when everything was still in comparative obscurity, shows that they were also expected to exercise a ministry of service: "The presbyters should be compassionate, merciful to all, bringing back those who are astray, caring for the weak, neglecting neither widow nor orphan nor poor man."[72] But it was not until rather late in the patristic period that the presbyterate began to assume an identity somewhat independent of the episcopate, and this was caused by the force of circumstances, namely by the increasing demands on the bishop's time, which compelled him to share his ministry with others, and by the development of parishes in the countrysides, which were inaccessible to bishops on a regular basis and which had to be served by priests.

With the deacon we are once again in a more clearly defined ministry. *The Apostolic Tradition* relates that the deacon was ordained specifically to assist the bishop, "to do those things that are commanded by him,"[73] and the *Didascalia apostolorum* calls the deacon "the hearing and the mouth and the heart and the soul of the bishop."[74] In this capacity a deacon was frequently his bishop's secretary and closest advisor, as well as the one whom the bishop would send on missions to represent his views or to be the bearer of important messages.

The deacon's ministry, like that of the bishop and the priest, with some exceptions, was essentially twofold, namely liturgical and charitable. We learn something of the deacon's liturgical activities as early as the middle of the second century from Justin Martyr, who says that, after the Eucharist was celebrated, the deacons would bring Communion to those who were absent.[75]

Other sources tell us that deacons maintained order in the church, guarded the doors, recited or chanted certain prayers, instructed catechumens and proclaimed the Gospel. This last office came to be particularly associated with them. At the same time it was recognized that the deacon had some special relationship to the eucharistic chalice. An anonymous Gallic work of the fifth century tells us that a bishop may not even lift the chalice from the altar unless it has first been handed to him by his deacon.[76] Deacons also assisted at the baptism of men, while there were deaconesses to assist at the baptism of women in some of the churches.

In his letters Ignatius of Antioch is constantly comparing the deacons to Christ. "The deacons, who are very dear to me," as he says in one place, "are entrusted with the ministry of Jesus Christ."[77] He is probably referring in such passages to the ministry of service or charity, which was the deacon's chief function. He was in fact *the* minister of service in the ancient Church. This meant that he assisted the bishop in every charitable work that he undertook. In Rome a deacon was in charge of the cemeteries, which required an administrative skill second only to that of the bishop himself. It was not untypical of what deacons were customarily expected to do.

These were the three major orders of Christian antiquity, and they are still the central orders in many Christian Churches. Sometime in the fifth or sixth century the mysterious Pseudo-Dionysius attached a mystical significance to each of them. The episcopal order, he wrote, which is refulgent with the most splendid qualities, has the task of interpreting divine realities and teaching them to those who are already advanced. The presbyteral order has an illuminating function: priests introduce the initiated into the sacred mysteries and admit them into their communion. Finally, the diaconal order is responsible for discerning who is to approach these mysteries: it has a cathartic function, purifying those who are as yet unclean and drawing those who have been purified to be illuminated.[78] There is a certain beauty to this concept, which was characteristic of the Eastern Church (Pseudo-Dionysius himself was probably Syrian) and which had been in the making over the course of two or three centuries. It represented, however, a tendency to under-

stand the three orders primarily in cultic or mystical terms and
to neglect the idea of the ministry of service. To that extent,
despite its value, it was an unfortunate development, and it was
a development that was ultimately not restricted to the Church
in the East.

There were other orders as well, each one having a specific
function. We hear of subdeacons, lectors or readers, who apparently occupied a very high position in the Syrian hierarchy,[79]
acolytes, cantors or psalmists, exorcists, porters and grave-dig-
gers, who were responsible for burying the poor and strangers.
All these appear, along with the three great orders, at one
moment or another in the ancient Church. It was traditional to
count seven such, including the episcopacy, presbyterate and
diaconate, since seven was a number of considerable mystical
significance, although they sometimes existed in groupings other
than seven.

It is not unusual to read that Christ himself exercised each
of these ministries in some fashion. A sixth-century work written
in Gaul, called the *Chronicon palatinum,* gives an example of this:

> Christ was a porter when he opened the door of the ark and
> closed it again. He was a grave-digger when he called forth
> Lazarus, already stinking, out of the tomb on the fourth day.
> He was a lector when he opened up to the ears of the people
> the book of the prophet Isaiah in the midst of the synagogue
> and read and, when he had finished, handed it back to the
> minister. He was a subdeacon when he poured water into a
> basin and humbly washed the feet of his disciples of his own
> accord. He was a deacon when he blessed the chalice and
> gave it to his apostles to drink. He was a presbyter when he
> blessed the bread and gave it to them in the same way. He
> was a bishop when, as one having power, he taught the peo-
> ple in the temple about the kingdom of God.[80]

At the basis of schemes like this was almost certainly an attempt
to establish the legitimacy of these orders in the most striking
way possible, and to show that Christ had sanctified each of
them by having exercised their functions, just as Irenaeus
wanted to show that Christ had sanctified the different ages of
human life by having passed through all of them.[81] More impor-

tant than this, though, is the idea that the present holders of these offices are thus continuing the ministry of Christ in carrying out their duties: it is not their own work but his that they are doing.

The Selection of Ministers

One of the most consistent themes to appear in patristic literature with regard to the ministry is that of the candidate's hesitation or even refusal to take an ecclesiastical office upon himself, primarily out of a sense of unworthiness. Among those stricken with such a sense were some of the most illustrious of the Fathers. Ambrose fled from Milan rather than answer the call of the people to be their bishop.[82] Gregory Nazianzen ran away from his hometown immediately after having been ordained to the priesthood, so onerous did he consider its duties and so incapable himself of fulfilling them.[83] Augustine was made a priest unexpectedly and against his will, and he wept freely during the ceremony.[84] John Chrysostom, for his part, composed his entire treatise *On the Priesthood* as a justification for refusing ecclesiastical rank. Among the otherwise unknown was a certain Ammonius, a monk of the Egyptian desert, who cut off an ear so that he could not serve as bishop; but when he saw that even this would not dissuade some from their purpose he threatened to cut out his tongue as well, and it was only then that he was left in peace.[85]

In one of his letters, written at the end of the fourth century, Epiphanius of Salamis relates the remarkable story of how he ordained Paulinian, a brother of Jerome, to the diaconate and the priesthood. While visiting Jerome's monastery at Bethlehem he saw that Jerome himself and another priest were unwilling, "on account of modesty and humility, to offer the sacrifice that was permitted them and to labor in that part of the ministry that is of the most saving benefit to Christians." He wanted to ordain Paulinian, who was a monk there, for the sake of the other monks, who had been without the celebration of the Eucharist for a long time. But Paulinian always used to go into hiding when he suspected that this was the intent of the bishop. "Consequently I was surprised," Epiphanius writes,

> when by the disposition of God he came to me with the deacons of the monastery and a number of other brethren in order to make amends for something or other that I had against them. When therefore the collect was being celebrated in the church of the villa near our monastery, while he was completely unaware and suspected nothing, I ordered him to be seized by several deacons and his mouth to be covered, lest perhaps in his desire to be set free he might adjure me in the name of Christ. And first I ordained him a deacon, admonishing him with the fear of God and forcing him to minister, although he struggled a great deal, crying out that he was unworthy and protesting that it was a heavy burden beyond his powers. I was just barely able to bring him to this and to persuade him with proofs from the Scriptures and the setting forth of the divine commandments. And when he had ministered at the altar, again with great difficulty, with his mouth closed, I ordained him a priest, and with the same arguments that I had previously used I now insisted that he take his place among the priests.[86]

This narrative, for all its disconcerting aspects, permits us at least to catch a glimpse of a principle dear to the ancient Church that was often subsequently overlooked, namely, that ecclesiastical offices existed to minister to needs, and that the will of those experiencing the needs had decisive force in determining who was to exercise an office. The preference of the person being considered for the office, on the other hand, was hardly as significant.

In the choosing of a bishop, priest or deacon, therefore, the consultation and approval of the laity was integral. "We see that this comes from divine authority," Cyprian writes,

> that the bishop be chosen in the presence of the people, before their eyes, and that he be approved as worthy and fit by public judgment and testimony. . . . The Lord commands that the bishop be ordained in the presence of the whole synagogue. That is, he instructed and showed that episcopal ordinations must not take place except with the knowledge

of the people so that, with the people present, they would either discern the crimes of the wicked or proclaim the merits of the good, and that the ordination that has been examined by the suffrage and judgment of all might be just and valid. . . . And we notice that the apostles observed this not only in the ordinations of bishops and priests but also of deacons.[87]

None of what has been said here is to imply that all the occupants of the different ministries of the ancient Church were without reproach. We read constantly in acts of synods and elsewhere of sanctions being imposed on ministers who have fallen in one way or another, and we know too that to be a bishop or priest was often a lucrative possibility: hence the frequent admonitions against the love of money that are addressed to them in patristic literature.[88] We may in fact be moved with shame upon reading the pagan historian Ammianus Marcellinus' account of the luxury and power that was at the disposal of the clergy in late fourth-century Rome,[89] which is an account seconded by Jerome in the most scathing terms.[90] It was on account of infidelity on the part of priests and bishops, after all, that the Donatist schism began and that Augustine had had to evolve the tragic distinction between the personal morality of the ordained official and the validity of the sacraments that he administered. But the implication even in so many spoiled expectations is that the standard of ministry was high indeed.

VII

Martyrdom and Virginity

Thus far we have devoted ourselves to what might be considered "official" or "institutional" aspects of patristic thought—to the Fathers' reflections on Scripture, God, Christ, the human condition and the Church. These were things that demanded some sort of faith or assent on the part of the Christian. With this chapter, however, we enter a new realm, which might be characterized as "unofficial" or, better yet, as "charismatic." But what we shall touch on here and in the following chapter was, to the ancient Church, as truly and as uniquely Christian as any of the great mysteries. This was certainly the case with martyrdom in particular. By likening it to both baptism and the Eucharist (as we shall see that they did), the early Christians demonstrated that, indeed, they considered it somehow to be one with those mysteries.

When speaking of martyrdom, it seems worthwhile to begin by briefly dispelling the perhaps still popular notion that the Church was constantly and universally subject to persecution in the course of its first three centuries. There were comparatively large spaces of time—between the death of the emperor Septimius Severus in 211 and the accession of Decius in 249, for example—when there was no general persecution and when the Church experienced a considerable amount of freedom. Even when there was an official policy of persecution it was not carried out everywhere with the same thoroughness; that depended on the mood of the local authorities and the local citizenry. Rome itself and the provinces of North Africa seem to have suffered particularly, while those of present-day Turkey often remained relatively unscathed. On the other hand, not every martyr perished during a time of general persecution: Ignatius of Antioch, perhaps the most famous of all the early Church's martyrs, suffered under the emperor Trajan, who was rather fair-minded in his attitude toward Christianity. Likewise, while it is true to say that persecutions ended in the Roman Empire with the accession of Constantine at the beginning of the fourth century, isolated attacks on Christians still occasionally took place for centuries afterward, usually in out-of-the-way rural locations. And in Persia, outside the Empire, state persecutions that claimed many lives occurred from time to time throughout virtually the whole of the patristic era.

What we know of the martyrs comes from court reports preserved in Christian narratives, from eye-witness accounts and from subsequent accounts. Even what may not be historically accurate, however, reveals the Church's mentality, or at least that of the average Christian, and that is of prime importance.

From the point of view of that mentality the martyr was a privileged individual indeed, for he bore witness to Christ by the most complete conformation to his suffering and death. In fact the restriction of the term "martyr" (meaning "witness") to those who died for Christ, or who were about to do so, indicates that they were considered to be his witnesses in an unqualified manner, par excellence. As such they merited a veneration, both in life and in death, which was unique to them. Those who had suffered torment in prison and been released were called "confessors" (or sometimes "martyrs") and earned the right to a similar veneration. According to the Syrian *Didascalia apostolorum*, they were to be regarded as "an angel of God or a god upon earth, spiritually clothed with the Holy Spirit of God."[1] The Roman writer Hippolytus tells us about the beginning of the third century, in a remarkable passage, that those who had been imprisoned for the Lord could claim the honor of the presbyterate for themselves without submitting to the rite of the imposition of hands.[2] These were the "saints" of the ancient Church, and it was generally believed, at least in the first two centuries, that they alone experienced the vision of Christ immediately upon death.[3]

If we want to catch a glimpse of the honor that was paid to the martyrs in their lifetimes we could do no better than turn to the second-century pagan writer Lucian of Samosata, who describes an incident in the life of a professional charlatan named Peregrinus, who pretended to be a Christian teacher while traveling through Palestine. Lucian's chief interest in recounting the tale is Peregrinus himself, but he also gives what we have every reason to believe is an accurate portrayal of the early Christian attitude toward those suffering for the faith. For his supposed Christianity, Lucian writes, Peregrinus was thrown into prison,

> which itself gave him no little reputation to help him in later life and gratify his passion for posture and notoriety. Well, when he had been imprisoned, the Christians, regarding the incident as a calamity, left nothing undone in the effort to rescue him. Then, since this was impossible, every other form of attention was shown him, not in any casual way but with assiduity; and from the break of day you could see aged women lingering about the prison, widows and orphans, while their officials even slept inside with him after bribing the guards. Elaborate meals were brought in, and sacred books of theirs were read aloud, and excellent Peregrinus . . . was called by them "a new Socrates."
>
> Indeed, people came even from the cities of Asia, sent by the Christians at their common expense, to succor and defend and encourage the hero. They show incredible speed whenever any such public action is taken; for in no time they lavish their all. So it was in the case of Peregrinus, then; much money came to him from them by reason of his imprisonment, and he procured not a little revenue from it.[4]

Lucian concludes by saying that, after he had been removed from prison by the order of the governor of Syria, who recognized that he was only a charlatan looking for notoriety, Peregrinus continued to take advantage of the Christians' kindness (and gullibility) until they too finally discovered that he was an impostor.

So great was the influence of the confessors or martyrs by the middle of the third century, at least in North Africa, that they began to interfere in affairs that were not their concern. Many of them felt that they had the right to readmit to communion in the

Church other Christians who had in weakness renounced the faith in time of persecution, although the sacrament of reconciliation was at that period reserved to the bishops and could only be received once in a person's life; others simply pestered the bishops until they gave in to their demands. Thus they effectively threatened episcopal authority with their claims to a special position within the Church, and we see Cyprian of Carthage inveighing against them for just this reason. What is tragic, however, is that some of the martyrs whose demands were not met and who were all too aware of the esteem in which ordinary people held them entered into schism. In his treatise *On the Unity of the Catholic Church* Cyprian points out that such persons are not really martyrs at all:

> Those who have refused to be of one mind in the Church of God cannot be abiding with God. Though they be burned in the flames and cast into the fire, or lay down their lives exposed to wild beasts, this will not be the crowning of their faith but the punishing of their unfaithfulness, not the glorious consummation of religious valor but an end put to foolhardiness. A person like this can be put to death, but crowned he cannot be.[5]

The opposition of Cyprian and other bishops to the encroaching claims of the martyrs was so forceful that the phenomenon was not repeated, at least on any important scale, in the next great series of persecutions at the end of the third and the beginning of the fourth centuries.

It was his experience with the Donatists at the beginning of the fifth century, when they were calling attention to their own "martyrs," that gave Augustine the occasion to draw a distinction that is implicit in Cyprian: "It is not suffering but rather the reason for it that makes the martyr."[6] The reason for it could only exist within the body of the Church.

Although suffering and death of itself was insufficient to make a person a true Christian, nevertheless, according to Irenaeus, it was one of the very marks of the Church:

> And so the Church everywhere, by reason of that love which it has for God, in every age sends forth a multitude of mar-

tyrs to the Father. All others, however, not only have nothing of this kind to point to among themselves but even maintain that such witness-bearing is unnecessary. They say that the true witness is to hold to their opinions, although occasionally one or two of them have, during the whole time since the Lord appeared on earth, borne the reproach of the name [of Christ] along with our martyrs . . . and been led forth with them [to death]. . . . For the Church alone sustains with purity the reproach of those who suffer persecution for the sake of justice and endure all sorts of punishments and are put to death on account of their love for God and their confession of his Son.[7]

In the well-known phrase of Tertullian, it was precisely martyrdom that made the Church grow: "The blood of Christians is seed."[8] It was a commonplace in patristic literature, too, to advance martyrdom as a proof of the truth of the Christian religion, as Athanasius does when he says that, since Christ's coming, not only men but even women and children have gone eagerly to their deaths for his sake.[9]

Since martyrdom was a charism, a grace, it could not be demanded as a right; it was a free gift of God. Consequently the Church discouraged people from offering themselves to be killed. "Blessed, then, and noble are all the martyrdoms that have taken place according to the will of God," writes the anonymous author of the second-century *Martyrdom of Polycarp*,[10] and he speaks a little later of a would-be martyrdom that failed because it was entirely a personal venture:

> A certain Quintus, a Phrygian recently arrived from Phrygia, lost heart on seeing the beasts. But he was one who had forced himself and some others to come forward of their own accord. The proconsul persuaded this man with many entreaties to take the oath and offer sacrifice. On account of this, then, brethren, we do not commend those who give themselves up, since this is not what the Gospel teaches.[11]

Clement of Alexandria says that those who provoke martyrdom are accomplices in the crime of the persecutor,[12] and the Synod of Elvira, held in Spain at the dawn of the fourth century, has for one of its canons: "If anyone breaks idols and is killed on the spot, since this is not written in the Gospel nor will it be found that it ever happened in the days of the apostles, he shall not be received into the number of the martyrs."[13] It was for this reason that a person like Cyprian would flee from the authorities until he felt sure that his time for witness had come.[14]

It was characteristic of the martyr to be able to recognize this moment of witness and to see the rightness of it: it was frequently a moment of transformation, of inner peace or of spiritual exaltation, reflected in his actions or his features. The narratives of the martyrs recount almost invariably that they greeted their sentences of death with praise and thanksgiving. The reaction of one Nartzalus, who died with eleven others in the year 180 in North Africa, is typical. On hearing that he was to suffer he exclaimed: "Today we are martyrs in heaven! Thanks be to God!"[15] Polycarp of Smyrna astonished those around him by a composure remarkable for a man of eighty-six years. Having been granted permission to pray just after his capture, he falls into a trance and for two hours prays aloud without stopping.[16] During his interview with the proconsul, who threatens him with death by fire, Polycarp, we read, "was filled with courage and joy, and his countenance was suffused with grace."[17] This physical transformation is classic in the narratives of the martyrs. We see it in the earliest one of all, that of Stephen in Acts 6:15, where he is described as having a "face like the face of an angel." The author of a letter that recounts the massacre of Christians in Lyons and Vienne in the year 177 says that the martyrs went forth to death with joy, "with glory and much grace blended on their faces."[18] In *The Passion of Perpetua and Felicity*, written perhaps by Tertullian at the beginning of the third century, those about to die proceed into the arena "as if to an assembly, joyful and with shining countenances."[19] So great is the martyrs' joy conceived to be that it is possible to speak of their suffering as an inebriation. Thus, in a hymn probably composed by the Syrian bishop Rabbula of Edessa at the beginning of the fifth century, we read:

> Blessed martyrs, you are like grapes on God's vine, and the Church is drunk with the wine you make. You are God's

lamps, and how brightly you shine! You welcomed your sufferings as though they were pleasures: yours is the triumph,
not theirs who put you to death.
    Glory to the Power who helped you in the struggle!
    May the God who came to save us have pity on us.
When the saints were preparing for their feast of suffering,
they drank the wine that the Jews had made in the winepress
of Golgotha, and so they came to know the mysteries of
God's house.
    Therefore we sing: Praise be to Christ, who made the
martyrs drunk with the blood that came from his side![20]

At the root of the physical and psychological transformation
attributed to the martyrs was the firm conviction that they were
not suffering alone. They were following Christ as closely as
possible and experiencing his presence in their sufferings. In *The
Martyrdom of Polycarp,* as elsewhere, this union with Christ is
understood to be so overwhelming that it obliterates any sense
of pain: in the very act of martyrdom the sufferers are already
out of the flesh—"no longer human beings but already angels":

Can there be anyone not in awe of their nobility of character,
their patient endurance and their devotion to their Master?
Some, for example, even through they were so severely torn
by scourging that their deeper veins and arteries were visible,
endured, becoming objects of pity and lamentation to the
onlookers. Others attained such a degree of heroism that not
a grumble or a groan escaped from their lips, demonstrating
that the martyrs of Christ had passed out of the flesh even in
the very moment of being tortured—or rather, that they were
in the company of and in conversation with the Lord. Their
attention fixed on the grace of Christ, they downplayed the
tortures of this world, in the space of a single hour purchas-
ing unending life. The fire that their torturers applied felt
cold to them, for they concentrated on the fact that they were
escaping from an unending and unquenchable fire. With the
eyes of their heart, their vision was on the good things in
store for those who would persevere—goods of which ear
has not heard nor eye seen nor the human heart ever conceived. These things were revealed to them by the Lord

because they were no longer human beings but already angels.[21]

Polycarp himself does not simply follow Christ to his death. The whole course of his martyrdom is a re-enactment of Christ's own suffering. The author tells us at the very beginning of his narrative that "everything that led up to it [his death] happened in such a way that the Lord might show us anew a martyrdom in accordance with the Gospel."[22] In this vein his death is described in eucharistic terms as "a holocaust prepared and acceptable to God," a sharing in the cup of Christ, "a rich and pleasing sacrifice";[23] and as the flames rage around him, Polycarp stands at the center, "not as burning flesh, but as bread being baked."[24] Yet Polycarp is merely the most striking example of a theme that recurs throughout patristic literature. In the bodies of the martyrs, the *Didascalia apostolorum* says, the sufferings of Christ are renewed, and in them one can see the Lord himself.[25] Thus in the body of Sanctus, one of the martyrs of Lyons, it is said that Christ suffered and accomplished mighty wonders.[26] And several other of these martyrs are compared in various ways to Christ.

As in *The Martyrdom of Polycarp*, where the experience of Christ's presence brings relief from suffering, so it is with one of the martyrs of Lyons, who finally loses consciousness after having suffered severe torment; this release from pain is granted to her "on account of her hope, her grasp of what she believed and her converse with Christ."[27] In *The Passion of Perpetua and Felicity* a vision of Christ brings solace to Saturus and Perpetua, destined to die in the arena, who are led by angels into the Lord's presence: "And the four angels raised us up, and we kissed him and he stroked our faces with his hand."[28] Finally, in the prolonged suffering of the early fourth-century Vincent of Saragossa, as described later in the century by the poet Prudentius, the martyr is in an ecstasy, his face transparently joyful, for he is consoled by the presence of Christ.[29]

According to Cyril of Jerusalem, on the other hand, it is the Holy Spirit, acting in his capacity as Comforter, who aids the martyr in his suffering. He whispers words of hope to the sufferer and gives him a glimpse of paradise, so that the sufferer despises his torments.[30] In fact, the strength bestowed on the martyr to witness on behalf of Christ is a gift of the Spirit for, as Cyril says, quoting 1 Corinthians 12:3, "no one can say Jesus is Lord except by the Holy Spirit."[31]

Such narratives of the martyrs' sufferings as *The Martyrdom of Polycarp* and *The Passion of Perpetua and Felicity*, whose essential veracity we have no reason to doubt, provide us with a kind of rudimentary theology of martyrdom. It is a theology of the imitation of Christ and of the glory of the cross, which are Pauline and Johannine themes. The narratives are marked by what one might call an unblinking look at the martyrs' suffering, totally unabashed by any of the horrid details, yet not dwelling on them. There is none of the psychological drama involved in the anticipation of a cruel death; in early literature we find that only in the letters of Ignatius of Antioch, and in them it exists in sublimated form. Ignatius' self-expressed desire, among other things, to be ground to bits by wild beasts in the Roman arena so that he may prove to be "Christ's pure bread"[32] represents, according to one biographer, "not morbidity, the brooding of self-hate and contempt for life, but the fear that he might betray his dearest convictions."[33] Everything that the martyrs do is characterized by an austere single-mindedness that is typical of the Gospels themselves: as Jesus' life is directed toward Jerusalem and is there fulfilled, so that of the martyrs is directed toward the supreme moment of their own death. We can see this particularly in Ignatius, whose final months on the road to Rome and the death awaiting him there are a journey to God that must not be obstructed in any way, particularly by the misbegotten kindness of Roman Christians who might try to save him from his destiny.[34]

Complementary to this is the nuance of a certain inevitability in martyrdom. The good seems invariably to attract to itself the malice of the wicked. Such at least is the thought of Tertullian, who draws upon the Old Testament for his proof:

From the beginning, indeed, righteousness suffers violence. Immediately, as soon as God has begun to be worshiped, religion is dealt out ill-will. He who had pleased God [namely Abel] is slain, and by his own brother. Having started at home, so that it might all the more easily seek out the blood of strangers, wickedness finally went after not only that of righteous persons but even of prophets as well. David is harassed, Elijah put to flight, Jeremiah stoned, Isaiah sawn apart, Zachariah butchered between the altar and the temple, covering the pavement with enduring stains of his blood. He who is at the close of the law and the prophets [John the Baptist], who is called not a prophet but a messenger, is beheaded, dying ignobly as the price for a dancing girl. And indeed they who used to be led by the Spirit of God were accustomed to be directed by him to the shedding of their blood.[35]

Finally, in these narratives there is often a strong element of the ecstatic manifesting itself in dreams, visions and the experience of the presence of Christ and the Holy Spirit. Nowhere else do we find this on such a scale in the orthodox Christianity of the second and third centuries, which tended to suspect ecstasy on account of its appearance in certain pagan cults and heterodox sects.

Other Aspects of Martyrdom

If we turn to Tertullian's treatise on baptism we see there the first explicit mention of the familiar notion that martyrdom is a baptism in blood for those who have never been baptized in water: this is symbolized by the streams of blood and water that flowed from Christ's side on the cross. More than that, it offers the remission of sins to those who have lost their baptismal innocence.[36] Since there existed only one other opportunity for forgiveness of sins after baptism in the early Church, this was an important aspect of martyrdom. In Origen's treatise on martyrdom this idea has been expanded in a rather remarkable way: martyrdom profits not only the martyr himself but atones for many others as well. In this respect Origen suggests a daring comparison between the death of the martyr and the death of Christ: "Baptism in the form of martyrdom, as received by the Savior, is a purgation for the world; so too, when we receive it, it becomes a purgation for many."[37] And later on he continues still more forcefully in the same vein: "Perhaps just as we have been purchased by the precious blood of Jesus, when Jesus received the name that is above every name, so some will be purchased by the precious blood of the martyrs; for they themselves are exalted higher than they would have been if they had only been justified and not also become martyrs."[38] Small wonder that with this kind of mentality martyrdom eventually came to be regarded as greater than baptism. Chromatius of Aquileia, writing toward the end of the fourth century, says that "baptism in water is certainly good, but better and best of all is the baptism of the martyr. The former is forgiveness, the latter a reward. The former is the remission of sins, in the latter a crown of virtues is merited."[39]

There are also parallels with the Eucharist in the words of Origen that have just been cited, as the connection is drawn between the blood of Christ and the blood of the martyr. The idea is still more striking in the prayer that Polycarp offers on his funeral pyre, which was alluded to earlier. This is remarkably similar to a eucharistic prayer, even containing an epiclesis and a doxology, which are typical elements of such a prayer.[40] In fact, however, the parallel certainly goes back to Jesus himself, whose eucharistic words anticipate his suffering and death.

One of the most interesting aspects of the early treatises on martyrdom is their use of themes and images that will later be associated with the monastic vocation. In Tertullian the prison in which the martyrs await their death is described as if it were actually a monastery. At the gate of the prison, he tells the martyrs,

> you were cut off from the world, and how much more from worldly life and its concerns! Do not be alarmed that you have been separated from the world, for if we reflect that the world itself is more truly the prison we shall understand that you have left a prison rather than entered one. . . . [There] you are free from causes of offense, from temptations, from the remembrance of evil things and from persecution too. The prison offers the Christian the same thing that the desert offered the prophets. The Lord himself frequently went into seclusion, that he might pray more freely, that he might be

apart from the world. It was in solitude, too, that he showed his glory to his disciples. Let us drop the name of prison; let us call it a retreat. Even if the body is shut in, even if the flesh is confined, all things are open to the spirit.[41]

In Origen we find both Matthew 16:24 ("If anyone will come after me, let him deny himself and take up his cross and follow me") and Matthew 19:27–29 ("Everyone who has left houses or brothers or sisters or father or mother or children or lands for my name's sake will receive a hundredfold and inherit eternal life") applied to martyrdom.[42] These two passages were later claimed by the monks as their own. Indeed, as has been pointed out any number of times by other writers, monasticism may be seen as the succesor of martyrdom.[43] The monastic life was a daily martyrdom of asceticism, a heroic substitute for the heroism of the martyr. "Let us not think," Jerome says in a homily addressed to his monks, "that there is martyrdom only in the shedding of blood. There is always martyrdom."[44] But the monk could hope, as did Anthony of Egypt, the father of monasticism who yearned to die for Christ, that one day he might be given the opportunity of actually shedding his blood.[45]

Of all the Fathers, the one who, along with Ignatius of Antioch, writes about martyrdom with the most beauty and conviction is Origen. We may even say that his treatise on the subject, the *Exhortation to Martyrdom*, represents a kind of theory or theological investigation of martyrdom, which complements the "practical" narratives of the martyrs' actual suffering. While Origen was still a rather young man his father Leonides was put to death in the persecution of Septimius Severus at the beginning of the third century, and his son's desire to join him was so great that his mother had to hide his clothing in order to prevent him from appearing in public and bearing witness to Christ before the civil authorities.[46] He finally attained his wish as an old man of about seventy, dying after severe torture inflicted during the persecution of Valerian at the middle of the third century. Thus his words carry a greater weight when he writes, encouraging others to die: "What other day of salvation is comparable to the day of our glorious departure from here below!"[47]

We have already seen how for Origen martyrdom is a participation not only in Christ's sufferings but in his redemptive work as well, since he advances the idea that some are ransomed by the blood of the martyrs. Thus nothing that the martyr does is for himself alone. His struggle is not merely personal; it has, in fact, a cosmic significance: "A great assembly is gathered to watch you as you do combat and are called to bear witness. . . . The whole universe and all the angels on the right and on the left, all human beings, those on God's side and the others—all will hear us doing battle for Christianity."[48] Therefore the martyr's victory, like his struggle, is not merely personal but cosmic also: it is a joining with Christ in defeating the world of principalities and powers.[49]

In addition to this, Origen sees martyrdom in terms of a mystical journey to a knowledge of the divine secrets, secrets more profound than those into which Paul was initiated when he was caught up to the third heaven.[50] It is, too, a mystical return to paradise, from which the first parents had been expelled—a return that involves encountering the flaming and purifying fire of the sword of the cherubim who stand guard at the entrance to paradise.[51]

But perhaps the most sublime aspect of Origen's teaching on martyrdom is that he shows it to be demanded by the love of God; it is a gift offered to God out of the abundance of the martyr's heart, and not extracted unwillingly from him under torture.

> A saint is a person with a zeal for doing what is right; his desire is to repay the many good things that God has previously done for him. He is in quest of something that he can do for the Lord in return for all that the Lord has done for him. He learns that for a person of even the best intentions there is no act that can match the Lord's generosity—except to end one's life in martyrdom. Scripture says: What shall I give back to the Lord for all that he has given me? The answer comes immediately: The cup of salvation I will take, and I will call upon the Lord's name. Now, as we find in the Gospels, martyrdom is usually called a cup of salvation.[52]

In Origen's thought, martyrdom is the most precious offering that a human being can make to God.

As the age of persecutions drew to a close in the Empire and the number of martyrs diminished to relative insignificance, the Church realized that in some way something had been lost to it. So central had martyrdom been to the Church's spirit that it seemed inconceivable that it should be without this charism. For this reason, it would appear, by the end of the third century the terms "martyr" and "martyrdom" begin to be used with a certain looseness. More than that, however, these terms were undoubtedly believed to confer an added luster on the things and persons to which they are attached. We have already seen the monastic state referred to as a martyrdom, and it becomes increasingly the case that holy persons who have not in fact suffered a violent death are spoken of as martyrs. Thus, for example, Sulpicius Severus writes of his contemporary, Martin of Tours, who died near the end of the fourth century, that

> although the temper of the age was unable to offer him martyrdom, nonetheless he will not lack a martyr's glory, since by both desire and virtue he could have been a martyr and was willing to be one. . . . Even though he did not endure these things [namely, the actual pains of martyrdom], still he attained to martyrdom, albeit in unbloody fashion. For what agonies of human sorrows did he not bear for the hope of eternity, in hunger, in vigils, in nakedness, in fastings, in the hard words of the envious, in persecutions of the unrighteous, in care for the sick, in concern for the imperiled?[53]

Much the same is said of Honoratus of Arles, who died in 430, by his biographer, Hilary of Arles. Addressing the dead saint, Hilary writes: "Indeed, I think that no one would doubt that it was not courage that failed you for martyrdom but rather the occasion for it."[54] And a certain deacon writes to Cyril of Alexandria just about the time of the Council of Ephesus in 431 and unhesitatingly tells Cyril that, after having endured some slight harassments from the Nestorians, he has merited "a richly-flowered crown adorned with all the glory of martyrdom."[55] The instances could be multiplied.

Virginity

With this we come to virginity, which by the end of the third century was being compared to martyrdom. It is then that Methodius of Olympus writes that virgins will be the first to follow in the Lord's train into the kingdom of heaven,

> into the repose of the new ages. Their martyrdom did not consist in enduring things that pain the body for a short period of time; rather it consisted in steadfast endurance throughout their whole lifetime, never once shrinking from the truly Olympian contest of being battered in the practice of chastity. Because they stood firm against the torments of pleasure, fear, sorrow and other vices, they carry off the highest honors of all by reason of their rank in the land of promise.[56]

This notion is repeated any number of times among the Fathers. Ambrose qualifies the relationship between the two, martyrdom and virginity, when he remarks that "virginity is not praiseworthy because it is found in martyrs but because it itself makes martyrs."[57] Virginity is not seen to be like martyrdom simply because it involves a comparable struggle but also because it produces the same effect, death to self, expressed through the image of bodily death. Thus virginity, like monasticism, succeeds to the martyr's mantle, even though, as Augustine says, no one would dare consider virginity greater than martyrdom.[58]

To speak of virginity as a kind of martyrdom is already to understand something of its attractiveness to the early Church, since the martyr exerted such a tremendous fascination on it. To understand more it is necessary to see virginity in its relationship to married life.

Here it has become far too easy the criticize the Fathers in an unthinking sort of way. Almost invariably they seem to demean the married state as a matter of course, or at best to damn it with faint praise. It was a commonplace, in writing of virginity, to speak of the disadvantages attendant upon marriage—the uncertainties about the future of one's children, to say nothing of the agonies of childbirth that a mother underwent;

the constant fear that one's spouse would die at a young age or in some unexpected manner; the sorrow of widowhood. In comparison with this, virginity would necessarily look much better.

It must be said in the Fathers' behalf, however, that marriage in ancient times was not an easy vocation, and this was so almost precisely for the reasons that the Fathers advanced and that could be elaborated. Moreover, as Gregory of Nyssa writes in his treatise on virginity, marriage had no need of defenders, whatever its drawbacks may have been:

> The human nature that we all share is quite adequate to the task of speaking in defense of marriage. By itself, human nature instils in all of us a lower inclination to enter into marriage in order to beget, whereas virginity stands in the way of our natural proclivity in a certain manner. Since this is the case, writing a treatise praising or encouraging marriage is an unnecessary task. Its own pleasures are its best advocate and champion of its merits.[59]

But Gregory goes on to admit that there are in fact those who deny the goodness of marriage and that something has to be said to them too, and so in the end he devotes some effort to defending the legitimacy of the married state.

When marriage actually was in danger in the early Church—as it was occasionally from gnostic groups and extreme ascetics—it did not lack writers to come to its support. Clement of Alexandria gives over a whole book of his *Miscellanies* to an argument in favor of marriage, and in so doing he shows a remarkable sympathy for his subject, perhaps because he himself was married.[60] Even the somber Tertullian, who was married, could describe marriage in the most beautiful terms, as the deepest and most complete sharing of two lives, in a treatise addressed to his wife[61] and written before he fell prey to the harshness of Montanism, which could hardly distinguish between marriage and fornication.[62] Some lines of Gregory Nazianzen in one of his poems are as splendid as anything ever written by the Fathers about marriage. Gregory makes those who are married speak for themselves:

We whose concerns are the bonds of marriage and of life
follow the law of human generation
established by the Son of the eternal Father
when he joined the first Adam to the woman drawn from his
      side,
so that man might be born as the fruit of man and,
throughout the generations,
might dwell in his offspring as in an ear of grain.
In carrying out this law and union of love
we aid one another mutually and,
since we are born of the earth,
we follow the primitive law of the earth,
which is also the law of God. . . .
See what prudent marriages offer to the human race:
Who has taught wisdom, sought the depths,
the things on earth, in the sea, under the heavens?
Who has given laws to the cities and, before these laws,
who established the cities and discovered the arts?
Who has filled the public places, the houses, the arenas?
Who has supplied the army in time of war
and the tables in time of feasting?
Who has set up the choirs singing in the temple?
Who has calmed the exigencies of primitive life,
tilled the soil, cultivated gardens,
sent dark ships into the seas in the face of the winds?
Who has joined the earth and the moist paths of the ocean
in one and brought together what was remote, if not marriage?
And there is still more.
Those things that are higher are nobler by far.
In our living together we are one another's hands, ears and feet.
Marriage redoubles our strength, rejoices our friends,
causes grief to our enemies.
A common concern makes trials bearable.
Common joys are all the happier,
and accord makes riches more pleasant;
it is even more delightful than riches for those without wealth.
Marriage is the key of moderation and the harmony of the
      desires,
the seal of a deep friendship . . .
the unique drink from a fountain enclosed,
inaccessible to those without.
United in the flesh, one in spirit,

they urge each other on by the goad of their mutual love.
For marriage does not remove from God
but brings all the closer to him,
for it is God himself who draws us to it.[63]

In this respect mention should also be made of the mid-fourth-century Synod of Gangra in Asia Minor, which excommunicated a group of ascetics called Eustathians who condemned marriage. The canons of the synod are typical of the church's response to that phenomenon. The first, for example, reads: "If anyone despises marriage and blames and despises the woman who sleeps with her husband, even if she is a believer and devout, as if she were unable to enter the kingdom of God, let him be anathema." The tenth canon is complementary to it: "If anyone of those who remain unmarried for the Lord's sake lifts himself up in pride above those who are married, let him be anathema." This warning against pride on the part of virgins vis-à-vis the married is nearly as old as the practice of Christian virginity itself and is one of the most common themes in patristic literature touching on virginity.[64]

Yet, despite such sentiments and precautions, it must be said that, by and large, marriage got short shrift in comparison with virginity in the ancient Church. For one thing it was felt, as Gregory of Nyssa maintained, that the pleasures of married life, uncertain as they may have been, were sufficiently evident to warrant that marriage not be made much of. For another, Christian writers had picked up some of the attitudes of the pagan philosophers toward marriage. Jerome quotes one of them, a certain Theophrastus, with approval. "A wise man," Theophrastus had written, "must not take a wife. For in the first place his study of philosophy will be impeded, and it is impossible for anyone to give equal time both to his books and to his wife." He goes on to complain about women's demands, to say that it is more convenient to have a slave than a wife, and to remark that, when a man is alone, he can best hold converse with God.[65] But to the credit of Jerome and others, they saw with some clarity that what distinguished pagan from Christian celibacy was ultimately grace. That is to say, for the pagans celibacy or virginity was either a kind of heroic achievement or simply an escape from the burden of married life, whereas for Christians it was primarily a divine gift with the love of God and Christ as its object, and only in that context did they speak of what they felt were its other "advantages."

Underlying this view of the incompatibility of married life and the pursuit of anything serious on a husband's part, it goes without saying, is the demeaning attitude toward women in classical antiquity. A woman's overarching reason for existence was to bear children; for companionship it was usually assumed that a man would seek out the company of another man. Augustine expresses the position well in commenting on the creation of Eve from Adam's side:

> If the woman was not made for the man in order to help him in begetting children, for what purpose was she made to help him? If it was to till the earth together, the work did not yet exist so that he was in need of help; and if such had been necessary, a man would have been a better helper. The same thing may be said about friendship, if perhaps he was growing weary of solitude. For how much better do two male friends live together, enjoying one another's company and conversation, than do a man and a woman! But it is was necessary to live together with one issuing commands and the other obeying (lest wills at variance with one another disturb the peace of those living together), an arrangement for such would not have been lacking, by which one man would have come first and another after—especially if the latter was created from out of the former, as was the case with the woman. Would anyone say that God was only able to make a woman from the man's side and not also a man if he had so willed it? Consequently I do not see what help a woman is to a man if not for childbearing.[66]

In addition to this, marriage was seen by many of the Fathers as only a remedy for concupiscence, permitted by Paul but hardly encouraged by him when he wrote in 1 Corinthians 7:9: "It is better to marry than to burn with passion." Since a woman could not be a man's intellectual or social equal, the sole source of married pleasure consisted in the enjoyment of sexual activity; this is certainly the impression that Jerome gives.[67]

Then, for a number of the Fathers the sexual act was inextricably caught up in the original fall: it was only after Adam and Eve had been expelled from paradise that Eve conceived and bore Cain. There was thus something "unclean" about sexual intercourse that had to do with its very origins, to say nothing of the shamefulness of lust that was always associated with it in practice. Gregory of Nyssa has an interesting idea that makes marriage ultimately responsible for all the evil in the world. He connects it with pride, the root of every vice, and demonstrates (rather unconvincingly) that were it not for pride no one would ever get married. Thus pride and marriage together constitute the first link in a long chain made up of all the vices that pride draws after itself, and whoever marries must almost surely bear this chain about with him continually.[68]

Small wonder, if looked at from this vantage point, that marriage suffered in comparison with virginity. The Fathers insist that they do not intend to deprecate marriage, yet in fact they do just that. Ambrose writes, for instance: "I am not, to be sure, seeking to dissuade anyone from marriage, but merely setting out the benefits of virginity." But then he proceeds immediately to enumerate all the familiar annoyances of married life.[69] It seems that very few of the Fathers could look at marriage and virginity together without making the inevitable and invidious comparison.

Yet virginity did not need to be compared with marriage in order for it to be seen as a value in itself. Nor was it merely an over-reaction to pagan mores, which were notoriously slack. Its similarity to martyrdom in the eyes of the early Church has already been noted. And there was more to it than that.

One could begin with the relationship of virginity to God. Methodius of Olympus shows that the very word "virginity" *(parthenia)* becomes "nearness to God" *(partheia)* simply by changing one letter, and this demonstrates that virginity "alone makes divine the one who possesses it and who has been initiated into its pure mysteries,"[70] Gregory of Nyssa elaborates on this aspect of deification. Virginity, he says, is called "the uncorrupted" *(to aphthoron)*; as such it is a participation in the uncorruptedness of God himself. For the Father has a Son, but has begotten him in a virginal way, without passion; and the Holy

Spirit is virginal as well. Virginity is therefore deifying: "It enjoys communion with the whole celestial nature; since it is free from passion it is always present to the powers above."[71] But besides being a participation in or a likeness to God himself it is also the means whereby this participation or likeness is attained: "Virginity bestows a certain disposition and power with regard to the divine life, furnishing those living in the flesh with the ability to assimilate themselves to spiritual reality."[72] This it does by turning the soul away from earthly beauty and toward the contemplation of divine beauty, toward the contemplation of a beauty that lies within the human soul itself once it has achieved the utmost possible purity and so is able to mirror the purity and beauty of God.[73]

Ambrose emphasizes a complementary aspect, the incarnational, while not ignoring that of deification. For him virginity ascends into heaven in order to find there the Word of God and draw him from the bosom of the Father into itself. The pattern for this is of course the Virgin Mary, in whose chaste body "the Word became flesh so that flesh might become God."[74]

All this represented a development of the most primitive Christian insight, which had been a part of the pagan Greek heritage as well, namely that virginity of its very nature established a relationship with the divine. This is stated as something taken quite for granted in Athenagoras' *Embassy for the Christians*, written before the year 180: "To abide as a virgin or a eunuch unites one to God, while a mere [unclean] thought or evil desire turns one away from him." There are in the Christian community, Athenagoras says, "both men and women who are growing old in virginity in the hope of being united more closely to God."[75]

This relationship with God becomes, so to speak, more personalized as the virgin comes eventually to be characterized as the bride of Christ. This was a title that had, in the New Testament, been reserved to the Church alone; it was the bride of Revelation 19:7: "The marriage of the Lamb has come, and his bride has made herself ready." By the beginning of the third century, however, we see that concept being applied to virgins by Tertullian, when he admonishes them to wear the veils that married women were accustomed to wear:

Wear the garb of a married woman in order to preserve the standing of a virgin. Belie a little of what you keep within yourself so as to show the truth to God alone. And yet there is no question of an untruth about being married, for you are in fact married to Christ: to him you have given rights over your flesh, to him you have wedded your maturity. Walk in accordance with the will of your husband.[76]

While the first commentators on the Song of Songs, Hippolytus and Origen, had understood this book of the Old Testament to be referring mystically to the marriage of Christ and the Church or to that of Christ and the soul of the Christian, by the end of the third century, with Methodius of Olympus, it is taken to have special reference to the virgin's relationship with Christ.[77] So we find it in the later Fathers. The virgin has become Christ's own and follows the Lamb wherever he goes with a joy that is uniquely her own—with the joy of the virgins of Christ, Augustine says, almost in rapture, "of Christ, in Christ, with Christ, after Christ, through Christ, for Christ."[78] And this is as it should be, for Christ is the "Archvirgin" and "the leader of the choir of virgins," as Methodius calls him.[79] He is the object of all the virgin's desires. "If you have disdained marriages with the sons of men," Augustine writes, " . . . love with your whole heart the one who is fairer than the sons of men. . . . Look upon the beauty of your lover. . . . The very thing that the proud deride in him, see how beautiful it is!" His wounds, his scars, his blood—all of this is lovely to the virgin.[80]

In the course of the first few centuries it was natural that the virgin, with her marital relationship to Christ, should become a figure of the Church, and indeed so she appears, for example, in Ambrose's treatise *On Virgins*.[81] It was natural too that, precisely on account of this relationship, the virgin should have been thought of increasingly in feminine terms, although in the first few centuries virgins were spoken of as both masculine and feminine. Gregory of Nyssa is almost alone in emphasizing that the possibility of a spiritual marriage applied to both men and women, for "there is neither male nor female" (Galatians 3:28), but "Christ is all, and in all" (Colossians 3:11).[82]

The explicitation of a special relationship with Christ (or with God, as Gregory of Nyssa has it in his treatise on virginity) brought certain consequences with it for women. It meant that virgins could do nothing that might be construed as pleasing men. Tertullian said that a virgin wearing a veil would simply be taken for a married woman; no one need realize that she was a virgin. But by the middle of the third century an evolution has occurred here. "A virgin ought not only to be such," writes Cyprian; "she should also be perceived and believed to be such. No one on seeing a virgin should have any doubt as to whether she is one."[83] Thus all sorts of "safeguards" became the norm. In his famous letter to Eustochium, Jerome outlines how his addressee, a Roman virgin, should live. These few lines are typical:

> Let your companions be those whom fasting has made thin, whose countenance is pallid, and who are approved by their long years and their manner of life. . . . Be subject to your parents: imitate your spouse. Rarely go out in public. . . . There will never be lacking a reason for going out if you are always finding some necessity for doing so. Take food in moderation and never fill your stomach. There are many women who, although they are sober with respect to wine, are intoxicated by the amount of food they have eaten. When you arise at night for prayer, belch not from indigestion but from hunger. Read often and learn as much as possible. Let sleep creep upon you as you hold a book, and let the sacred page catch your head as you nod.[84]

When he has concluded his advice Jerome draws a parallel between this life of deprivation and an idea that we have already noticed applied to martyrdom and that appears elsewhere in patristic literature on virginity, namely the return to paradise. We see in virgins, Ambrose says, the life that we left behind in paradise.[85] Jerome explains that the bringing forth of children in pain and sorrow fell to women only after Adam and Eve had been expelled from paradise, but in paradise they had been virgins. Thus the virgin attains to the same state as her first parents.[86] Gregory of Nyssa develops the theme differently: for him the practice of virginity is the first step toward the restoration of all that was lost in the fall. Now marriage was the culmination of the series of events connected with the fall. It had begun with pleasure; after that came shame and fear; then Adam and Eve hid from God; finally they were cast out of paradise and "sent forth into this pestilential and burdensome land in which marriage was instituted as a compensation for having to die." Thus, Gregory writes, marriage represents the final moment of humanity's departure from the life that was lived in paradise, and so it must be the first thing done away with by those who wish to return thither.[87]

"But since paradise is the home of the living and will not admit those who are dead by reason of their sins, and since we are fleshly, mortal and sold under sin, how can one who is in the power of death dwell in the realm of the living?"[88] The theme of the return to paradise immediately evokes for Gregory that of virginity as release from death. For virginity conquers death by bringing forth deathless children—life and immortality—into the world, whereas marriage continues death's work by producing children who will die, for "the physical bearing of children . . . is as much the beginning of death for human beings as it is of life, since at the moment of birth death takes its start."[89] Thus it is that virginity effects a radical transformation of those who practice it, and virgins may be said to be living another life entirely than those who are not virgins. "What we shall be you have already begun to be," Cyprian writes to the virgins of Carthage. "You possess already in this world the glory of the resurrection."[90] And Ambrose will say, in fact, that whoever disdains virginity disdains the resurrection itself, so much is the one the image of the other.[91] "You pass through the world," Cyprian continues, "without the contagion of the world. As long as you remain chaste and virgins you are equal to the angels of God."[92] The idea of virginity as angelic reappears constantly. "Those who do not marry and take a spouse for themselves are like angels on earth: they do not feel the trials of the flesh, they know no servitude, they are removed from the contagion of earthly thoughts, they are intent upon divine things," writes Ambrose.[93] Indeed, for Peter Chrysologus, the angel is in one sense inferior to the virgin: "If you wish to know," he tells his congregation in one of his sermons, "it is a greater thing to acquire angelic glory

than to possess it already. To be an angel has to do with beati-
tude; to be a virgin has to do with virtue. For virginity obtains
by its own powers what an angel has by nature."[94] The angelic
passionlessness of the virgin, which was really a control of the
passions rather than an absence of them, is highly reminiscent
of the state of the martyrs who, in the midst of their sufferings,
were "no longer human beings but already angels."[95]

As an image of the resurrection, virginity was not viewed
from only one perspective, namely freedom from physical defile-
ment. There were virgins who had been violated but who still
retained their spiritual virginity uncorrupted (although Ambrose
suggests that a virgin may kill herself to avoid being sexually
abused, so sacred even is physical virginity[96]). For virginity was
a thrust of life rather than just a single virtue. In a poem of Gregory Nazianzen in its praise he makes virginity say: "For me there
is only one law, one thought—that, filled with divine love, I
might journey from here to the light-bearing God who reigns in
heaven."[97] As Gregory of Nyssa explains, virginity is like a pipe
in which a heavy flow of water is contained, and which, despite
immense pressure, does not permit any of the water to escape,
but pushes it upward, denying the pull of gravity. Thus virginity
collects all the energies of the soul in a single great drive, rather
than permitting them to be dissipated in a vast array of smaller
drives, and so by the very strength of these energies the soul
is pushed upward to an exalted love.[98] This drive simply ex-
cludes everything else in the force of its Godward movement
and makes marriage, with its concerns and preoccupations,
impossible.[99]

For the Fathers, virginity touched everything, and for this
reason its enemies were everywhere—unchastity of course, but
also avarice, intemperance in food and drink, disobedience, and
especially pride, to which Augustine devotes a large part of his
treatise on virginity. For him the two virtues that must accompany virginity are love and humility: "Nothing guards the good
of virginity except God himself who gave it, and God is love.
Therefore the guardian of virginity is love, but the place of this
guardian is humility. For there he lives, he who said that his
Spirit rests on the lowly and the meek and on the one who trem-
bles at his words."[100] In the literature of the desert, conversely,

pride traditionally brings down upon itself a visitation from the demon of fornication. "When a person is swollen with pride," the monk Paphnutius tells some visitors, as Palladius recounts it, " . . . then God removes the angel of providence from him. When he has been removed, then he is oppressed by the adversary and, exalted by his own natural ability, he falls into impurity through his arrogance."[101] And Palladius has a picturesque story elsewhere that serves to illustrate the point:

> I was acquainted with a virgin in Jerusalem. For the space of six years she clothed herself in sackcloth and was shut up inside a wall, without access to anything that might bring her pleasure. In the end her excessive arrogance tripped her up and she fell. When she opened the door and received the fellow who had been taking care of her needs she had intercourse with him; for her ascetical practices were undertaken not for a godly purpose and out of love for God but simply to be noticed by people. Such is the result of vainglory and unsound intention. With her thoughts preoccupied with looking down on other people, she was bereft of the guardian of temperance.[102]

Gregory of Nyssa's treatise on virginity is the occasion for him to speak about the virtuous life and the harmony of the virtues and the passions, since they must all be mustered to protect virginity. Indignation and anger are its watchdogs, courage and confidence its weapons, hope and patience its staffs to lean upon, while sorrow is there for repentance; even desire for possession plays its part in the defense of virginity. It is a remarkable synthesis of the moral life, all centered about virginity.[103]

A word has already been said about the virgin as a type of the Church. More than that, virginity, like martyrdom, appears from time to time as a kind of mark of the Church. Before Christ came and the Church was established there was no virginity, although the Old Testament gradually prepared the Jewish people for it: so says Methodius.[104] Now that the Church has been established, Athanasius writes, it exists nowhere else, and this "is a very strong argument that the genuine and true religion exists with us."[105] Athanasius could not have been unaware of the fact that virginity did actually exist elsewhere, among pagans and heretics, but for him virginity must have seemed to flow, like martyrdom, from the very nature of the Church, which was itself a virgin.

Springing up from a sort of inner necessity within the Church, drawn on by the desire for Christ and the yearning to be one with God in the sharing of his incorruptible nature: thus virginity, which with martyrdom was the early Christian's fullest possible expression of love. And thus the reason for its extraordinary esteem in the early Church.

VIII

Monasticism

On a certain day sometime toward the end of the 260's, in a town in Middle Egypt, a young man named Anthony was visiting his local church, and as he entered the Gospel was being read. He was a pious young man, and on his way to church he had been reflecting on the life of the Christian community in apostolic times, when, as Acts 4:34–35 has it, all the members used to lay their property at the feet of the apostles. Consequently he took it as something directed right to him when the words of Matthew 19:21 caught his ear: "If you would be perfect, go, sell what you possess and give to the poor, and you will have treasure in heaven; and come, follow me." Feeling inspired to observe literally this saying of the Lord, Anthony immediately sold the rather sizable property that he had inherited from his recently deceased parents and gave the price of it to the poor, only keeping back a little for the support of his sister.

Shortly thereafter he entered the church a second time, and now he was struck by the words of Matthew 6:34: "Do not be anxious about tomorrow." This time he gave to the poor the money that he had saved for his sister, placed her in a community of nuns and at once entered upon a life of asceticism and self-denial near his house.[1]

Thus begins *The Life of Saint Anthony* by Athanasius, which was written by the great bishop of Alexandria shortly after Anthony's death in 356 at the age of one hundred and five. The effect that this book had upon virtually the whole ancient Church, both in East and West (for shortly after it appeared it was translated into Latin), can hardly be overestimated. Athanasius himself had intended the *Life* to be a kind of rule and model for monks in the form of a narrative,[2] but it proved to be more than that: it became the very inspiration of monasticism and, to those who read it, Egypt was transformed from the land of pharaonic oppression into a new paradise of spiritual perfection. Although monasticism had already taken firm hold in the Egyptian desert at least three decades before Athanasius wrote his book, with its publication there began a monastic golden age. And even though Anthony had been for the most part a hermit, it was to him that both hermits and cenobites (monks who live in a community) turned as their ideal.

Anthony's abrupt conversion to asceticism was perhaps the most famous part of Athanasius' biography, but the pattern of the rest of Anthony's life was also quite familiar. He first pursued asceticism in a spot near his home, and there too he had his first encounters with demons—encounters described in remarkable detail and destined to provoke the imagination and to influence painting and literature to our own day. After these initial conflicts with demons he went to live in a tomb on the outskirts of his village, and there he stayed, struggling with the enemy, until he was about thirty-five years old. Then he moved again, this time going to an abandoned fort in the so-called Outer Desert. Here he remained for twenty years, receiving bread sufficient for his needs from a benefactor every six months. At the end of the twenty years Anthony was forcibly removed from the fort by some friends, and with this a more active and public part of his life began. Suddenly many people were attracted to him and monasteries sprung up about him: it was now that he became what future generations would call him, the "Father of Monasticism." This seems to have been a relatively short period in his life, however. In 311, when he must have been sixty years old, Anthony left the desert and went to Alexandria, where he hoped to die a martyr in the persecution of Maximin Daia. Unsuccessful in this, he returned to the desert, but he eventually left the location where he had been and, in a search for complete solitude, went to a place designated in his biography as the Inner Mountain. With the exception of some brief journeys (including one again to Alexandria, where he opposed the Arian heretics), the Inner Mountain was to be his home for the remainder of his life. Here he had visions and received visitors for whom he occasionally performed miracles, here he gathered a few disciples around him, and here at last he died and was buried in a spot unknown to all but two of his disciples.

Themes in Monastic Writings

Inasmuch as Athanasius meant the *Life* of his hero to be a sort of model, he included in it certain themes that he understood to be characteristic of monastic life, all of which found their way into subsequent literature, perhaps having filtered through Athanasius' book. The first of these, which runs through the whole biography, is the notion of the life of the monk as a spiritual journey, which is reflected in Anthony's own progress from his native village through various stages to the Inner Mountain, a place deep in the desert. This movement, from civilization to an almost absolute solitude, is symbolic of the journey of the individual, the monk, from exteriority to an increasingly profound interiority, a journey that is not made without painful opposition from demonic forces. The most famous exponent of the journey theme in ancient Christian literature was Origen, and almost certainly Athanasius was familiar with and had been influenced by his twenty-seventh homily on Numbers 33, which has been cited earlier at some length.[3] Seeing in the Israelites' march through the desert, with its forty-two stages, an image of the interior journey, Origen could write that when a person

> has overcome one temptation and his faith has been tried in it, thereupon he comes to another, and he passes as it were from one stage to the next; and when he has mastered whatever may befall him, and faithfully endured it, he goes on to another. And thus he is said to have proceeded by stages as he submits to each of the trials of life and the tests of faith, and in them the virtues are acquired one by one. Likewise in them there is fulfilled what has been written: They shall go from strength to strength—until the final stage is attained, which is the summit of the virtues, and the river of God is crossed and the promised inheritance is received.[4]

The anonymous first Greek *Life of Pachomius,* written at the end of the fourth century, combines interestingly the theme of pilgrimage with the rich imagery of the East.[5] Theodore, the disciple and successor of the great monastic founder Pachomius, tells a monk that monastic life is a symbolic journey to the East, which begins at baptism. The road is narrow and precarious, and the monk cannot afford to deviate even slightly to one side or another lest he lose his way completely. To the left of the road is fleshly desire, and pride is to the right. But "if one journeys well and with fear, once one has arrived at the East he finds the Savior upon his throne, and all around him are hosts of angels and eternal crowns, and they crown the one who journeys to him well."[6]

Since the East is synonymous with paradise, we are made to recall still another monastic theme, which is that of monastic life as a return to paradise. Anthony's settlement on the Inner Mountain is highly reminiscent of the situation in which the first parents lived before their fall from grace. Athanasius tells us that Anthony planted a garden there, which is doubtless symbolic of Eden, and that he successfully rebuked the wild animals that had come into the garden and disturbed his plantings, just as Adam and Eve had had dominion over the wild creatures with whom they lived.[7] This sway over animals is a relatively common idea in early monastic literature, as has already been noted.[8] The monk Amoun, for example, was known to have summoned two large serpents from the desert waste to stand guard at his hermitage and protect him from robbers; by prayer he killed another serpent that was threatening the neighboring countryside.[9] The great Macarius, a disciple of Anthony, was once approached by a hyena, who licked his feet and then took him gently by the hem of his garment to a cave where her cubs were, which had been born blind. He cured the cubs of their blindness and the mother, as a token of gratitude, gave Macarius the skin of a large ram.[10] Another anonymous monk was said to have fed figs to a lion as he might have to a dog.[11] Such stories could be multiplied indefinitely. They indicate that at least among the monks something of the original paradisal state was felt to have survived or been recaptured.

Another side of the paradise theme is the (obviously) exaggerated description of the desert as a place of beauty, such as we may read in Jerome's letter to Heliodorus, written to dissuade the latter from leaving the monastic life: "O desert, verdant with the flowers of Christ! O solitude in which are born those stones from which the city of the great king in the Book of Revelation is built up! O wilderness rejoicing in intimacy with God!" A few lines later, however, Jerome is rather more realistic in his approach to Heliodorus: "Does the boundless vastness of the desert frighten you? Then take a stroll in paradise in your mind!"[12] Yet another aspect of this theme is that which sees monastic life as a figure of the paradise to come. Here we may turn to the Syrian monastic writer Philoxenus of Mabbug, who compares at some length the life of the monk and that of the angels, and who concludes the comparison by remarking: "You are seen with the eyes as corporeal beings, but your service is completely spiritual. You are angels with bodies, spiritual beings clothed in flesh. Your habitation is clean, ordered, pure and holy, and what we know of the habitation of spiritual beings on high is borrowed from it."[13] In this the monk is the successor of the martyr and the virgin, who were also compared to angels, as we have seen in the previous chapter.

The monk was interested not only in recapturing or attaining paradise, however, but also in gaining back the spirit of the apostolic Church. This, indeed, is how Anthony's own story begins—with a nostalgia for the life of community and poverty that was supposedly practiced by the earliest Christians. Cassian is certainly the strongest representative of the view that monastic life is the most perfect reproduction of the life of the primitive Church. For him, in fact, the monks may be traced in a direct line back to the apostles. In one of the most famous passages of his *Conferences* he sets out his conviction in this regard. He begins by remarking that "the discipline of the cenobites took its rise from the time when the apostles preached," and he goes on to cite the passages from the Acts of the Apostles that describe the apostolic community at Jerusalem. Then he continues:

> This, I say, was how the whole Church was then, although it is difficult to find even a few such persons in the cenobia

[i.e., monastic communities] now. But when the multitude of believers began to grow lukewarm after the death of the apostles, and particularly those who had come to the Christian faith from foreign and diverse peoples (from whom the apostles, out of consideration for their rude faith and ingrained pagan customs, looked for nothing more than that they should abstain from things sacrificed to idols and from fornication and from things strangled and from blood), and when the freedom that had been conceded to the Gentiles on account of the weakness of their new belief had gradually begun to contaminate the perfection of the Church at Jerusalem, and as the fervor of that first faith was cooling with the daily increase of both natives and foreigners, then not only those who had come to the faith of Christ but even those who were leaders of the Church fell away from that [initial] strictness. For some, thinking that what had been conceded to the Gentiles for the sake of their weakness was also licit for them, believed that it would not be detrimental if they adhered to the faith and to the confessing of Christ while holding onto their property and possessions. But those who were still imbued with the apostolic fervor, remembering that earlier perfection, abandoning their cities and the companionship of those who believed that the negligence characteristic of a lax life was permitted to them and to the Church of God, began to live in rural and somewhat out-of-the-way places and to exercise in private and as individuals those things which they remembered had been passed on from the apostles to the whole Church. And thus there grew up what we have been speaking about—that discipline of disciples who kept themselves from others' contagion. As time went on, having been cut off from the crowds of believers, they abstained from marriage and turned from the society of their relations and the life of the world and were called monks or solitaries on account of the strictness of their singular and solitary life. From their common life they were called cenobites, and their cells and lodgings were called cenobia. This alone, then, was the most ancient kind of monks, which is first not only in time but also in grace, and which alone continued untouched to the days of Abbots Paul and Anthony. Even now we still see traces of it surviving in strict cenobia.[14]

This remarkable passage, which makes the monks the direct descendants of the first Christians gathered around the apostles, is also illustrative of a certain elitism that was attaching itself to monasticism by the end of the fourth and the beginning of the fifth centuries. This tendency, which cannot be seen in *The Life of Saint Anthony*, is perhaps the most unfortunate development to have occurred in ancient monasticism. It relegated those who were not monks to a sort of secondary status: they were the luke-warm, the less blessed, or at least the imperfect. It was the prac-tice of virginity and poverty in particular that seemed to raise the monk or nun above the common level. We have already seen in the previous chapter the esteem that the virgin enjoyed in the early Christian community—an esteem so enviable that warn-ings against pride were frequent. Much the same esteem was granted to the poor person as to the virgin, for in giving up his possessions entirely the monk was believed to have fulfilled the word of Jesus in Matthew 19:21 and become "perfect." Thus it is that Jerome, who probably more than anyone else is the great theorist of ancient monasticism, can tell the wealthy widow Hedibia, after having cited the Matthean verse in question: "If you wish to be perfect and to stand at the summit of excellence, do what the apostles did: sell all that you possess and give to the poor and follow the Savior." There was an alternative, however: "If you don't wish to be perfect but would rather hold the second degree of virtue, get rid of all that you have and give it to your children and your relatives. No one will look down on you if you pursue lesser things, so long as you realize that the one who has chosen higher things is superior to you."[15]

Poverty was in some ways the truest touchstone and the most typical quality of the monk. It was the call to poverty, as it had been practiced in the apostolic Church, that had trans-formed Anthony himself from a pious young man into a monk. And when Anthony died he had but four possessions to bequeath to others—two sheepskins, a cloak and a hair shirt.[16] Cassian tells us that the monks of the East owned nothing but an undergarment, an outer garment, a pair of shoes, a sheepskin and a small rush mat. Everything else was held in common, and no one would ever say: "This is mine"; if someone did, he would be obliged to perform a penance.[17] The acceptance of voluntary poverty was, moreover, a regular part of the great conversion stories of Christian antiquity, just as it was of Anthony's. We read of it in the cases of Ambrose,[18] Augustine[19] and Paulinus of Nola,[20] to name only a few of the most famous instances.

Poverty, however, was but one aspect of the broader life of asceticism that the monk embraced, and it is the ascetic struggle as a whole that constitutes another major monastic theme, which is sounded clearly in *The Life of Saint Anthony*. Anthony's asceticism consisted in fasting, continual prayer (of which we shall hear more in the following chapter), solitude and a number of other practices, such as not bathing. All of this was for him a kind of martyrdom, since it was not permitted him to die violently for the faith.[21] In Syria the asceticism of the monks was considerably more extreme: it was there, for example, that the practice of spending years on the top of a pillar, exposed to the elements, originated. We know that Anthony learned his asceticism from others: he would observe how different persons were skilled in different forms of asceticism, and then he would attempt to imitate them. Indeed, it was his aim not to be inferior to anyone else in this domain.[22] This "pious rivalry," typical of the desert, was a characteristic of the legendary Macarius of Alexandria in particular. When he discovered that some monks, for instance, fasted on uncooked food during the forty days of Lent, he did so for seven years. On hearing that another monk lived on only a pound of bread a day, he managed to get by on four or five ounces, surviving thus for three years.[23]

But, however it may have been carried out, the monk's entire ascetic struggle may be characterized by one image, which is that of combat with the demons. Our concern here is not whether these are the demons that rise up from within a person or the demons that assault him from without; they are portrayed as if they were the latter, but that does not exclude the possibility of their having been the former. This combat, in any event, was an ever-present reality to the monk. Anthony, in fact, as much as invites it by living for years in a tomb, which he knew would have been a haunt of demons.[24] The demons not only attack their victims physically but also, and more usually, employ the tactic of subtle temptation. A common story in desert and other monastic literature concerns a monk who has been approached by a demon disguised as a beautiful woman, who often appeals to him for help or shelter.[25] Or, even more deceitfully, a demon would appear to the solitary in the form of the Savior, surrounded by lights and angels.[26] As a result, a great deal of this literature is devoted to how one may recognize demons for what they are and deal with them adequately. At least a quarter of *The Life of Saint Anthony* is taken up with a lengthy discourse that Anthony holds for his monks, and most of this is in turn occupied with the demons and their power.[27] In *The Shorter Rules*, written for his monks, Basil the Great would try to put the demonic into some perspective by remarking that the demons in fact only take advantage of what they have already found in a person and that they cannot force anyone to commit sin.[28] As widely understood as this may have been, however, no one would have dared to underestimate how a demon might take advantage of a person's failings.

Success in the ascetic struggle, which would nonetheless continue to a greater or lesser degree through the course of a lifetime, meant the monk's acquisition of a remarkable self-control, known in the Greek-speaking world as *apatheia*. To the pagan philosophers *apatheia* signified passionlessness, or the complete eradication of the passions, a goal that Christians rejected.[29] To Christians, rather, it indicated an ordering and directing of the passions by the faculty of the intellect, this latter itself working from Christian principles. Anthony is a striking example of such self-control, which is reflected in the state not only of his soul but of his body as well. When, at the age of fifty-five, Anthony emerged from the abandoned fort in which he had hidden himself for nearly twenty years, his friends were astonished at his appearance and his demeanor.

> His body was in its former state, and it was neither obese by reason of lack of exercise nor emaciated by reason of fasting and his struggle with the demons. They recognized him as the same man that he had been before his departure for the desert. The condition of his soul, too, was pure. It was neither contracted by sorrow nor dilated by pleasure nor taken up with hilarity or dejection. Nor was he disturbed at seeing the crowd nor elated by the many who were there to receive

him. He was completely even-tempered, as one would be who was governed by reason, and in him everything was in its natural state.[30]

So in harmony was Anthony's body with his peaceful soul that he could not fail to attract people to himself by an appearance that could only be described as charming.[31] And even when the time came for him to die, at the age of one hundred and five, he was in the best of health, with eye undimmed and not having lost a single tooth.[32]

This *apatheia* or equanimity is also known as being "dead to the world," which is a concept that recurs frequently in monastic writings. We may see it, for example, in the story of the monk Sarapion who, while visiting Rome, went to see a woman who had been living in seclusion for twenty-five years. He convinced her that if she were really advanced in the spiritual life—"dead to the world" is the phrase that is used—she would leave her hermitage and go out into the city, since it would no longer make any difference where she was. This she did, then, although with reluctance. But once this had been accomplished, he spoke to her again, this time saying that if she were really dead to the world she would walk nude through the middle of the city. When she refused because such a thing would be scandalous and would damage her reputation, he replied that she could not consider herself dead to the world. He himself would do it, he said, "without embarrassment and without feeling. And so he left her humbled and broke her pride."[33] To such odd and seemingly unvirtuous behavior might one be led by practicing death to the world.

A further monastic theme which appears in *The Life of Saint Anthony* is that of the higher wisdom of the ascetic. Anthony apparently could not read, but his memory was so sharp that it retained everything he heard.[34] (A certain Ammonius, we are told, not only memorized the Old and New Testaments but also six million lines of Origen and other Fathers![35]) If Greek philosophers happened to visit him, as they occasionally did, he was prepared to joust with them, armed only with common sense and the knowledge that he had garnered from the Scriptures. He would astound them with his acuteness, as when he once asked some whether the mind or letters came first, and which was the cause of which. When they replied that of course the mind had come first and that it had invented letters, he said by way of rejoinder: "In that case, one who has a good mind does not need letters."[36] Otherwise he would preach to them about the cross and the foolishness of this world's wisdom.[37] Such encounters with philosophers were frequent enough in the desert, and it was always the philosophers who were bested.[38]

The shadow side of this higher wisdom, which otherwise we can hardly fail to applaud, was the danger of anti-intellectualism and of scorn for the intellect. Anthony himself at least comes close to this in his conversations with the philosophers, which have the ring of diatribes to them. Worse than this, however, was the simple ignorance of so many monks, which could often exist side by side with undeniable holiness of life. Such was the case, for example, with two monks, one of whom denied that the Eucharist was truly the body and blood of Christ and had to be convinced of the fact by a vision. The other monk was certain that Melchizedek was the son of God, but he was cleverly deceived into discovering the truth of the matter.[39] Related to this was a tendency to take Scripture literally, of which Anthony is a notable instance. He, of course, took at their face value the passages from Matthew that he had heard read in church. A less happy result of this literalism was the belief of many monks that God had a body; this was a great problem in the Egyptian church toward the end of the fourth and the beginning of the fifth century, when different monastic factions took different sides of the issue. We even sometimes find a certain suspicion of Scripture precisely because it was so susceptible of being misunderstood. Thus we read of a rather startling exchange between the monks Poemen and Amoun in which the latter asks the former if, when engaged in conversation, he should speak about Scripture or about the sayings of the elders (namely, monks who were reputed to be wise). Poemen replies: "If you are unable to keep silence, it is better to speak about the sayings of the elders than about Scripture. For the danger therein is not little."[40]

The immanence of divine power is another monastic theme to which the biography of Anthony bears witness. The consciousness of the divine, as of the demonic, was universal in the ancient world and in the ancient Church, as has already been noted.[41] In a monastic setting—in a desert, with its sense of infinity and eternity[42]—this was considerably heightened. If demons in all shapes and forms made themselves present to the monk, so did angels and God himself, although usually in more subtle ways. So it is that Anthony is the recipient of numerous visions—of the soul of a devout monk ascending to heaven, of himself struggling with the invisible powers but ultimately being saved, of other souls after death.[43] Visions like these served as a compensation for the trials of monastic existence.

Perhaps the most frequent indication of the presence of the divine, however, is the miracles of which monastic narratives are full. Anthony heals diseases and casts out demons simply by calling on Christ's name, and his reputation in this regard is so great that he attracts not only Christians but pagans and their priests as well.[44] Sulpicius Serverus' life of Martin of Tours, a work nearly as influential as Athanasius' life of Anthony and written only a few decades later, seems little else than a catalogue of the wondrous things accomplished in the holy man. He raises the dead, controls the movement of a crowd from a distance and makes a tree that is about to fall on him turn in the opposite direction, to cite only some of his more extraordinary deeds.[45] Nothing appears to be beyond such a person's power.

A final theme sums up many of the others. It is that of the monk as the personal recapitulation of the qualities of the saints of old. Anthony resembles Adam in his regaining of paradise, Moses in his communion with God on the mountain and also in the circumstances of his death,[46] the three young men of Daniel 1:15 in his good health after severe fasting,[47] Elisha in his visionary abilities[48] and Elijah in his general demeanor.[49] In Gregory the Great's biography of Benedict the comparisons are still more pronounced, and in the event that the reader may have missed them they are specifically drawn to his attention. Benedict, we are told, is like Moses, Elisha, the apostle Peter, Elijah and David. Nevertheless he possesses the spirit of only one person, namely Christ himself.[50] It was natural, however, that the monk should be compared most frequently with Elijah, since this Old Testament prophet had spent so much time in the desert. This sort of comparison, daring in its way, gives us some indication of the esteem and even awe in which the monastic call was held. The monk gathered up in himself the ancient patterns of holiness, and in so doing he became the model for future holiness. Indeed, for nearly a millennium after the origins of monasticism in the fourth century, the life of a monk was the ideal form that sanctity took in both East and West, and whoever was recognized as saintly was believed to have cultivated monastic habits and virtues.

Styles of Monastic Literature

A word must be said about the styles of monastic literature. There are, first of all, biographies of a number of the greatest figures, such as, of course, Athanasius' *Life of Saint Anthony*, the anonymous *Life of Pachomius* and Jerome's *Life of Paul*. All of these constitute a new and significant genre of literature, which is hagiography, or the biography of a holy person. Invariably many liberties are taken with strict historical truth in ancient hagiography, but the embellishments that were made were part of the expected. It was taken for granted that a saint would behave in such and such a way, would have such and such habits, and so forth. We cannot, then, speak of real deception here. In many ways the hagiography has its antecedents in the Greek and Roman lives of pagan heroes and sages, although the miraculous substitutes for the feat of strength or daring, and peasant cunning (most monks were peasants) and a background in Scripture take the place of scholarship. The major difference, however, is that ultimately the monk accomplishes by grace what the hero or sage accomplishes by his own prowess or intellectual ability. The hagiography, as a result, points to God. It is intended, too, to serve as a model of sanctity, as has already been indicated: it is thus a rule of life in biographical form.

A second style of monastic literature is the rule explicitly as such. The most famous examples of this are the so-called longer and shorter rules of Basil and the *Rule of Benedict*; but there are numerous others. These set down the norms of monastic life in a certain juridical and detailed manner, although by no means in the ordered fashion that we would expect of a modern legal document.

A third style of this literature might be described, for convenience's sake, in terms of history or reminiscence, under which guise monastic teaching is conveyed to the reader. The *Conferences* of Cassian would qualify in this respect, since they purport to be the record of a visit that the author made to some of the most notable Egyptian monks; so would the anonymous *History of the Monks in Egypt* and Palladius' *Lausiac History*. These works often contain considerable biographical and hagiographical material, but they are not biographies or hagiographies in the usual sense.

A fourth style can perhaps be categorized in a general way as exhortatory. Here we could catalogue a large number of letters by Jerome, for example, in which the glories of monastic life are set out and extolled.

Throughout these other categories there appears a fifth and final style, and this is undoubtedly the one that is most closely associated with the early monks. It is the apophthegm, usually a short and highly charged statement or story that is meant to teach a lesson about the monastic and the Christian life. The occasion for the didactic content is often a question posed by a disciple to his abba, his spiritual father, or by one abba to another. Typically it goes like this:

> One of the brethren asked the abba Isidore, an elder of Scete: "Why do the demons fear you so much?" The old man said to him: "Since the time I became a monk I have taken care that anger not rise as far as my gorge."[51]

In an exchange such as this the wisdom of a lifetime seems to be contained, and a whole monastic rule is distilled into the fewest possible words. For what appears on the surface to be merely a question about demons, which is answered with some useful advice about not getting angry, is in actuality an extremely succinct spiritual treatise about the struggle between good and evil. If the apophthegm is reflected upon closely, it becomes clear to the reader that the spiritual life can in fact be reduced to controlling one's anger, all things being equal, since control of one passion will bring with it control of others; this is the way that the demons, the evil influences in one's life, are thwarted. Much the same may be said of nearly all the apophthegms (or apophthegmata) that have come to us from the early monks, many of which are only as long as a single sentence. Thus, for example: "I have never either spoken a worldly word or wished to hear one."[52] Or: "You cannot be a monk unless you become all aflame like a fire."[53] These are deceptively simple master-pieces, and they sum up the monastic genius as nothing else can, for their austerity and often slightly disquieting manner mirrors the austerity and often disquieting sanctity of their authors.

IX

Prayer

If martyrdom, virginity and the monastic life were the extraordinary means by which a few attained to the experience of God, prayer was the ordinary way of touching the divine, and it was enjoined upon all. So we must now speak of prayer. One of the most important problems with which the Fathers grappled in this regard was that raised by Paul in 1 Thessalonians 5:17, where he tells his readers to "pray without ceasing." It is an admonition that is repeated in different ways a number of times in the New Testament. The question of how Paul's words were to be observed provoked an interesting variety of responses in the ancient Church, and to study these different responses is to be struck by the seriousness with which the Church took the words of Scripture.

Prayer Without Ceasing

The earliest patristic treatment of prayer that we possess, part of the seventh book of the *Miscellanies* of Clement of Alexandria, is obviously occupied with precisely this issue, although Clement does not specifically mention Paul. He speaks of the "gnostic," the perfect Christian, as one who enjoys the uninterrupted presence of God and who does not restrict his prayer to the several times daily that were customary in the early Church.[1] Thus he finds himself continually at prayer, whether he is plowing the ground or sailing the sea[2] and, although he is used to praying together with his fellow Christians at the traditional times, he is not limited to this. "His whole life is a sacred festival.

For example, his sacrifices are prayers and praises and the study of the Scriptures before meals, Psalms and hymns at mealtime and before retiring, and prayers again at night. In this way he joins himself to the heavenly choir by his constant absorption in contemplation."[3] When one reads this in conjunction with some other thoughts of Clement on the gnostic's prayer—that it is always answered, for instance, and that it always partakes of the most lofty contemplative quality[4]—then one realizes that what he has to say is of necessity restricted to an elite and is to a great degree unfeasible.

In large part the ancient Church understood that Paul's precept could be accomplished in one way by the observance of the set hours of prayer that Clement tended to pass over as somewhat inadequate. Each hour would at least have consisted in the recitation of the Lord's Prayer, perhaps accompanied by some Psalms, spontaneous prayer and a hymn. In the beginning there seem to have been six such hours or times of prayer (until two more were added in the fourth century), and it was understood that all Christians would observe them. Hippolytus' *Apostolic Tradition* contains the earliest explanation of them; although written at the beginning of the third century, it purports to hand on customs that were much older.

> If you are at home, pray at the third hour [nine o'clock in the morning] and bless God. But if you are elsewhere then, pray to God in your heart. For at that hour Christ was seen fixed to the wood. Hence even in the Old Testament the law ordered that the bread of proposition should be offered at the third hour as a type of the body and blood of Christ; and the immolation of the irrational lamb is a type of the perfect Lamb. For Christ is the shepherd, and he is also the bread that came down from heaven.
>
> Pray likewise at the sixth hour [noon]. For when Christ was fixed to the wood of the cross the day was broken and there was a great darkness. So let a powerful prayer be offered at that hour in imitation of the voice of him who prayed and caused darkness to overshadow all creation because of the unbelieving Jews.
>
> Let a great prayer and a great blessing be offered also at the ninth hour [three o'clock in the afternoon] to imitate the

manner in which the soul of the righteous praises God who does not lie, who remembers his holy ones and has sent his Word to glorify them. At that hour Christ, pierced in his side, poured forth water and blood and, illuminating the rest of the day, brought it to evening. And so, when he began to fall asleep, while causing the following day to begin, he imaged the resurrection.

Pray as well before your body rests on its bed. But toward midnight rise up, wash your hands and pray. . . . It is necessary to pray at that hour. For the ancients who have recounted the tradition to us told us that at that hour the entire creation rests for a moment in order to praise the Lord: the stars, the trees, the waters stop for a short space of time, and the whole army of angels who serve him praise God at that hour along with the souls of the righteous. That is why those who believe should hasten to pray then. And the Savior bears witness to this when he says: Behold, a cry is heard in the middle of the night of one saying: Behold, the bridegroom is coming; rise up to meet him. And he continues: Watch, therefore, for you do not know the hour when he is coming.

And at cockcrow rise up and pray once more. For at that hour, at cockcrow, the children of Israel denied Christ, whom we know by faith. In the hope of eternal light at the resurrection of the dead, our eyes are turned toward the day.[5]

Some of the Fathers give different reasons for praying at these times. Tertullian, for example, relates the third hour to the descent of the Spirit, which occurred then, the sixth to Peter's having gone up to the housetop at noon to pray when he was in Joppa (cf. Acts 10:9), and the ninth to Peter's and John's visit to the temple in Jerusalem (cf. Acts 3:1), and he remarks that, even though one should pray always and everywhere, nonetheless these times are particularly sacred.[6] Cyprian agrees with this and also, along with Tertullian,[7] links the commemoration of these three hours to a confession of faith in the Trinity.[8]

In reaction to those who omit prayer at midnight, Cyprian is most explicit in connecting the observance of fixed hours with the idea of unceasing prayer. Reminding the readers of his treatise *On the Lord's Prayer* that Scripture refers to Christ as the Day and the Sun, he says:

There should be no hour in which Christians do not frequently and always worship God, so that we who are in
Christ—that is, in the Sun and in the true Day—ought to be
constant throughout the day in petitions and prayer. And
when by the law of nature the night comes around again,
those who are praying cannot be harmed by the nocturnal
darkness because, for the children of light, day exists even
during the night. For when is he without light who has the
light in his heart? And when is he without the sun and the
day whose sun and day is Christ?

We who are in Christ—that is, always in the light—
ought never to cease from prayer during the night. For the
widow Anna used to persevere in deserving well of God,
always praying without ceasing and keeping vigil. As the
Gospel says: She did not depart from the temple, worshiping
night and day with fasting and prayer. Let the Gentiles who
have not yet been enlightened look to this, or the Jews who,
having deserted the light, have remained in darkness. Let us,
dearest brethren, who are always in the light, who remember
and keep hold of what we have begun to be by grace, consider the night as day. Let us realize that we are always walking in the light, let us not be hindered by the darkness that
we have left behind. Let there be no lack of prayers during
the hours of the night, let there be no idle and shameful
waste of the times of prayer. By God's good pleasure let us
who have been spiritually recreated and reborn imitate what
we shall be in the future. As those who will live in the kingdom, enjoying the day without the intervention of night, let
us thus keep vigil at night as if it were light; as those who
will always be praying and offering thanks to God, let us not
cease here as well to pray and offer thanks.[9]

It is Origen who summarizes the teaching of many of those
who had gone before him and at the same time succeeds in
broadening the concept of prayer considerably. Other Fathers
seem to have understood prayer in the strict and classical sense
of a conscious elevation of the mind and heart to God in the form
of praise, thanksgiving and petition. Only Clement of Alexandria
spoke of prayer explicitly as a constant interior event, but for this
a leisure and concentration were required of which most Christians were incapable. The observance of fixed hours of prayer

made such formal prayer possible for ordinary Christians within a restricted scope. Origen, however, introduces something completely new into the discussion. In his treatise *On Prayer* he explains what he means by unceasing prayer:

> Praying without ceasing means uniting prayer with the works that we are obliged to perform and joining fitting works to our prayer, since virtuous deeds and the fulfillment of what we are commanded to do are included as a part of prayer. If praying without ceasing means anything humanly possible, it can only mean this: that we call the whole life of a saint a great synthesis of prayer. What we normally call prayer is only a small part of praying, something that we are obliged to do at least three times a day.[10]

Toward the end of the fourth century Jerome elaborates this idea a little in a discourse intended for his monks. Commenting on Psalm 1:2, which speaks of the righteous person who meditates on the law of the Lord day and night, Jerome remarks that it seems impossible to do this, just as it seems impossible to pray always.

> Am I able to pray during the time that I sleep? Therefore, meditation on the law consists not in reading but in doing. For it is said in another place: Whether you eat or drink, or whatever you do, do everything in the name of the Lord. If I give an alms, I meditate on the law of God; if I visit a sick person, my feet meditate on the law of God; if I do those things that are commanded, I meditate in my body what others meditate in their mouths. . . . Our meditation is our work.[11]

In a homily preached by Jerome's contemporary, Theodore of Mopsuestia, the notion of prayer as the practice of good works is emphasized perhaps even more strongly, so much so that prayer is seen to be the fruit of good works rather than good works the fruit of prayer. Commenting on the Lord's Prayer, Theodore says that Christ

> made use of these short words as if to say that prayer does not consist so much in words as in good works, love and zeal

for duty. Indeed, anyone who is inclined to good works, all his life must needs be in prayer, which is seen in his choice of these good works. Prayer is by necessity connected with good works, because a thing that is not good to be looked for is not good to be prayed for. More wicked than death by stoning is the death that would come to us if we asked God to grant us things that contradict his commandments. He who offers such prayers incites God to wrath rather than to reconciliation and mercy. A true prayer consists in good works, in love of God and diligence in the things that please him.[12]

The possibility of work as prayer, as well as the observance of formal hours of prayer, was at the foundation of cenobitic monasticism. A monastery could hardly survive if the monks felt that prayer and work could not be combined and yet were sure that they had to pray constantly. Basil the Great, in some conferences given to his monks about the year 360, speaks of the dangers of idleness in monastic life and says that a monk must never use piety as an excuse for laziness. He goes on to unite the two ideals of unceasing prayer and work:

> The way to achieve stability in our soul is to beseech God that in each of our undertakings we might have a successful outcome, to give him full gratitude for having provided us with the power to perform what we have done, and to persevere in our goal of pleasing him, as I have remarked. For unless we adopt this approach, how can we possibly reconcile the two texts of Paul the apostle—"Pray without ceasing" and "At work night and day"? Nevertheless, even though the law requires us to give thanks at each and every moment and both nature and reason show thanksgiving to be one of life's necessities, we should not overlook the fixed times for communal prayer; for these times have been selected with an eye to the necessity that each has its own distinctive way of remembering God's good gifts.[13]

Apart from cenobitic monasticism, represented by Basil, among solitaries the ideal of constant formal (conscious) prayer continued to be pursued, however. This was especially the case with many of the Desert Fathers. Sometimes this prayer could be practiced while working, but only if the work were of such a kind as to permit it. Thus it had to be simple, allowing the mind to soar of itself: consequently the weaving of baskets and the plaiting of mats, which required only mechanical movements, were much in favor. A monk could sit in his cell the whole day through, weaving baskets out of reeds and reciting Psalms. Sometimes, however, the prayer was so engrossing that it seemed to leave no place for work. What Palladius tells us of a certain Paul, an Egyptian monk, is typical in this regard: "He engaged in no work or business and he took nothing except what he ate. But constant prayer was his work and his asceticism. Therefore he had three hundred prayers memorized, and gathering the same amount of pebbles and putting them in his lap, he would cast one pebble out of his lap at each prayer."[14] Yet this Paul does not represent the monastic ideal, and Palladius mentions that he was later rebuked by another monk who said only one hundred prayers a day but who also supported himself and was available to his fellow monks for consultation in spiritual matters.[15]

Another story from the desert, recorded elsewhere, shows how some of the more sober and balanced monks tended to regard the claim that one could pass one's life exclusively in prayer, doing nothing else. Some men called "Euchites," or "Men of prayer," approached an old monk named Lucius, and the following dialogue ensued:

> The old man asked them, saying: What work do you do with your hands? And they told him: We touch no kind of handiwork but, as the apostle says, we pray without ceasing. The old man said to them: And do you not eat? But they said: Yes, we do eat. The old man said the them: And when you eat, who prays for you? And he asked them again, saying: Do you not sleep? And they replied: We do sleep. And the old man said: And who prays for you while you are sleeping? And they were unable to answer him when he said this. And he said to them: Forgive me, brethren, but behold, you do not do as you said. But I shall show you how I pray without ceasing while working with my hands. For, with God's help, I sit down, steeping my few palm fronds, and from them I make a mat, while I say: Have mercy on me, O God, accord-

ing to your great mercy, and according to the multitude of your mercies blot out my iniquity. And he asked them: Is that prayer or not? And they said to him: Yes, it is. And he said: When I have spent the whole day at work, praying in my heart or with my lips, I earn about sixteen coins, and I put two of them at my door and I eat with what remains. Whoever finds these two denarii prays for me while I am eating or sleeping, and thus by the grace of God there is fulfilled in me what is written: Pray without ceasing.[16]

It was at least partly in trying to bring together work and prayer that the so-called "prayer of the heart" was developed. As Lucius makes clear, this involved the constant repetition of a particular phrase, which would eventually make its way into the heart of the one praying. It was possible so to interiorize one's prayer that one could in fact even overcome the obstacle of sleep, which is frequently mentioned as insuperable by writers on the subject. Thus we read in the early fifth-century *Life of Saint Honoratus* that the saint's lips used to pronounce the name of Christ even while he lay asleep. "While his body found its rest on his bed, his mind found it in Christ."[17] In the intimacy with the Lord of which this anecdote speaks, and which is typical of the saint in general, we discover the solution to the problem of unceasing prayer as it was more literally understood. This was the hoped-for goal of the prayer of the heart.

But Augustine, as is his wont, brings a wholly new insight to bear on the question of prayer without ceasing. In fact he puts prayer into another context entirely, redefines it and removes from it a certain aspect of formality. His view can be summarized in a passage from one of his homilies. Commenting on Psalm 38:9 ("All my desire is before you"), he says:

Desire itself is your prayer, and if your desire is continuous your prayer is unceasing. For the apostle did not say in vain: Pray without ceasing. Is it possible that we should unceasingly bend the knee or prostrate our body or raise up our hands, that he should tell us: Pray without ceasing? Or if we say that we pray in this manner I do not think that we are able to do it unceasingly. There is another prayer that is unceasing and interior, and it is desire. Whatever else you do,

if you desire that sabbath [namely, eternal life] you do not
cease to pray. If you do not wish to stop praying, do not stop
desiring. Your unceasing desire is your uninterrupted voice.
You will grow silent if you stop loving.[18]

And in another homily he tells his congregation: "Desire always
prays, even if the tongue should be silent. If you are always
experiencing desire you are always praying. When does prayer
sleep? When desire has grown cold."[19] Far from demeaning
prayer at particular hours during the day, as one might perhaps
expect, Augustine valued it as a tool for stirring up this interior
desire.[20]

Thus we may say that the problem of how to pray without
ceasing was resolved in one of four different ways: by the
observance of set hours during the day, which effectively served
to sanctify the whole cycle of the day; by considering all good
actions as prayer, as Origen and others suggested; by the practice
of the prayer of the heart, which was especially the method of
the Desert Fathers; and by the equation of desire with prayer, as
Augustine says. It is important to remark that Clement of Alexandria's approach, with its nearly impossible ideals, is at least
implicitly rejected in favor of something more human. The
Euchites too represent a distinctly minority position. To this
extent the problem of constant prayer provides a study in mini-
ature of how the Church generally seeks to avoid extremes in
the cultivation of spiritual goods and encourages lines of pursuit
that are accessible to all Christians rather than to just a few.

The Atmosphere of Prayer

A prayer that was "accessible" also demanded a certain
atmosphere in which it could be carried out more easily. The
early Church's continual fostering of the observance of particular
hours of prayer shows a profound awareness of the relationship
between prayer, which is a spiritual event, and time, which is a
measure of something material. Likewise, the Fathers were very
conscious of position, or posture, and nearly every treatise on
prayer has at least a few words to say about this. Origen notes

that the posture of the body images the qualities of the soul in prayer, and he says that standing with hands extended and eyes elevated is by far the best way to offer prayer.[21] Tertullian explains that the hands are to be extended, "not too high, but temperately and moderately uplifted,"[22] after the fashion of the Lord's hands outstretched on the cross.[23] One was not to look boldly upward in the manner of the Pharisee in the temple, nor to pray in anything other than a subdued voice.[24] Pagans, on the other hand, prayed with hands raised up high above the head, eyes heavenward and with loud voices. The difference between the two modes was the difference between supplication, on the part of the Christians, and imperious demand. Standing, in turn, was meant to recall the resurrection, and hence it was especially appropriate on Sundays and during the Easter season; in fact kneeling was forbidden then,[25] although it was proper on days of fasting[26] and when confessing one's sins.[27] Tertullian considered prayer while sitting to be a mark of laziness: "If it is irreverent to sit down under the eyes of or over across from someone whom you should greatly honor and venerate, how much more irreligious is it to do this under the eyes of the living God, while the angel of prayer is still standing by, unless we are complaining to God that prayer has worn us out!"[28] Origen, however, could approve of prayer while sitting or even lying down if a person were sick.[29] In addition to this, on account of the rich symbolism of the East, it was customary to pray facing in that direction.[30] Each of these gestures, then, was rich in meaning, and each was integral to the more spiritual aspect of prayer, which was the movement of the heart, or the mind, to God. Moreover, according to Basil, many of them were aspects of an unwritten tradition that was handed down by the apostles and that had equal authority with the Scriptures themselves.[31] Consequently they were not simply gestures that corresponded to a psychological need (or techniques of prayer, as we might call them today) but actions that carried with them a divine approbation.

It is Augustine, though, who qualifies the sometimes rather rigid position of many of the earlier Fathers and explains that ultimately a person is not obliged to follow the tradition regarding posture when praying. In responding to the inquiry of a certain Simplicianus, he shows how Scripture speaks of standing, kneeling, sitting and lying prostrate during the act of praying. Yet, in the end, how one prays is a matter of indifference.

> For when someone wants to pray he arranges his body just as it suits him at that moment with a view to moving his soul. But when the desire to pray is not looked for but is stirred up of itself, when something suddenly comes into the mind so that the desire to pray is activated with unutterable groans— however we find ourselves then, our prayer must certainly not be put off until we have the opportunity of sitting or standing or falling prostrate. For the desire of the mind pro- duces a kind of emptiness around it and frequently forgets either where it is or in what position the body is at the time.[32]

That Augustine should not have been satisfied with the tradition regarding posture in prayer and should have felt obliged to break with it and to seek the underlying reality—namely, that gesture was at the service of the spirit and could not always adapt itself to the swift movements of that spirit—is typical of him. Yet at the same time something is lost when Augustine seems to see in gesture no more than a merely ancillary part of prayer; so he contributes unwittingly to the diminution of the role of the body in the life of the spirit.

Besides bodily position, location was also an important con- sideration in prayer. Here the early Church was confronted with two apparently contradictory teachings from the Scriptures— that prayer should be offered "in every place" (1 Timothy 2:8), and that prayer in public was forbidden (cf. Matthew 6:5–6). The earliest writers on prayer grappled with this discrepancy, the solution to which depended on how one viewed prayer. Tertul- lian, for example, never speaks of prayer as a purely interior event or as a more or less continual state that occasionally man- ifested itself in gestures; it is rather a formal discipline with a number of observances or gestures invariably attached to it. For this reason there can be for him no praying outside the Christian community or the privacy of one's home, unless "opportunity or necessity" demands it. Thus it is not to be imputed against the apostles that they prayed and sang to God in prison while their jailers overheard them, or against Paul that he offered thanks to God in the presence of all while on board ship.[33] For Clement of Alexandria and Origen, however, although they stress the posture of the body as Tertullian does, prayer is principally a constant disposition of the soul that seeks a certain externalization in gesture. Consequently Clement's gnostic prays everywhere, without its necessarily being apparent to anyone else, and Origen can write that, "for one who prays well, every place is appropriate."[34] Nonetheless, some places were more fitting than others, and Origen recommends a special corner in one's own house that could serve as a sanctuary; it should be a section of the house in which nothing bad has ever occurred, lest God shun both it and the one who uses it.[35] He questions whether prayer may suitably be offered in the bedroom of a married couple, since sexual intercourse is performed there.[36] Yet Hippolytus sees no difficulty in this whatsoever. When speaking of the hour of prayer at midnight he says simply that, "if your wife is present, pray both of you together." But if one of the spouses is not a Christian, then the one who is should retire to another room.[37]

The best place of all to pray, however, is, as Origen says, "where the faithful meet together."[38] There not only the faithful themselves congregate but also the spirits of the dead and the guardian angels of those present as well. It is an assembly whose prayers are all the more effective for its being so numerous.[39] Whether Origen is referring to an actual church building here or more generally to any place in which Christians might have gathered from prayer in the third century—the large home of a wealthy person, for example—is uncertain. There is no doubt, in any event, that church buildings already existed at that time, but whether individual Christians then would come to such churches to pray outside of the regular hours seems unlikely. When Origen mentions praying "where the faithful meet together" he is most probably speaking not of individual but of communal, liturgical prayer. What we would today call "private prayer" almost certainly originally took place at home. It must not have been until the fourth century or even later that there was any such thing as "devotional prayer" in church; the church was designed specifically for the public prayers of the Christian assembly.

The early Christians were also familiar with the idea of making pilgrimages to places associated with the life of Christ, as well as to the tombs of holy persons, especially martyrs. By the middle of the fourth century nearly all such spots of any importance had had *martyria*—church-like buildings where the remains of a holy person could be approached conveniently by large numbers—constructed over or near them. There people might seek a cure to some illness; there they might obtain for themselves a modest relic, which was often, until the fifth or sixth centuries, nothing more than a piece of cloth that had been touched to the tomb of the saint or some oil from a lamp that had burned near it; there, too, they might want to be buried. The faithful would visit living persons also, to look for advice, to ask for miracles or simply to be in the presence of sanctity. In this respect the Fathers of the Desert were especially popular, and some of them would attract great crowds. On account of the dangers involved, however, pilgrimage did not become a general practice until the fourth century, when Christianity was no longer subject to persecutions. Then quite a number of pilgrimage places began to flourish: there were the Holy Land, Rome, Antioch, Constantinople and Carthage, and also Kal'at Sim'ān in Syria, famous on account of Simeon Stylites, Nola in Italy, where the martyr Felix was buried, and the grave of the martyr Menas, located southwest of Alexandria. The best known and certainly the most interesting account of a pilgrimage that has come down to us from patristic times is *The Journey of Egeria*, the narrative of a trip to the Holy Land written by a late fourth-century French or Spanish nun for her sisters who could not accompany her. She describes what would occur at every holy place where she and those who were with her would stop: the passage from the Scriptures associated with that place would be read, a Psalm sung and a prayer recited; in addition, if possible, the Eucharist would be celebrated.[40] For Jerome, who moved from Rome to Bethlehem and there ended his days, the experience of living in proximity to places made holy by Christ and other figures of the Old and New Testaments partook of the mystical. In a letter to Marcella, one of his spiritual daughters at Rome, he implores her to join him and speaks rapturously of what they might do together:

Will the day never come when we shall be permitted to enter the Savior's cave, to weep in the Lord's sepulcher with his sister and his mother, to kiss the wood of the cross, to be raised up in prayer and in spirit with the ascending Lord on Mount Olivet, to see Lazarus come forth bound in his shroud and to gaze upon the waters of the Jordan purified for the Lord's baptism? . . . We shall go to Nazareth and see, as its name means, the flower of Galilee. Not far from there Cana will be visible, where the water was changed into wine. We shall travel to Mount Tabor and see the tabernacles of the Savior, where he dwells not with Moses and Elijah, as Peter once wished, but with the Father and the Holy Spirit. From there we shall come to the Sea of Genesareth, and we shall see five and four thousand men filled with five and seven loaves of bread. The town of Nain will appear, at whose gates the widow's son was raised up. Hermon will also be seen, and the torrent of Kishon, where Sisera was vanquished. And there will be Capernaum, famous on account of the Lord's miracles, and all of Galilee round about. And when, with Christ as our companion, we have visited Shiloh and Bethel and other places, where churches have been built, so to speak, as victory standards, we shall return to our own cave, and there we shall sing constantly, weep copiously, pray unceasingly and, wounded by the Savior's dart, say together: I have found him whom my soul has sought. I will hold him and not let him go.[41]

Not all the Fathers, however, felt the same way about pilgrimages or felt the lure of the holy places. In a famous letter Gregory of Nyssa raises a number of objections to pilgrimages—that at the last judgment the Lord will not ask whether one has traveled to Jerusalem, for example, and that such voyages are occasions of moral danger to many—and he remarks that, despite a journey that he himself had made to the Holy Land, his own faith remained unaffected: it was no deeper after he had seen Jerusalem and Bethlehem than it had been before. This leads him to conclude that

coming close to God is not a question of simply changing the place where we pray. No, no matter where you may be, as long as your soul forms the sort of resting place in which God can dwell and linger, he will visit you. But if you fill your inner self up with base thoughts, then you could be standing on Golgotha or on the Mount of Olives or the monument of the resurrection and you would still be as far from welcoming Christ into yourself as someone who has never begun to confess him.[42]

The Interior Life

These were some of the customs amidst which the prayer of the ancient Chruch flourished. Fasting may be mentioned as well, since it was often recommended as an accompaniment to prayer.[43] There were other customs, too, that we can read about in such authors as Hippolytus and Tertullian—the use of the sign of the cross,[44] the blessing of oneself with one's own breath and saliva, symbolizing the gift of the Spirit and the water of baptism,[45] the preliminary washing of the hands,[46] to name but a few. All this constituted the "atmosphere" in which prayer was offered, and where these things were observed, as has been suggested, they were no less a part of the act of praying than was the interior lifting up of the mind and heart.

What strikes us in reading about these customs is, perhaps more than anything else, a certain sobriety. Tertullian is especially careful to stress this when describing the stance of the Christian at prayer; everything is meant to bespeak humility and moderation, whether it be the position of the hands, the elevation of the eyes or the tone of the voice. Extravagant gestures or motions, the element of the Dionysian or the irrational, were characteristic not of orthodox Christianity but of heretical groups and the pagan cults. This sobriety was reflected in both public and private prayer. For its first two or three hundred years the liturgy everywhere was very rich in symbolism but rather severe in execution, although, typically, it gradually grew more elaborate, particularly in the East. The Eucharist that Justin Martyr speaks of in the middle of the second century as well as the one described in Hippolytus' *Apostolic Tradition* at the beginning of the third could hardly have lasted more than twenty minutes each.[47] Not until about the middle of the fourth century—with the Christianization of the empire, the appropriation of some imperial imagery by the Church and the need to express in liturgical fashion the divine majesty of Christ that the Arians had denied—did the liturgy of the Eucharist begin to lose its primordial simplicity. Even then, however, it was not extravagant in any Dionysian sense; it merely accumulated ceremony and still more symbolism.

This external simplicity appears to have reflected, by and large, an austerity in the early Christians' approach to God in non-liturgical or "private" prayer. Needless to say, it is a rather daring task to try to gauge the spiritual life of a people who lived sixteen or seventeen centuries before our era and who have left us relatively little material from which to make such a judgment. Even the most mystical of the Fathers, men like Origen and Gregory of Nyssa and Augustine, are sparing in what they have to say of their interior lives. We are amazed, for instance, when Origen reveals in a homily on the Song of Songs that he has occasionally felt the presence of Christ in a most intense way, but that such an experience of him has also always been highly elusive.[48] The vision of Monica and Augustine at Ostia, perhaps the most famous mystical event recorded in patristic times, is famous at least in part precisely because Auustine writes of it in such rare detail in his *Confessions*.[49] This reticence seems to be in keeping with the *gravitas*, the seriousness or even severity, of the classical Roman mentality and with the moderation and balance of what was best in Greek culture as well, although it would not necessarily be true of the Syrians, who tended to be more emotional.

The way of the Fathers, ultimately like that of all Christians, including those who have sometimes experienced special graces in connection with prayer, was the way of faith and not of vision. With some exceptions (Origen is the greatest), their mysticism was expressed primarily in terms of darkness, and their prayer corresponded to this, we may be sure. Some lines of Gregory of Nyssa typify this in general perception, if not in the choice of language that he uses:

> The more the spirit makes progress, attains to a knowledge of the One-who-is through an ever greater and more perfect

concentration and comes closer to vision, the more it sees that the divine nature is invisible. For when it has left all appearances behind—not only what sensual perception grasps but also what the intellect thinks that it sees—it presses more deeply into what is most profoundly within, until with great spiritual effort it attains to the invisible and inconceivable, and so sees God. For therein lies the true knowledge of the one who is sought, therein lies the seeing in not-seeing, in that the one who is sought surpasses all knowledge and is cut off on every side by his incomprehensibility. Therefore the sublime John, who penetrated into this luminous darkness, says: No one has seen God. By this negation he teaches us that the knowledge of the divine essence is unattainable not only by human beings but indeed by every intellectual nature.[50]

What a passage such as this tells us is that the Fathers' grasp of union with the divine through prayer is both very deep and marked by a strong sense of human limitation.

If, as we may believe, unusual spiritual gifts or states of prayer were not frequently granted, neither were they sought after. Ecstasies, illuminations and the like were the objects of suspicion rather than of desire; they smacked too much of the frenzied pagan cults and of splinter groups of Christian enthusiasts to be attractive to the Church at large. Prayer had rather to be rooted in the ordinary living out of Christian life, which was characterized by the practice of good works. This was the insight of a Father such as Theodore of Mopsuestia, whose words on the subject have been quoted earlier, who insisted that good works not only had to accompany prayer but were a part of prayer. It was the insight also of Basil of Caesarea, who exalts the life of the cenobite, the monk who lives in community, over that of the hermit because the latter, although enjoying the benefits of solitary prayer, cannot minister to others. If you live alone, Basil asks in a well-known passage, "Whose feet will you wash? For whom will you care? In comparison with whom will you be the least?"[51] Indeed, the call of charity in the form of ministry and service was more imperative than the call of prayer. A story from the Egyptian desert illustrates this in pungent language:

> A brother questioned a certain old man, saying: Suppose that there are two brothers, and one of them stays quietly in his cell, extending his fasting over six days and imposing heavy labor on himself, but the other one cares for the sick. Whose work is more pleasing to God? The old man replied to him: If the brother who keeps a fast for six days were to hang himself up by his nostrils he could not be the equal of the one who tends the sick.[52]

Almsgiving or good works legitimized one's prayer, so to say, and also made that prayer acceptable to the Lord. "If we wish our prayers to be heard by the Lord," Augustine tells his congregation, "we ought to commend them with good works and alms."[53]

This is not to deny that the ideal of a life exclusively given over to prayer and contemplation was profoundly attractive to the early church. We can see in Augustine's commentary on the story of Martha and Mary in Luke 10:38–42 how easily Mary would come to symbolize the contemplative and Martha the active life, and how, although both were good, the former was better. Yet Augustine realizes that Martha's part, which is that of ministry and service, belongs to this world and is both necessary and demanded by justice, while Mary's foreshadows the world to come.[54] There is a tension here between the two possible orientations of Christian existence that Augustine himself, always occupied with pastoral duties but always nostalgic for the peace of contemplative prayer, experienced in his own life in sometimes poignant fashion.[55] But in this respect Augustine is merely the most notable example of such a tension: it was shared by many of the Fathers who found themselves engaged in pastoral activity or works of mercy. In the end, the recognition is that, except for some specially chosen by the Lord, the sabbath rest of contemplation is reserved for heaven; and even those specially so chosen are obliged to come to the aid of their brothers and sisters when the need arises.

From the Fathers, then, we can expect profound insights about prayer, but no easy methods. Their wisdom in this regard is perennial, traditional, extremely balanced, sober like their prayer itself.

X

Poverty and Wealth

In his book entitled *The True Word*, sections of which Origen includes in his treatise *Against Celsus*, the pagan author Celsus, writing sometime in the late second century, accuses Christians of being credulous and illiterate and gives the impression that they all come from the lowest stratum of society: they are wool-workers, shoemakers, washer-women, he says, who succeed in attracting to their absurd beliefs only those who are equally ignorant and low-born.[1] Yet it seems that Celsus' prejudice has gotten the better of him, for already by the end of the first century Christianity was drawing in people from every social class and had probably even penetrated the imperial household itself. Certainly, by the end of the second century and the beginning of the third, Paul's words addressed to the recently baptized in 1 Corinthians 1:26–28 must have lost a good deal of their pungency: "For consider your call, brethren; not many of you were wise according to worldly standards, not many were powerful, not many were of noble birth; but God chose what is weak in the world to shame the strong, God chose what is low and despised in the world, even things that are not, to bring to nothing things that are." It was toward the end of the second century that Clement of Alexandria produced his *Who Is the Rich Man That Shall Be Saved?*—perhaps at the behest of a rather large number of wealthy Alexandrian Christians who were worrying that they would have to divest themselves of all their material goods in order to be saved. We know that by then there were well-established communities of rich Christians not only in Alexandria but in every major city in the Roman Empire. The Church thus had to deal with the problems and discrepancies that inevitably arise when a single body of persons with common goals exists on several different social levels. More than that, though, it had to come to grips with what appeared to be a certain sentiment against the wealthy implicit in its own constitution and spelled out for all to see in several places in the New Testament.

The Christian Use of Wealth

The possibility of being both wealthy and Christian was consequently one of the first things that had to be established. That the wealthy person had a genuine place in the Christian community and a real function to fulfill there is brought up at length for the first time in the middle of the second century in *The Shepherd* of Hermas. Hermas warns the rich about vainly spending their resources on their own pleasures: God gave wealth to the rich, he says, not for luxury but in order that they might come to the aid of the afflicted and of widows and orphans.[2] Then he goes on to explain how rich and poor need one another and support one another; the thought, if not Hermas' imagery, is classic among the Fathers. Seeing a vine curling about an elm tree, Hermas is led to reflect how well the two growing things complement each other, for the elm bears no fruit of itself, while the fruit of the vine would be rotten if it lay upon the ground. The elm holding up the fragile vine and the vine supplying for the elm's lack of fruit with its own abundance turn into a symbol of the relationship between rich and poor:

> The one who is rich has much wealth, but he is needy with regard to the Lord since he is busy about his riches and has little time for intercession or confession before the Lord, and what he does is weak and small and without any other power. When therefore the rich person rests upon the poor and gives him the things that he needs, he believes that what he does for the poor person is able to find him a reward before God, because the poor person is rich in intercession and confession, and his intercession has great power with God. And so the rich person unhesitatingly helps the poor in all things. But the poor person, being helped by the rich,

intercedes to God and thanks him for the one who gave to him, and the rich person is still zealous for the poor so that he may not be wanting in his life, because he knows that the intercession of the poor is acceptable and rich before the Lord. Both of them, then, bring the work to its end. The poor person labors in the intercession in which he abounds, which he received from the Lord; this he pays to the Lord who helps him. And the rich person in like manner unhesitatingly provides the poor with the wealth that he received from the Lord; and this work is great and acceptable before God, because he is understanding with regard to his wealth and has acted well toward the poor person with the gifts that the Lord has given him, and he has discharged his ministry well. As far as human beings are concerned, therefore, the elm tree does not appear to bear any fruit, and they do not know or realize that when there is a drought the elm, which has water, nourishes the vine, and the vine, having an unfailing supply of water, gives double fruit—for itself and for the elm. Likewise the poor, when they intercede with the Lord for the rich, make up for what is lacking in their wealth, and again, when the rich help the poor in their need they complement their prayers. Thus both share in the righteous work.[3]

More than two centuries later Augustine speaks succinctly in one of his sermons of the relationship between rich and poor. "Who made both?" he asks. "The Lord. He made the rich in order to come to the aid of the poor, and the poor in order to prove the rich."[4] Each exists for the other and each has a role to play, although, in the balance, the role of the poor is superior to that of the rich because the former offers spiritual goods to the latter in return for material ones. "What are the poor to whom we give if not our carriers, by whom we are brought from earth to heaven?"[5] "Let the one who is poor be fed here below, where I am rich but he is in need," Paulinus of Nola writes in a letter, "so that he may feed me in heaven, where I shall be in need but he will be filled."[6]

The consensus of the Fathers is that wealth of itself is not a bad thing so long as it is properly used, just as poverty, pure and simple, is not virtuous of itself. "For not all poverty is holy,"

Ambrose writes, "nor are all riches criminal. But as luxurious living corrupts wealth, so holy living commends poverty."[7] "The crime is not in possessing worldly goods but in not knowing how to use them."[8] Clement tells the Christians of Alexandria that it would be irresponsible of them to think of throwing away their possessions when so much good can be accomplished with them: "What kind of sharing would there be among people if no one had anything? . . . How would one be able to feed the hungry, give drink to the thirsty, clothe the naked and shelter the homeless—for the not doing of which a person is threatened with fire and the outer darkness—if one were himself divested of all these things?"[9] In the first exposition of a particular scriptural passage that has come down to us from the early Church, Clement shows that the narrative of the rich young man in Mark 10:17–31 is to be understood in a spiritual sense, as we have already seen in a previous chapter.[10] Jesus did not intend the young man to abandon his property but rather "to drive from the soul the vain thoughts about wealth, the excitement and distress related to it, the worries that are the thorns of existence and that suffocate the seed of life."[11] By arguments such as this, which Clement was the first to utilize, the legitimization of the position of the wealthy Christian in the Church was accomplished.

Yet sentiments hostile to wealth survived and exerted their influence elsewhere. Cyril of Jerusalem, among others, reports that the Manicheans said that gold and silver belonged to the devil, to which he replied, citing Haggai 2:8: "God says plainly by the prophet: The silver is mine and the gold is mine, and I will give it to whomever I desire."[12] The Synod of Gangra, held in Asia Minor toward the middle of the fourth century, had to condemn a sect of heretics called Eustathians who insisted that the rich who did not forsake their property had no hope of being saved.[13] The Pelagians held the same opinion, and Augustine counters it by pointing out that the patriarchs of the Old Testament were all wealthy and were not on that account denied salvation.[14] But the tremendous misuse of wealth—so evident particularly in the later empire, when Rome could no longer control its economic destiny and the middle class had effectively been destroyed, leaving behind virtually nothing but the extremes of wealth and poverty—drove the Fathers themselves to say some things about wealth that may be considered exaggerated or unrealistic, or at least exceedingly pessimistic. Thus Irenaeus writes that everything a person possesses comes ultimately from the mammon of iniquity:

> For where do the houses in which we live come from, and the clothing that we wear, and the vessels that we use, and all the other things that we employ in our daily lives, except from what we acquired out of avarice when we were still unbaptized, or from relatives or friends who obtained it unjustly? Even now, while we are in the faith, we acquire. For who sells and does not wish to make a profit out of the one who buys? And who buys and does not wish to be treated to his own advantage by the one who sells? What businessman carries on his business if not to be fed by it?[15]

Jerome expresses the same thought in one of his letters: "All riches come from iniquity, and unless one person suffered loss another would not make gain. Hence the popular saying seems to me to be very true: A rich person is either wicked himself or the beneficiary of someone else's wickedness."[16] And Eucherius, bishop of Lyons in the second quarter of the fifth century, cites another such proverb in a letter of his: "What is wealth but a token of wrongdoing?"[17]

Yet even what seems exaggerated often has the ring of being based upon hard experience. Ambrose describes the extravagance and thoughtless cruelty of the rich in northern Italy at the end of the fourth century in a manner that is probably not hyperbolic, given what we know of conditions at the time: "You clothe your walls," he tells the rich, "and strip human beings. A naked person cries out before your house and you neglect him. A naked person cries out, and you are concerned with what sorts of marble you should cover your floors. Someone who is poor looks for money and has none. Someone asks for bread, and your horse champs on a golden bit."[18] Gaudentius of Brescia, writing a few years later, uses the same harsh language: "Certain women weigh down their own limbs and those of their daughters with gold and pearls, while they pass by with empty hands the crowds of poor begging for alms. They even have delicate ornaments made of silver and gold for brute animals, horses and mules, while to human beings made in the image of God they give not the crudest clothing or food."[19]

The Fathers' condemnation of lending money at interest, at least among Christians, is so oft-repeated that this practice must have been very common. Always the usurer is excoriated in the strongest language. Basil finds money-lenders worse than dogs: at least a dog is pacified when it receives something, but a money-lender is only further provoked and wants still more.[20] In his commentary on the Book of Tobit, which is really a treatise against usury, Ambrose speaks of children being sold at auction to pay off their father's debt and of usurers refusing burial to their debtors.[21] It is true that the wealthy themselves sometimes suffered from this, but primarily usury represented an oppression of the poor.

The Sharing of Goods and Money

The abuse of wealth, which was so widespread, provided the impetus for a number of the Fathers to propose a form of communism as a model for Christian living. Indeed, this had been an ideal from the very origins of Christianity, as we read in the Acts of the Apostles, and it appears as an ideal that is still viable and permeated with the spirit of the apostolic community in a chapter of Tertullian's *Apology*, written toward the beginning of the third century. Tertullian tells how the pagans say "See how they love one another" when they observe the fraternity that exists among Christians, and a few lines later he goes on to speak of the sharing of goods that is practiced in the Church: "We who are united in mind and soul do not hesitate at all to share our property. Among us everything is in common except our wives."[22] This description is probably not merely an idealization: the persecutions from which the Christians in North Africa were suffering as Tertullian wrote his *Apology* in their defense would certainly have served to cast them upon each other's resources. A half century after Tertullian, Cyprian of Carthage could write that it was the very breakdown in the

sense of shared property and common goods which was responsible for the Christians' dismaying weakness in the face of the
Decian persecution of 249–251. In the years of peace preceding
the persecution, Cyprian asserted, both clergy and laity had
spent their energies on making money and acquiring land. When
the years of trial came upon them, they were unwilling to abandon their material gains; rather than do so, they denied their
faith.[23]

For many, the Church of the Acts of the Apostles was a
golden age that was to be looked back on with nostalgia and
regret. Chromatius of Aquileia, speaking to his congregation
toward the end of the fourth century, is not the only one to draw
an unfavorable comparison between that age and his own day.
"I fear," he tells his listeners, "that the unanimity and charity of
the believers under the apostles might be our condemnation—
we who in our avaricious zeal hold to neither unanimity nor
peace nor charity. They considered their own property to be in
common, but we want to make other people's property our
own."[24] And Jerome proposed to write a history of the Church
(a project that he never got around to accomplishing) in which
he would demonstrate how the Church had declined in virtue
from apostolic times to his own, although it had increased in
power and wealth.[25]

Among the Fathers who preach and write in the centuries
of peace following the persecutions, it is now a sense of frustration with the indifference of the rich to the plight of the poor
that causes them to speak in terms of community of goods or
communism. This is apparent in the idea's greatest proponents,
Chrysostom in the East and Ambrose in the West. In one of his
sermons on 1 Timothy we can see how Chrysostom is led to
develop his line of reasoning in this regard:

> Tell me then, how did you come by your wealth? Did you
> receive it from someone? Where did he get it from? From his
> grandfather, you say, or from his father. Are you able to
> show, as you go back through the generations, that it was
> justly acquired? It cannot have been. No, the beginning and
> root of wealth must lie in injustice of some sort. And why?
> Because, in the beginning, God did not create one person

wealthy and another to go wanting; nor did he, at some point later in time, reveal great heaps of gold to one person and cheat another searcher. He gave one and the same earth to all alike. And, inasmuch as the earth is a common possession, how is it that you have acres and acres of land, while your neighbor has not the tiniest fraction of the earth? It is an inheritance from my father, you say. And from whom did it come to him? From his ancestors, you say. Yet you must go back and search out the origin of your claim. Jacob grew wealthy, but it came as what he earned from his own toil. Still, I will not quibble too much over details. I grant you that your wealth may have been gathered honestly and without any taint of larceny—that the gold he had somehow just gushed up out of the earth. What of it? Is wealth something good? Not at all. Still, he argues, it is not something evil. No, it is not something evil—so long as it is not hoarded and is shared out with those in need. Unshared, wealth becomes something evil, a trap. But not doing a good work, he goes on, is not tantamount to doing an evil one or being an evil person. True enough, but isn't the fact that you claim sole ownership of what belongs to the Lord, of what is common property, something evil? Or do you deny that the Lord's is the earth and its fullness? And so, if whatever we have belongs to our one common Lord, it belongs also to those who are his servants along with us. Whatever belongs to the Lord belongs equally to all. Isn't this the arrangement established in great households, where all get an equal share of food since it comes from the store of their master? The master's house is available to all. Whatever kings own—cities, marketplaces, public walks—is common property, shared equally by all. Now look at God's loving plan. In order that they might put humankind to shame, he created certain things as common property—the sun, the air, the earth and water, the sky, the sea, light and the stars—and shares them out equally as with members of a single family. He has fashioned us all with the same eyes and body and soul, the same equipment in all respects, all things that come from the earth, all human beings from a single parent and all of us in one dwelling place. But none of these shames us. Other things as well he made common property—baths, cities, marketplaces, walkways. And notice that no one argues over what belongs to all in common; all is peaceful. Strife comes on the scene only when someone tries to gain possession of something and make it his own. It is as if human nature itself grows wroth when, in spite of God's uniting us in every way, we are bent on dividing and standing apart by owning things and using phrases like "This belongs to me" or "That is yours"—chilling words indeed. This is the occasion of quarreling and turmoil; without this sort of conduct there can be no quarrel and no contention. It is rather the state of common property that is our inheritance which is more in keeping with our nature. Why do we never argue over who owns the market-place? Is it not because it belongs to all alike? It is rather over houses and possessions that we see each other always at each other's throats. Whatever is necessary for life is given to all alike; yet even in the smallest matters we cannot seem to keep things common to all. God has made these great gifts available to all in common so that we might learn to share lesser things. Nevertheless, we have not learned this lesson.

To return to my earlier questions: how can a rich person be a good person? He is a good person when he shares his wealth; by no longer being wealthy he becomes good—by giving his wealth to others. As long as he hoards it for himself he is not good.[26]

A section from his great diatribe against the rich, *On Naboth,* is typical of Ambrose:

How long, O you wealthy, will you draw out your insane desires? Shall you alone live upon the earth? Why do you cast out those whom nature has made your companions and claim for yourselves the possession of nature? The earth was established in common for all, rich and poor. Why do you alone arrogate an exclusive right to the soil, O rich? Nature, which brings forth everyone poor, knows no rich. For we are not born with clothing, nor are we conceived with gold and silver. Naked she brings us into the light, needing food, covering and drink. Naked the earth receives those whom she brought forth, not knowing how to enclose their property in the sepulcher. The narrow sod is equally generous to both rich and poor, and the earth, which did not contain the desire of the rich when he was alive, now contains him whole and entire. Nature therefore is unable to distinguish when we are born, nor can she do so when we pass away. She creates all alike, all alike she encloses in the bosom of the sepulcher. Who can tell the forms of the dead? Uncover the earth and pick out the rich man if you can. When the rubbish has been somewhat cleared away from the tomb and you recognize the poor man, prove it. Perhaps the only difference is that when a rich man dies more things perish with him.[27]

Between these two long passages several themes appear that recur in patristic literature on poverty and wealth, namely, the evil origins of wealth, the inability of the rich to contain their avarice, nature's even-handed bestowal of her goods on all and, finally, the desirability of possessing all things in common.

Nevertheless, despite the vehemence of their feelings on the abuse of wealth, the Fathers never demand unconditionally that the rich distribute everything that they possess to the poor; that was the teaching of heretics, not of the orthodox, and characteristic of their extremism. In the end the Fathers fall back on the position that rich and poor exist for one another and mutually benefit from one another. Nor, in the final analysis, despite certain extreme statements, do they condemn wealth outright; following the view first set down by Clement of Alexandria, they ask only that the rich be detached enough from their wealth that they be willing to share it with the poor. At the same time they incessantly warn of the temptations that the possession of wealth brings with it. The greatest such temptation was to avarice, so frequently pictured as the root of all sins, creator of insatiable desires that would afflict rich and poor alike with equal fury. "O blindness of the human mind!" says Zeno of Verona in a sermon preached about the year 370. "How each pushes on to the same death in his own way—the poor person when he unhappily seeks after wealth that happily he does not have, and the rich person when he does not think that he has wealth that he does have! In the one avarice burns, in the other it rages, in both it waxes, in neither does it die down."[28]

Yet, however much the Fathers may accept the fact that rich and poor alike have a place in God's plan, they find themselves obliged at least to try to elucidate why God should have permitted certain persons to be rich and others to be poor. Why, especially, are the wicked rich? Augustine is one who addresses himself to this mystery and works out all the possibilities in it: "You see wealth among thieves, among the impious, among criminals, among the wicked. . . . God gives these things to them because of their share in human nature, on account of the abundance of his overflowing goodness, he who makes his sun to rise on good and bad and lets his rain fall on just and unjust."[29] Elsewhere he develops another thought in a sermon to an audience that apparently finds it very difficult to understand:

> That God gives good things to the wicked is—if you want to understand why—for your growth and does not indicate a divine perversity. Yet I see that you still do not grasp what I said. Listen therefore to what I was telling you who blame and accuse God because he gives these earthly and temporal goods even to wicked persons, which according to your way of thinking he ought not to give except to the righteous alone. . . . Gold, silver, every type of money, clothing, clients, relatives, cattle, honors—all these are externals. If these lower, earthly, temporal, transitory goods were not given to the wicked as well, they would be considered great by the righteous. And so God, who gives these things to the bad, teaches you to long for higher things.[30]

Finally, in still another sermon, he expands this idea, explaining that wealth is distributed indiscriminately to good and bad alike—to the good in order to console them on their journey through life, but not to the good alone, lest the wicked think that God should be worshiped for that reason; and to the wicked in order to show the good how insignificant wealth is and to teach them to desire other things, but not to the wicked alone, lest the good who are weak should hesitate to be converted for fear that they would lose their earthly possessions. But both good and bad are afflicted with poverty as well—the good as a kind of trial and purification, and the wicked so that the good who are hesitant might be moved to conversion.[31] As Ambrose remarks, since poverty and wealth are completely fortuitous, wealth cannot be seen as a reward for virtue nor poverty as a punishment for sin.[32]

Almsgiving

Although the wealthy were not expected to divest themselves of all their material possessions, nonetheless it was frequently impressed upon them that whatever they had of superfluity was to be given to the poor in alms. This excess of wealth, in fact, belonged to the poor by right, for "the superfluities of the rich are the necessities of the poor," as Augustine says; "whatever you have in excess is not your own property."[33] Consequently the person who gave alms was simply carrying out the will of God. But almsgiving was not without its benefits for the giver: it was, with prayer and fasting, one of the three great acts of religion to obtain the forgiveness of sin, and as such it appears constantly in the writings of the Fathers. In what is perhaps the oldest sermon that we possess, delivered sometime toward the middle of the second century, an anonymous preacher compares the three: "Almsgiving is good as penitence for sin. Fasting is better than prayer, but almsgiving is better than both."[34] The traditional connection with fasting made almsgiving a frequent topic of Lenten sermons, in which we may read scores of exhortations to generosity. "In these days of holy fasting, then," Leo the Great tells his congregation, for instance, "the works of mercy, which ought always to be pursued, should be carried out with still more vigor."[35] Almsgiving could even be compared to baptism itself, as Maximus of Turin says about the end of the fourth century, expressing a common opinion in striking fashion:

> Almsgiving is another kind of washing of souls, so that if perchance anyone has sinned through human frailty after baptism there is still the possibility of being cleansed by almsgiving, as the Lord says: Give alms, and behold, everything is clean for you. But, with due regard to the faith, I would say that almsgiving is more indulgent than baptism. For baptism is given once and provides pardon once, whereas as many times as alms are bestowed pardon is granted. These are the two founts of mercy, which give life and forgive sins. Whoever holds to both shall be endowed with the honor of the heavenly kingdom, but whoever, having sinned after baptism, has betaken himself to the rivers of mercy [namely, almsgiving] shall himself obtain mercy.[36]

Because the poor are identified with Christ, according to Matthew 25:40 ("As you did it to one of the least of these my brethren, you did it to me"), to give alms to them is to give alms to him. "Although he is the Lord, and a real Lord who has no need of our goods, yet he has deigned to be hungry in his poor so that we might do something for him," Augustine tells his congregation. "I was hungry and you gave me to eat, he says. Lord, when did we see you hungry? When you did it to one of the least of mine, you did it to me. In a word, let everyone hear and consider worthily how great is the merit for having fed the hungry Christ, and how great is the crime of having scorned the hungry Christ."[37] For this reason, as much as for the sake of sheer justice, almsgiving was an obligation from which no one could be excused. Even poverty, Jerome writes, must not prevent a person from at least giving a cup of cold water to someone who asks for it.[38]

To speak of the identification of the poor with Christ is to begin to touch upon the aspect of the spirituality of poverty. Occasionally the Fathers romanticize the condition of the poor, speaking of their freedom from the burdens of wealth, the peaceful sleep that they are able to enjoy under the open skies while their rich neighbors toss restlessly on their beds of ivory and gold.[39] But more often than not, by far, they recognize that poverty is a bitter trial for most people and cannot be characterized as a good unless it is voluntarily accepted out of love for Christ. So the poor were counseled to resign themselves to their lot and to realize at least that their poverty gave them a certain advantage before God, since they were less subject to temptations to pride and luxury and more prone to be meek and humble. The truest poverty was ultimately spiritual: for the poor this meant detachment from the desire to possess what they did not have; for the rich, detachment from what they already possessed. This notion of detachment is at the heart of Clement of Alexandria's *Who Is the Rich Man That Shall Be Saved?* which stands as a model of the moderate approach to the problem of poverty and wealth in the ancient Church.

Yet this moderate—perhaps one would even call it "bourgeois"—approach was not for everyone. The very same passage from the Gospels about Jesus and the rich young man, which

Clement interprets in such a way as to convince the wealthy that they need not abandon their possessions, is also interpreted by the Egyptian peasant Anthony, as we have already seen, in a very radical way.[40] This interpretation is the basis for monastic poverty, which ideally intends to be absolute, although the concession of common ownership of a minimal amount of property is made. Despite the rather severe poverty that they embraced, however, the monks were well within the spectrum of the Church's views, for they did not condemn the possession of wealth in itself. Cassian, for example, who was one of Western monasticism's greatest and most influential figures, considered wealth to be something indifferent that could be used for either good or bad ends; in this respect it was like marriage, or even like customs that were often held to be holy in themselves, such as fasting and keeping vigil.[41]

It is safe to say that, for the Fathers, the problem of poverty and wealth was the most important specific social issue that the early Church faced—as, indeed, it has perennially been. From the attention that they devoted to it we may even say that it was more important than war and peace. Their attitude in this regard is characterized by the same tendency to strike a balance between extremes that is typical of their approach to doctrine. The tension of maintaining both humanity and divinity in Christ, for instance, when the unorthodox would emphasize one at the expense of the other, or the need to understand how the Church could be holy in itself and sinful in its members: this is paralleled in the Fathers' concern neither to condemn wealth on the one hand nor to idealize purely material poverty on the other; neither to deny (however reluctantly) the right of individuals to possess property nor to deny the right of the poor to have what was necessary for their subsistence. In these positions there is not absolute consistency, and it is undoubtedly the immediacy of the suffering of the poor and the failure of the rich to respond to it that drives the Fathers into making statements from which they must occasionally draw back. However much they may have expressed an attraction for radical solutions to the problems of poverty and wealth—and we know that the sympathies of many of them lay in the direction of radical solutions—they were ultimately moved by the desire that the Church be as inclusive as possible, that it be open to rich and poor alike and not to the poor alone. This may leave the reader with the impression that the Church of the Fathers somehow compromised the rigor of the Gospel. Or it may make the face of the Church all the more human and appealing.

XI

The Christian in the World

To speak of the relationship of the early Church to the world—or, somewhat more specifically, to the Roman Empire, for that was the world of the majority of the Fathers—is to be obliged to speak of the pagan cults. Until Christianity began to dominate, the glue that held the empire together was, perhaps more than anything else, the imperial cult: the worship of the emperor was the one practice that was universally observed, except by the Jews, who enjoyed a special privilege. To ask a person to take an oath or to swear by the emperor's genius (his "guardian angel," as it were) was not only to demand the ultimate surety from him; it was also the usual certain way of discovering where his loyalty lay. "Swear by the genius of Caesar," the pro-counsul advises Polycarp as he is being led to his death in the amphitheater at Smyrna. "Take the oath and I will set you free."[1] "Christians are public enemies on account of this," Tertullian writes, "that they do not give the emperors empty or false or unfounded honors."[2] The refusal of the Christians to participate in the imperial cult was one of the measures of their failure to be integrated completely into the life of the empire. In vain would Tertullian tell the pagan audience of his *Apology* that Christians reverenced the emperor second only to God because he occupied the highest place in society and that they prayed "unceasingly for all the emperors, for their long life, for a secure empire, an untroubled imperial house, brave armies, a faithful senate, an upright people, a world at peace—whatever the emperor himself, as man and Caesar, would pray for."[3] Anything less than total submission to the custom of the empire was insufficient.

Secular Powers and Demonic Powers

With respect to the honor due the emperor, as far as Christians conceived it, certain distinctions had to be made that were evidently impossible for the pagan mind to grasp or accept. Thus Christians could recognize the emperor's authority over nearly every sphere of life with the exception of religion. It seems that they would willingly fight for the defense of the emperor and the empire (it is difficult to know if and to what extent the early Christians practiced pacifism, despite a number of texts that indicate such a practice[4]), but they would not sprinkle incense, thereby rendering divine honor, before an image of the emperor as a token of reverence. None of their positive reactions to emperor and empire bespoke an attempt on the part of the Christians to ingratiate themselves somehow with the secular powers. These reactions were simply typical of the Christian respect for established authority, even when that authority was misdirected, and in this they mirrored the attitude of Paul in Romans 13:1–7 ("Let everyone be subject to the governing authorities . . . ") and in 1 Timothy 2:1–2 ("I urge that supplications, prayers, intercessions and thanksgivings be made for everyone, for kings and all who are in high positions . . ."). It is remarkable to see at the conclusion of Clement's *Letter to the Corinthians*, written either during or immediately after the reign of the tyrant Domitian at the end of the first century, a long prayer for the health and happiness of temporal rulers.[5] Even Lactantius, who wrote his virulent tract *On the Deaths of the Persecutors* at the beginning of the fourth century in order to show how God had deservedly punished the emperors who persecuted the Church, never questioned the imperial authority. The first Christians, then, were clearly not revolutionaries in the usual sense of the term.

But idols could not command the recognition that even bad emperors enjoyed in the Christian mind. There was no feeling here that loyalty to the empire and its rulers demanded a nod to those myriad deities upon whom the popular mind was sure that the foundations of society in all its aspects rested. The reaction of the Fathers to the pagan cults, of which the imperial cult was but one part, was marked by contempt and disdain.

Yet we cannot leave it at that. So permeated was society with idolatry that the gods were in fact a force to be reckoned with. Consequently, until the beginning of the fifth century, when the empire finally took on an irrevocably Christian cast, patristic literature was filled with polemic against pagan worship. It has been remarked[6] that the early Christians were extremely conscious of the presence of demons all around them; it was these demons that were at work in the pagan cults. For the gods, according to one school of thought, were nothing other than demons from the beginning.[7] A second opinion had it that they were originally human beings—heroes and kings, for example, but also such personages as the infamous Antinous, deceased lover of the Emperor Hadrian—who were deified after their death and who now existed in demonic form.[8] "These spirits," writes Cyprian,

> lurk beneath the statues and consecrated images. They inspire the breasts of the prophets with their suggestions, animate the fibers of the entrails, govern the flight of birds, rule the casting of lots, bring about oracles, always confuse false things with true (for they both deceive and are deceived), make life turbulent and disturb dreams. As spirits creeping about in bodies they also secretly terrify minds, distort limbs, destroy health, leave people so sick as to be compelled to worship them, so that when they are glutted with the fumes of the altars and the piles of cattle they may seem to have cured those whom they themselves pushed into sickness.[9]

Whether in human guise or under the form of inanimate objects, it was still always the demons who ultimately received the honor and who took pleasure in the smoke and blood of the sacrifices that were offered. And still more, as Augustine writes, did they take pleasure in the submission of the human will to them.[10]

Contemptible as they may have been, the demons nonetheless were by their nature remarkably clever, as Cyprian evidently recognizes. One of the first charges that Christian authors brought against idol worship was that it was in many cases an attempt to subvert the Christian religion by anticipating it in a number of instances. Thus Justin Martyr writes that, knowing from the prophets that Christ was to come and being informed about what kind of man he was to be, the demons devised gods who resembled him so that no one would be impressed with him when he did come. Bacchus, Hercules, Asclepios and Mithras, for one reason or another, were among those who in some respect imitated Christ.[11] In fact the demons imitated not only Christ himself but also the sacraments, demanding of their worshipers sprinklings and washings reminiscent of baptism and, in the case of the Mithraic cult, inspiring a ceremony with bread and a cup of water that was similar to the Eucharist.[12] This theme of imitation, initiated by Justin, was taken up by later writers.

As powerful and as original as this charge may have been, it was easiest for the Christian apologists to fall back on the most obvious line of attack and the one that most embarrassed the pagans, namely the blatant immorality of the gods. As we have seen,[13] the pagans themselves, even before the advent of Christianity, had sought to explain in allegorical fashion the adultery, incest and pederasty that were rife among their deities. Arnobius of Sicca, perhaps idolatry's most unrelenting critic, who wrote at the very beginning of the fourth century, has a pagan complain that Christians do not understand the deeper meanings in the stories of the gods:

> You err and are mistaken, and in your criticism of these matters you show yourself to be quite inexperienced, unlearned and crude. For all these stories, which seem sordid to you and unworthy of the gods, contain in themselves sacred mysteries, wonderful and deep principles that are not easily grasped by facile minds. For not what is written and is the first meaning of the words is what is intended and said, but everything is to be understood by way of allegory and in a mystical sense. And so, when someone says that Jupiter slept with his own mother, he is not talking about the incestuous and wicked embraces of physical love, but rather about the rain (under the name of Jupiter) and the earth (signified by Ceres). Likewise, when someone says that he acted lasciviously with his daughter, he is not at all speaking of base pleasures, but instead of the word "showers" he employs "Jupiter," and he uses "daughter" to indicate the crop that was sown.[14]

To this Arnobius, speaking for the Christians, makes a sharp reply:

> All this is nit-picking and cavilling, as is evident, and the sort of thing that is used to bolster up bad cases in the courts. . . . Since to accept these accounts as they stand is shameful and disgraceful, recourse is had to this expedient, that one thing is substituted for another, and a more becoming interpretation is squeezed out of something disgusting. But what is it to us if other senses and other meanings underlie these vain stories? For us, who contend that you treat the gods shamefully and impiously, it is enough to accept what is written and what is heard, and we need not be concerned about what may be hidden, since the insult to the gods is contained not in obscure meanings but on the surface. So that we may not appear unwilling to look into what is said, however, we ask you this first, if you will only be patient with us: How do you know, how was it intimated to you, that these things were written allegorically or intended to be understood as such? Did the writers call you into conference, or were you lying hidden in their bosoms when they were substituting one thing for another in order to cover over the truth? Moreover, if for some reason and out of religious fear they wished to hide these mysteries in shadowy obscurity, is it not audacious of you to seek to find out what they did not want to be known, to know yourselves and to make known to everyone what they concealed in vain by words that have no truth in them?[15]

Although many of the gods were disgraceful by reason of their immorality, sometimes they would appear as simply ridiculous. Tertullian remarks with truth that the pagan writers themselves would make fun of the gods to give pleasure to their audiences.[16] The late second-century apologist Theophilus of Antioch could mock the cult of Zeus because the god appeared under so many different titles: "In the first place there is the Zeus with the name Olympios, then Zeus Latiarios, and Zeus Kassios, and Zeus Kerannios, and Zeus Propator, and Zeus Pannychios, and Zeus Poliouchos, and Zeus Kapitolios. And there is also the Zeus who is the child of Kronos, who is king of the Cretans and has a tomb in Crete."[17] Equally worthy of mockery, at least for Theophilus and some others, were the Egyptian gods—"the reptiles and cattle and wild beasts and birds and river fishes, and even washpans and disgusting noises."[18] But for one anonymous third-century Greek homilist the religion of the Egyptians was not so much laughable as sinister. "Egypt is a vast and dark image of shadow and profound error," he says.

> It is the wellspring of error. There they have made idols and constructed theologies around heifers, fish, birds, wild beasts and all such creatures. But when the avenging anger was revealed from the heavens and the great wrath was unloosed upon the entire earth, then the error of superstition and idolatry was the first thing to be struck down. For it is written: On all the gods of Egypt I will execute judgment: I am the Lord.[19]

The ubiquity of the gods and their participation in the most mundane and insignificant affairs of daily life also made them subject to the apologists' scorn. Arnobius writes sarcastically of a certain Lateranus, god and genius of the hearths:

> He runs through the kitchens of the human race, seeing with what kinds of woods the heat is kindled on his hearths. He takes care that the flames do not crack the earthen vessels by their force. He sees to it that the savors of things in their original state reach the palate with all their delights, and he carries out the office of a taster so as to learn whether the sauces have been properly prepared.[20]

But Lateranus is only one of many such deities.

> Puta, you say, is in charge of pruning trees, and Peta of petitions. The god of groves is Nemestrinus. Patellana is a divinity, as is Patella, of whom one is in charge of things already made public and the other of things yet to be made public. Nodutis is called a god because he brings what has been sown to the sheaves, as well as Noduterensis, who sees to the treading out of grain. Upibilia shows us the way if we get lost on the roads. Parents whose children have died are under the care of Orbona, while Naenia looks after those

near death. She who strengthens and solidifies the bones of little children is called Ossilago. Mellonia is a goddess mighty and powerful among bees, guarding and preserving the sweetness of honey.[21]

Over against this proliferation of deities, so many of them concerned with inconsequential matters, the Christian God stood unique, and it was part of the apologists' armory to stress his oneness. Cyprian insists that deity cannot be divided among many gods, and he shows by examples from history that human beings do not willingly share supreme power: "One kingdom did not hold the Roman twins, although they came from a single womb. Pompey and Caesar were kinsmen, and yet they did not maintain the bond of relationship in their enviable position." Animal life too bears witness to the principle of a single ruler: "The bees have one king, and there is one leader in the flocks and one head in the herds."[22] Indeed, during this period in the empire, in the centuries just before Constantine, there was a growing inclination to think in terms of a single god. An apologist like Theophilus would point out certain inconsistencies in pagan literature, when the resolution between the monotheistic inclination, such as it was, and the traditional polytheism had not been achieved.[23]

The Sacred and the Secular

The involvement of the gods in every aspect of human life, whether banal or important, meant that in pagan society there was no differentiation between what we now call the "sacred" and the "profane" or the "secular." Instead everything partook of the sacred. "The squares and the forum and the baths and the stables and our homes themselves are not totally free of idols," Tertullian writes. "Satan and his angels have filled the whole world."[24] In this world the Christian had to exercise the greatest care lest he be polluted by the unclean spirits that lay in wait for him. Tertullian describes in detail how everything associated with idolatry must be abjured. The making of idols, needless to say, and all the professions related to idolatry might not be practiced; among these professions was that of teaching literature, for it was in the reading of poetry that the pagan myths were introduced to young minds.[25] Pagan holy days might not be observed,[26] nor certain dress connected with pagan worship be worn.[27] Christians should not attend public games and shows because they are tainted with idolatry both in their origin and in their performance; indeed, "the amphitheater is consecrated by more wicked names [of gods] than the temple of Jupiter itself: it is the shrine of all the demons."[28] (The tremendous lure of the games and shows was a constant source of vexation to the pastors of the early Church. Augustine's complaint, made in the course of one of his sermons, is typical: "How many of the baptized have chosen to fill the circus today rather than this basilica!"[29] It is almost impossible to overestimate the enthusiasm with which these events, provided without charge, were received by the people.) A Christian could hold public office only if it were possible—which it hardly was—to be free from every aspect of idol worship; likewise, one could assist public officials in the performance of their duties only in those things that did not touch idolatry.[30] To be a soldier, Tertullian asserts, is a near impossibility on account of the many connections between the military and the worship of the emperor and of idols.[31] Finally, in the treatise addressed to his wife, Tertullian speaks of the dangers that a woman who marries a pagan husband, "a servant of the devil," has taken upon herself: she will be expected to participate in pagan ceremonies and to accompany her husband to taverns and other low places.[32] Nonetheless Christians could not be completely removed from their surroundings; to the question of whether one could enter the amphitheater at some time other than when the games are being held, Tertullian responds quite reasonably:

> There is no prohibition with regard to places. For the servant of God may go not only to the places where the games are held but even to the temples themselves if he has a good purpose in mind—one that does not pertain to the proper business or function of the place. . . . It is not the fact that we are in the world that cuts us off from God but rather that we are touched by the world's wickedness. Hence I shall be sep-

arated from God if I enter the temple of Jupiter or that of Serapis to offer sacrifice or to worship, just as if I were to enter the circus or the theater as a spectator. Of themselves places do not contaminate us, but rather what is done in them, and we are sure that the places themselves are contaminated by what occurs in them. By association with what is unclean we are made unclean.[33]

To the pagans this refusal to have anything to do with the traditional cults, as well as the worship of a God who had none of the familiar human traits to which those who paid homage to the Roman pantheon were accustomed, was tantamount to atheism. From the middle of the second century we begin to hear the charge of atheism made: both Justin[34] and the anonymous author of *The Martyrdom of Polycarp*[35] mention it. Clement of Alexandria counters, as do others, by claiming that it is the pagans themselves who are atheists:

In my way of thinking, the name "atheist" belongs to people who know nothing of the God who really is, whose worship is directed to a child dismembered by the Titans [Dionysos] and a lamenting woman [Demeter], who shamelessly worship parts of the body that genuine shame would make unmentionable. People of this sort are caught up in a double atheism: on the one hand, they do not know God, ignorant as they are of his true nature; on the other, they commit a further error by believing in the existence of what does not exist and by calling what is not divine—even what has no reality but only a name—"god."[36]

The punishment for this atheism of the Christians was very frequently death, and, if it came to that, there could be no hesitation in choosing between idol worship and martyrdom. Tertullian writes: "Martyrdom fights against and opposes idolatry, but to fight against and oppose an evil cannot be anything but good. . . . Who would not call that a good which frees a person from something evil? What difference is there between idolatry and martyrdom other than death and life?"[37] For idolatry was, again in the words of Tertullian, "the principal crime of the human race, the highest guilt incurred by the world, the sole cause of judgment."[38] It was linked to adultery, fornication, fraud, contumely, murder, luxury, sexual excess, drunkenness, unrighteousness, vanity and lying. "Thus it is that in idolatry all wicked deeds are detected, and in every wicked deed there is an element of idolatry. . . . Whoever sins certainly involves himself in idolatry, for what he does pertains to the adherents of the idols."[39] For rigorists like Tertullian and others there could be no reconciliation with the Church for a baptized Christian who had offered sacrifice to idols. The first canon of the early fourth-century Spanish council at Elvira is unyielding in this respect: "If someone of mature age, after having been baptized, enters a pagan temple for the sake of worship and thus commits a capital crime (for it is the most grievous offense), he may not be accepted into communion even at the end of his life." This rigorism was perhaps not typical of the greater part of the Church, but it at least illustrates the extreme seriousness with which such lapses were viewed.

Inasmuch as the public welfare and the cult of the gods were intimately bound together in the life of the pagan empire, so that the Romans claimed that their devotion to the gods had made them the masters of the world,[40] Christians early were told that they were acting irresponsibly toward the empire. Their failure to offer worship provoked the gods to punish the earth with floods or the failure of crops or periods of drought or defeat in battle. "If the Tiber rises as high as the city walls," Tertullian writes in a famous passage, "if the Nile does not flood the fields, if heaven does not give rain, if the earth quakes, if there is famine or pestilence, immediately the cry is heard: The Christians to the lion!"[41] He responds by pointing out that there were catastrophes before Christ was born, and the gods did not save their worshipers from them. In fact, he continues, "if we compare tragedies that have occurred in the past, they are less unbearable now that God has placed Christians in the world; for from that time [when Christians first appeared], innocence has tempered the wickedness of the world and people have begun to call upon God."[42] The argument that the Roman Empire suffered from as many disasters before the coming of Christ as it did afterward is a theme that is developed particularly in the third book of Augustine's *City of God*, and it is the burden of all seven books of Orosius' treatise *Against the Pagans*, composed at the beginning of the fifth century at Augustine's instigation. Orosius writes that, until he had investigated the matter more thoroughly, he was thrown into confusion because "the calamities of the present age seemed to have exceeded all measure." His research, however, drew him to the same conclusion that Tertullian had reached— one that he backs up with an exhaustive catalogue of miseries, both historical and fabulous—namely, that "times past were not merely equally as oppressive but even more so, the further they were separated from the true religion."[43]

It would not be apropos to trace the history of the gradual decline of paganism in the empire and the triumph of Christianity to the point where, in many respects, Church and state could no longer be distinguished. By the time Augustine and Orosius were writing, of course, the empire was already officially Christian, but paganism endured as a significant factor until well into the fifth century, and in certain rural areas it even persisted considerably beyond that. Despite the vehemence and abhorrence with which the Fathers treated their pagan adversaries in the matter of the cults, paganism, at least in its decline, was capable of presenting a pathetic and sometimes even a noble facade. In the 380's, to give a famous example, the pagan Roman patrician Symmachus contended with Ambrose of Milan over whether the altar of the goddess Victory should be maintained in the Senate at Rome. Ambrose emerged the winner in the contest, but he appears harsh and shrill in comparison with Symmachus, who pleads that the ancient rites be permitted to exist side by side with the newer Christian ones: "Each person has his own way of doing things, each has his own religious observances. . . . That which all venerate should in fairness be considered as one. We all look at the same stars, we have the heavens in common, the same world surrounds us. What does it matter how a person searches for the truth? No one path leads to such a great mystery."[44] The Church had itself once called for religious freedom; Tertullian's words to the persecutor Scapula are ringing: "It does not befit religion to force devotion. . . . Even if you make us sacrifice it will profit your gods nothing, for they will not desire sacrifices from the unwilling unless they are obstinate."[45] There is something sad in the fact that toleration was not part of the Church's program once it had gained the ascendancy. Yet we can hardly realistically expect toleration from people who believed so firmly in the element of the demonic in the pagan cult and who saw idolatry as the worst of all possible sins.

Intellectual and Anti-Intellectual Influences

The struggle with the demonic gods and the ultimate triumph over them (a triumph that removed their real power and relegated them to the status of spooks and hobgoblins, for the most part[46]) represents perhaps the most important aspect of the Church's relationship to the world. A second significant aspect may be mentioned here, and it is in one way linked to the first. This is the ambivalent attitude of Christians toward learning in general and toward pagan literature in particular. The demonic consideration applies in the latter case because pagan literature was so frequently about nothing else than the Greek gods. Hence the prohibition of Christians' teaching such literature, as we have already seen, although this prohibition was probably not universal. But, more broadly, learning or literature of almost any kind was often subject to suspicion on account of its power to seduce the Christian soul, which was always too ready to be attracted either by the knowledge or by the beauty displayed therein.

From the point of view of grandeur of style and purely human interest the Bible could hardly compare with Plato or Virgil or Cicero. Augustine discovered this when, in late adolescence, he read Cicero's now lost *Hortensius*, which in turn inspired him to take up the Scriptures "so as to see what they were like." To his surprise and disappointment he came to the conclusion that Cicero was far more noble than they; their nobility, in any event, was not immediately accessible to the reader.[47] Pursuing another issue, Cassian speaks of a knowledge of literature as a hindrance to one's salvation. Even in the monastery the memories of what one may have read years before keep returning, and of his own experience Cassian writes:

Now my mind is corrupted with poetic songs so that even at the hour of prayer it meditates on those silly fables and histories of wars with which, in my childhood, it was filled from the time of its first lessons, and either the shameless memory of poetry insinuates itself to me when I am singing Psalms and asking mercy for my sins, or the image as it were of warring heroes comes into my mind's eye. The imagining of such phantasms constantly tricks me, so that it does not permit my mind to aspire to higher insights, nor can it be driven out with daily tears.[48]

Jerome, in a famous passage from his long letter to the virgin Eustochium, recounts how he was so taken up with the pagan authors that he would intersperse acts of devotion with the reading of Cicero and Plautus. When he would turn from them to the Scriptures, "their crude way of writing horrified me." He experienced a conversion when, in a fevered dream, he saw himself being brought before the heavenly tribunal; there he was accused in these words: "You are a Ciceronian, not a Christian; for where your treasure is, there also is your heart."[49]

Sometimes, however, the issue was not so much beauty as it was simply the learning contained in pagan works. Augustine was particularly conscious of the fact that the accumulation of knowledge was a danger, even if the knowledge itself was untouched by specifically pagan concerns, and he is fond of quoting 1 Corinthians 8:1: "Knowledge puffs up, but love builds up."[50] The human mind often desires to know just for the sake of knowing, and it does not matter whether the knowledge in question is beneficial or worthless. This is the vice of curiosity.[51]

More often than not, though, there was such a measure of idolatrous or erroneous thought compounded with otherwise useful information that one was liable to imbibe the former while taking in the latter. Consequently precaution had to be exercised, and a person had to be capable of sifting the good from the bad. In this respect Origen introduces an allegory into Christian literature that is employed by almost all the Fathers who subsequently treat of the problem. Interpreting Exodus 3:21–22 and 12:35–36, which treats of the Israelites despoiling the Egyptians of their gold and silver and other goods, Origen notes that these precious things—pagan in their origin—were used to construct the accoutrements of the Holy of Holies. In much the same way the valuable things to be found in pagan literature—geometry, music, grammar, rhetoric and astronomy—could be separated from the dross of idolatry and used for Christian purposes.[52] The idea at the basis of Origen's allegory, which may ultimately be traced to Justin's accepting attitude to whatever was good in pagan thought,[53] proved invaluable to the Fathers in their appropriation of certain aspects of pagan thought. These aspects belonged to the Christians anyway, Origen was suggesting, and could be seized by them with impunity. Gregory of Nyssa, who employs Origen's image,[54] also speaks of circumcision as a symbol of removing what is erroneous from pagan thought. Thus, for example, pagan philosophy teaches that the soul is immortal; but it also mentions a transmigration of souls, and that is an impure foreskin which must be cut off.[55]

Yet not everyone was open to such a balanced view of what pagan thought had to offer. There is a strain of almost violent rejection of secular—hence pagan—culture, which runs throughout a good deal of early Christian writing. The foremost example of this is Tertullian, who is accustomed to expressing himself in extreme language. The classic statement of his position may be found in his treatise *On the Prescription of Heretics;* after demonstrating to his own satisfaction that Greek philosophy has been the source of numerous heresies, Tertullian goes on to declaim:

> What then do Athens and Jerusalem have to do with one another? What the Academy and the Church? What heretics and Christians? Our learning comes from the Porch of Solomon, who himself had taught that the Lord was to be sought in simplicity of heart. What kind of Christianity can be produced from Stoic and Platonic and dialectic thought? After possessing Christ Jesus there is no need for us to be curious, nor, after the Gospel, for us to be inquisitive. Believing as we do, we desire no further belief. For this is our first belief, that we ought not to believe anything else.[56]

The monks too, as we have seen,[57] tended to disdain all aspects of learning. But the distinction must be made between persons such as Tertullian and Jerome and Augustine, who inveighed against learning or were at least suspicious of it but who were in fact themselves intellectuals of the highest caliber, and many monks of the desert, who for the most part could not even read and who knew nothing of secular culture. The former were in a position to make criticisms, however jaundiced, whereas it may be said that the latter ordinarily knew not of what they spoke and had no such right.[58] Against such as these latter the words of Gregory Nazianzen sound with particular force:

> I consider it to be accepted by all intelligent persons that learning is our first good. I refer not only to this more noble form of it, which is ours, which rejects all ornament and glory in speech and clings closely to the one salvation and to the beauty of things contemplated, but even to the external culture that many Christians mistakenly despise as treacherous and dangerous and keeping us far from God. For just as we ought not to reject the sky, the earth and the air and things of that sort because some people look at them in the wrong way, worshiping what is made by God instead of God himself, but ought rather to take advantage of them for our life and enjoyment while fleeing from what is dangerous; not raising creation in revolt against the Creator, as is the way of foolish persons, but acknowledging the Maker from the things that have been made and, as the divine apostle says, making every thought subject to Christ; and just as we know that neither fire nor food nor iron nor anything else is either most useful in and of itself nor most harmful, but is so according to the mind of the user; and as we use reptiles to make health-giving medicines—so also from secular literature we have received elements of judgment and insight, while we have rejected whatever is demonic, erroneous and leads to the pit of destruction. Indeed, we are even aided by these things in our religion, as we perceive what is worse and what is better, making the weakness of their doctrine the strength of our own. Therefore learning is not to be despised because it seems despicable to some people, but we are rather to consider these people to be boorish and uneducated, wishing that everyone would be like them, in order to hide in the commonality and escape reproach for their ignorance.[59]

The difference between an "intellectual" and an "anti-intellectual" Christianity is one of the themes that marks patristic literature throughout its history.

In this arena of letters, perhaps more than anywhere else, was played out the great struggle as to how much Christianity could accommodate itself to "the world." The struggle was ultimately resolved in favor of an accommodation in which the world that was accommodated to was one that was not in disagreement with Christianity's own rule of faith—a world that, in the thought of Justin Martyr, was Christian even unbeknownst to itself. In this world the Christian could walk at ease.

XII

Death and Resurrection

It is instructive to compare the pagan and early Christian concepts of death. There were exceptions, but by and large the pagans of the Mediterranean world regarded death as something terrible and looked forward to the afterlife—if they believed in an afterlife at all—with considerable apprehension. We need only glance over their grave inscriptions to catch a glimpse of the pagan viewpoint. Some of them imply no belief in an existence after death and counsel the reader to make the most of life. Thus: "Fortune makes many promises but keeps none of them. Live for the present day and hour, since nothing else is really ours."[1] And: "Live joyfully while you live. Life is but a little thing. Presently it begins, gradually grows stronger, and then gradually disappears."[2] Others do imply a belief in a life to come, but in that belief there is no gladness: the afterlife is an eternal sleep, a being committed to the dark earth and a being delivered over to gods who were characterized as *irati*—"angry."[3] The typical response to this was one of despair or rebellion, or an irreparable sense of loss. Death's great advantage was that it was a release, however joyless, from the sorrows of this life. Pagan antiquity had its noble deaths, to be sure (one thinks of Socrates and Seneca), but they were marked by a profound and almost inexplicable sorrow. In the end this, more than anything else, was responsible for the fatalism that the early Church devoted so much of its energies to overcoming.

What we learn from Christian grave inscriptions, on the other hand, tends to betray a different spirit. We find the words *in pace*—"in peace"—used very frequently. The idea of sleep, which the pagans also knew, has taken on another meaning: it is now a sleep from which one will awake to eternal life. The pagan emphasis on darkness, too, has been transformed into an emphasis on light—the *lux perpetua*. While the pagans inveighed against the fate that had dealt them death ("I lift up my hands against the god who has taken me away in my innocence," one inscription has it, using the language of cursing[4]), Christian inscriptions often reveal a wonderful serenity and even joy: "May you live in God! Rejoice forever!"[5] Or simply: "May you live!"[6]

.   This is not to suggest that Christians did not frequently have a fear of death themselves. There is no denying it in an inscription such as the following, which marked the grave of a young Egyptian deacon:

> O what a separation this is! O departure more distant than all others! O difficult passage in order to arrive at the other side! O death, bitter word in everyone's mouth, which tears apart, which separates fathers from their sons and sons from their fathers! May whoever knows how to weep over those who have died . . . come to this place to mourn deeply over the unhappiness of my youth. . . . Remember me, my dear friends, so that God might pardon me. . . .[7]

It would be too simple to imply that a sentiment like this was merely a carry-over from paganism, and that everybody should have experienced the élan of the martyrs. The dread of death and sorrow over the deceased are, after all, universal human experiences. But Christianity made it a part of its program, so to speak, to approach death in a new way.

In the first place the Fathers emphasized that, with Christ's own death and resurrection, the reasons for the fear and horror of death had been eliminated. "In times past, before our Savior had dwelt with us as God," Athanasius writes in the fourth century,

> even the saints were frightened of death; everyone lamented those who had died as being simply destroyed. After our Savior's bodily resurrection, however, death is no longer a reason to fear; those who believe in Christ tread upon death as if it were nothing, preferring to die rather than to deny

belief in Christ. For they are convinced that death does not mean destruction but life; through the resurrection they become indestructible. . . . A clear proof of this is that, prior to believing in Christ, people look upon death as an object of fear, as something that makes cowards of them. Once they have been converted to the faith and teaching of Christ, by contrast, they consider death to be such a small thing that they rush upon it with enthusiasm and make themselves witnesses of the resurrection that the Savior has accomplished against death.[8]

It was not only Christ's resurrection that showed to Christians that death had been conquered once and for all, however. The early Church stressed with almost equal weight his descent into hell, into the very dominion of death itself, just before his resurrection. Here the devil, portrayed as the prince of death, is despoiled of his victims and rendered helpless before the victorious Lord. The apocryphal *Acts of Pilate*, which date from about the fourth century, give a dramatic account of what is supposed to have happened in this encounter. As the hero Christ approaches, Hades is cast into fear. A voice like thunder is heard proclaiming: "Lift up your gates, O rulers, and be lifted up, O overlasting doors, and the King of glory shall come in," and Hades sends out Satan to do battle with Christ, while the demons lock the gates of brass and the bars of iron. But when Hades asks, as if he did not know: "Who is this King of glory?" angels respond: "The Lord strong and mighty, the Lord mighty in battle." "And immediately at this answer," the *Acts* continue, "the gates of brass were broken in pieces and the bars of iron were crushed and all the dead who were bound were loosed from their chains, and we with them. And the King of glory entered in like a man, and all the dark places of Hades were illumined."[9] This is quite different from anything pagan. In the myths of pagan antiquity, releasing someone from the underworld was occasionally ventured, but it never succeeded, or only for a short time at best.

In addition to seeking to alleviate the fear of death by proclaiming the redeeming work of Christ, some of the Fathers also attempted to give death its proper place in the natural scheme of things, to demonstrate its reasonableness in a somewhat more philosophical manner. In one of his sermons Peter Chrysologus develops this notion. He explains that the entire creation has to be dissolved and then be restored so that the human person, when he sees this, may realize that creation is a work of God and not itself divine. In the same way, a human being must die in order to understand himself and his relationship to God:

> O man, when your Creator fashioned you from the dust you did not see it, for if you had seen yourself being fashioned you would never have wept over the fact that you are going to die. You have seen yourself whole and entire, a living being, beautifully formed; you have seen yourself as the likeness of your Creator. But, having seen yourself neither be born nor die, how do you know where you are from or who you are? It is for this reason that you have attributed everything to nature and your own being to yourself, but nothing to God. Consequently God has brought you back by way of nature and has permitted you to be recalled from nothing into dust, so that you might see what you were and give thanks as one who shall be raised from the dead.[10]

One might say that in this perspective death appears as a decisive moment in the education of the human person.

The Transformation of Pagan Customs

A primary concern of the Fathers on a very practical level was to transform pagan mourning customs into something more Christian. In this they did not achieve the success that they might have been looking for, although they did at least put an end to the excesses of paganism—the loud wailing, the self-lacerations, the pulling out of the hair. For they themselves, in their own funeral orations and elsewhere, betray how hard they found it to be reconciled to the loss of a loved one. Ambrose, for instance, gave two long sermons on the death of his much loved brother Satyrus, the first at the funeral itself and the second seven days later, as was customary. In the first he dwells at length and with affection upon his brother. "This sermon is undertaken," he says,

> for the sake of accompanying him, so to speak, that in spirit I might be with him a little longer on his journey, that I might embrace with my mind him whom my eyes behold. Let me fix the intensity of my gaze upon him, let me linger with him and show him all the offices of the heart, let me address him with every form of endearment. Meanwhile my mind is numbed, and I do not believe that he whom I am still able to see before me has departed. I cannot realize that he is dead and that I am still not in need of those services of his to which I had attributed my life and my breath.[11]

He finds himself, as he tells his listeners, wanting "to temper my grief rather than remove my feelings of affection, so that my longings might be assuaged instead of being lulled to sleep."[12] It is only in the second sermon that he takes a different tack, having realized that in the first he had had to indulge his grief: "I gave into my longing somewhat," he begins, "lest the application of more severe remedies to a burning wound, as it were, might aggravate rather than relieve the pain."[13] So he goes on to point out that death should not cause excessive mourning inasmuch as it is, after all, something that every person must undergo and that frees one from the calamities of this life, and inasmuch as the resurrection demonstrates that nothing really perishes through death.[14] Yet it is evident that, despite his efforts to inspirit himself, Ambrose is still in sorrow.

We can see in these two sermons, and in similar works, an interior struggle that is reflected in some brave words inscribed on a Christian tombstone found near Vienne in France: *Non placeat gemere quod celebrare decet*—"It is not right to mourn what should be celebrated."[15] We come across the same ambivalence of feeling in Augustine's *Confessions*, when he describes what took place at the death of his mother Monica. "We did not think it fitting to hold that funeral," he says, "to the accompaniment of tearful cries and groans, since the misery of the dead, so to speak, or their (as it were) complete extinction is frequently bewailed in these ways. But she did not die miserably, nor did she die completely."[16] Yet Augustine continually finds it necessary to suppress his grief, which wells up spontaneously within him, and after he has described how, in the end, he did give way to weeping, he writes:

> Now, Lord, I confess to you in writing. Let him read it who wants to, and let him interpret it as he wants. And if he finds a sin in the fact that I wept for my mother for part of an hour, for the mother now dead to my eyes who for many years had wept for me so that I might live in your eyes, let him not mock me. But rather, if he is a person of great charity, let him weep himself for my sins to you, the Father of all the brothers of your Christ.[17]

But no matter how much the early Christians may have mourned their dead, and no matter how much they may have experienced some fear of death, nonetheless the basic attitude toward death was radically different from that of the pagans, and the pagans themselves did not fail to notice it. The difference was easiest to see, of course, in times of persecution, when scores of Christians went to their deaths with smiles on their faces. Justin Martyr remarks that the courage with which the Christians withstood torture and death made a great impression on him before he was converted to Christianity.[18] For many, a similar experience must have been a decisive motivation in conversion. Of course, not everyone died as a martyr. One may well believe that, for some time after the age of persecutions had passed, the Christians' funeral rites, with their sense of peace and hope, continued to be one of the most attractive aspects of the Church from the pagan point of view.

For those less susceptible of such attraction, however, skepticism was the response. In the *Octavius* of Minucius Felix, for example, a debate between a pagan and a Christian that was composed toward the end of the second century, the pagan Caecilius finds nothing at all admirable in the martyrs' contempt of death: "How amazingly stupid and incredibly insolent they are! They dismiss present torments while living in fear of uncertain future ones. And while they are afraid to die after death, in the meantime they have no fear of dying. Thus a false hope coaxes away their fear with the assurance of a rebirth."[19] Elsewhere, too, he berates the Christians for their belief that they would be born again into some new life at death, and he mocks the resurrection of the body as an impossibility. Finally he attacks again what he considers to be Christian credulousness: "All these figments of a morbid imagination, all the absurd consolations, all the ridiculous images used by deceiving versifiers to give charm to their poetry—all these have been dishonorably refashioned by you, gullible as you are, and applied to your God."[20] Octavius, who is defending the Christians, responds with arguments typical of the apologists. He shows how many of the pagan philosophers themselves seem to have hinted at the Christian teaching of a rebirth into new life; and for the resurrection of the body, always the hardest of all doctrines for a pagan to accept, he explains that it is easier for God to raise bodies from the dead than to create them in the first place. Besides that, he says,

> notice how all of nature rehearses our future resurrection and so brings us comfort. The sun sinks and is reborn, the stars disappear and return, flowers die and come to life again, shrubs burst into leaf after their decay, seeds do not sprout unless they have rotted. The body in this world resembles the trees in winter, which conceal their verdure beneath a deceptive barrenness. Why be impatient for it [the body] to come to life and return when it is still bitter winter? We too must await the springtime of the body.[21]

Arguments such as these for the resurrection of the body, as well as more philosophical and theological ones, were repeated and refined throughout Christian antiquity.

The pagans of the Mediterranean world generally had great respect for the bodies of the dead, and usually even gave the bodies of executed criminals over to their families for burial. But, knowing that for the Christians the resurrection of the body was one of the central tenets of their faith, they were sometimes perversely provoked to test this faith. The account of the martyrs of Lyons and Vienne, written in the late 170's, tells us that the bodies of the martyrs were thrown to the dogs or left unburied to be derided, while among the Christians themselves there was great grief "because we were unable to bury the bodies in the earth. The night did not make this possible for us, nor did money persuade or entreaty shame, but in every way they [the soldiers] kept guard, as though they were doing something important by preventing burial."[22] Finally the soldiers burned the bodies and threw the ashes into the Rhone River, "and this they did," the account continues,

> as if they could defeat God and rob them of their rebirth, in order, as they said, "that they might have no hope of resurrection, on account of which belief they have introduced a strange new cult into our country and are unafraid of tortures, going willingly and with joy to their death. Now let's see if they'll rise again and if their God can help them and take them out of our hands."[23]

The Christians were upset by these desecrations, but their faith remained unshaken. As Tatian had written at about this same time in explaining the resurrection to a pagan audience: "Even though fire should destroy my flesh . . . even though I should be dispersed through rivers and seas or torn in pieces by wild beasts, I am gathered up in the treasuries of a wealthy Lord. . . . And when he pleases, God, who is king, will restore the substance that is visible to him alone to its original condition."[24]

In what might such a restoration consist? The state of the resurrected body exercised the early Church's theologians throughout the patristic period. Origen was accused of having suggested that the bodies of the blessed would be spherical, undoubtedly because this was a perfect shape.[25] It seems that he held, in any event, that nothing resembling the earthly body would survive in heaven, and perhaps even that the body would eventually pass completely into non-existence.[26] Augustine, on the other hand, believed that the human body, even though spiritually transformed, would be fully recognizable as such, yet all its blemishes and imperfections would be done away with. Only the wounds of the martyrs might remain, because there is a deep and mysterious desire on the part of the faithful to see these tokens of their love for Christ; and "this will not be something unsightly in them, but honorable."[27]

The resurrection of the body and life with the Lord, along with attendant matters, provoked many questions, some of which are no longer being asked, while others still hold interest for us. What happened to souls before they were reunited with their bodies, for instance? Some felt that, until the general resurrection, only the martyrs were to see God.[28] Was the universe to be destroyed by fire at the last judgment? This was occasionally spoken of by the earlier Fathers—and with a cruel glee when Tertullian describes in lurid detail the burning up of the Church's enemies in the great conflagration, and the opportunity that Christians would have of enjoying the spectacle;[29] for the later Fathers, however, it ceased to be so important.

And how did purification take place after death? Gregory of Nyssa has some interesting words on this in his *Great Catechism.* He explains that the dissolution of the body into its original components upon death is necessary because wickedness has been mingled with it in the course of our lifetime; consequently it must be refashioned by the resurrection into its pristine beauty without any admixture of sin. It is as if a clay vessel that had held some poisonous substance were ground up and remolded, leaving no trace of the poison behind. Somewhat the same process is undergone by the soul, but it is extremely painful because a strong natural tendency to evil is inbred in it, and in the separation of this evil from the soul the latter experiences a profound laceration: "When the soul is tortured and melts away under the correction of its sins, as prophecy somewhere tells us, certain unspeakable and inexpressible pangs follow of necessity from its deep and intimate connection with evil." Yet this purification, no matter how painful, is the witness of God's abiding love.[30] Otherwise the purifying of the souls of the dead was assisted by the prayers, fasting and deeds of mercy performed by those who were still alive. "One may not doubt that the dead are aided by the prayers of holy Church, the saving sacrifice and the alms that are distributed on behalf of their spirits," Augustine says in a sermon. "On account of these, God acts more mercifully than their sins deserve." But such things are of value only to those who have deserved to be helped by them, not to those whose sins have merited them eternal punishment.[31]

Purification and the Afterlife

The most original and controversial idea of purification, however, was the famous one of Origen known as the *apokatastasis*, namely, the restoration of all rational beings by degrees to their original state, which was one of perfect spiritual union with God. According to this view, no punishment, not even that of the demons, was to be everlasting, but all would be restored to their primordial state. But this process was one that might take ages, lasting over the course of several successive worlds, as souls gradually ascended to a more sinless condition, all the while taking different forms upon themselves. Thus in one age a demon might become a human being, and in the next an angel; but by the same token a human being might become a demon in a succeeding age, depending on what he had done in his human condition.[32] Everything hung upon the docility of those who were being purified, for Origen was anxious to preserve the free will of rational creatures. Consequently the whole human family, he writes, will become subject to God not by force "but by word, by reason, by teaching, by the exhortation to better things, by the best methods of education, and by merited and appropriate warnings that are justly used to threaten those who disdain the care and well-being of their salvation and welfare."[33] Even the saints who had died were to be placed in "a kind of lecture room or school for souls, in which they may be taught about all those things that they had seen on earth, and may also receive an indication of the things that are to come." Eventually they would pass, according to the swiftness of their progress, into heaven itself.[34]

At the heart of this vast plan was Origen's own attempt to understand how, in the end, all things would be subject to Christ. "We are of the opinion," he writes,

> that the goodness of God through Christ will bring his entire creation to one end, with even his enemies conquered and subdued. For this is what Holy Scripture says: The Lord said to my Lord, Sit on my right, until I make your enemies your footstool. . . . Let us learn from Paul the apostle, who says

more openly that Christ must reign, until he puts all his enemies under his feet.[35]

No idea of Origen provoked more angry opposition than that of the *apokatastasis*. The thought that the devil himself would ultimately be saved was perhaps its most repugnant aspect as far as the rest of the early Church was concerned.[36] Also intolerable was the suggestion that those who had attained blessedness after a lifetime of struggle might in a subsequent age fall into another state and thereby be deprived of that blessedness.[37]

Origen's theory, of course, did away with the notion of an everlasting hell, a notion that Augustine in particular was anxious to preserve. The twenty-first book of his *City of God* is devoted exclusively to demonstrating the everlasting nature of hell by showing that it is neither unreasonable nor unjust. According to Augustine, hell was a place of real fire, whereas Origen indicates that the fire there was only metaphorical.[38] Consequently Augustine was obliged to prove that bodies could burn forever. This in turn led him to draw his readers' attention to numerous other phenomena that seemed to be at odds with what was known of nature.[39] Augustine's emphasis on the everlastingness of hell is of a piece with his pessimism about the afterlife, for he is certain that the number of the damned outweighs that of the saved. After speaking in the twenty-first book of *The City of God* about the original sin, which merited an eternal punishment for the whole human race, he goes on to say:

The human race is divided up in such a way that what a merciful grace can accomplish might be demonstrated in some, while in others it is a question of the justice of retribution. For both are not shown forth in all since, if everyone were to remain under the punishment of a just condemnation, merciful grace would appear in no one; on the other hand, if all were transferred from darkness to light, the harshness of retribution would appear in no one. On this account there are many more in the former than in the latter, so that there might be made manifest what was due to all. For if all had been punished, no one could justly blame the justice of the punisher; but inasmuch as so many are freed from that, there

is reason for giving very great thanks for the gratuitous gift
of the redeemer.[40]

Another question attendant upon the theme of death and
resurrection was that which asked whether, after a first resurrection following the last judgment, the saints were to enjoy a thousand year period of rest with Christ upon earth, in a paradise-
like state, before being transported, body and soul, into heaven.
This was an idea that had considerable support among the earliest Christians, who found it alluded to in Revelation 20:1–6.
The concept appears for the first time in patristic literature in the
mysterious Papias, who wrote toward the beginning of the second century and of whose writing only fragments remain. He
paints an extravagant picture of what it will be like in this period
of rest.

> Days are coming when vineyards will spring up, each one
> having ten thousand vines, and each vine ten thousand
> branches, and each branch ten thousand shoots, and each
> shoot ten thousand clusters, and each cluster ten thousand
> grapes, and each grape, when pressed, will give twenty-five
> measures of wine. And when any of the saints seizes one of
> these clusters another cluster will cry out: I am better; take
> me and bless the Lord with me. Similarly a grain of wheat
> will grow ten thousand ears, and each ear will yield ten thou-
> sand grains, and each grain will give ten pounds of the finest
> flour. And the other fruit trees, too, and seeds and herbs, will
> produce in appropriate proportions. And all the animals,
> feeding on these foods of the earth, will become peaceful and
> friendly to each other and be subject to human beings in all
> mildness.[41]

Even Augustine, nearly three centuries later, made use of this
concept, known as millenarianism or chiliasm (from the Latin
and Greek words for "thousand"), although in a much refined
version. For him it was part of an attempt to understand the
movement of history, divided into six ages corresponding to the
six days of creation. The present age was the sixth, and the seventh, the sabbath, being an age of rest, led into the eighth age,

that of heaven itself. The seventh or sab-batical age was to be the reign of God upon earth; but it was to be an entirely spiritual event, when "the great number of saints will appear, resplendent in dignity, outstanding in their merits, and bearing witness to the mercy of the Redeemer." After that, however, "we shall go," Augustine writes, "into that life and into that rest of which it is written: For eye has not seen nor ear heard, nor has it entered into the human heart, what God has prepared for those who love him."[42] But Augustine later modified this idea in *The City of God.* There he eliminated the notion of the sabbath, the seventh age, as a period of time; in its place "we ourselves shall be the sabbath, when we shall be filled and replenished with God's blessing and sanctification. There we shall be at peace and know that he is God." And this state will open up—imperceptibly, like a flower coming into blossom—upon the eighth day, the day of the Lord. "There we shall rest and see, see and love, love and praise."[43] In these noble thoughts there is nothing even vaguely reminiscent of the extravagant materialism of Papias and others.

A final question concerned the content of the heavenly existence, which has in fact already been hinted at. It was common to suggest, in this regard, that heaven was somehow a reattainment of the paradise that had been lost in the original fall.

> Behold, now there lies open to the faithful
> the luminous path to spacious paradise,
> and man is permitted to enter that garden
> which the serpent had snatched from him.[44]

Whatever good things characterized the place of earthly bliss might be expected to characterize heaven as well, and even to a higher degree.[45] It was, as well, a new Jerusalem, the true homeland of the blessed, whose citizens participated in the perpetual festival of divine contemplation.[46]

One might also speak of heaven in negative terms. Here on earth, Augustine says at the end of one of his sermons, as he urges his listeners to perform the works of mercy, we are obliged to feed the hungry, give drink to the thirsty, clothe the naked, take in the wayfarer, visit the sick. But there [in heaven] there shall be no hunger, there no thirst, no nakedness, no sickness, no wayfaring, no labor, no sorrow. I know that these things will not be there, but what will be there I do not know. For I have experienced those things that will not be there; but what we shall find there, neither eye has seen, nor ear heard, nor has it entered into the human heart. We are able to love, we are able to desire, we are able, in this pilgrimage, to sigh for so great a good; but we are unable to think of it in worthy fashion or to put it into words. In any case, I am unable. Therefore, my brethren, let him who can, seek it out. If you are able to discover it, take me along with you as your disciple.

He ends his sermon by saying: "There we shall find what today we have sung: Amen, it is true. Alleluia, praise the Lord!"[47] In another sermon Augustine resorts to a more positive description: There "our entire activity shall be Amen and Alleluia. . . . For what is Amen, what is Alleluia? Amen means: it is true. Alleluia means: praise the Lord!" For there we who here have seen only "as in a mirror, darkly," shall gaze upon Truth itself and say Amen, but with insatiable satiety. And "burning with love of the Truth and held by it in a sweet and chaste embrace that is also incorporeal, we shall praise it with a loud voice and cry out: Alleluia. For all the citizens of that city, exhorting one another to a like praise, and on fire with love for each other and for God, shall cry out: Alleluia, because they shall say: Amen."[48]

All of this of course represents a highly rhetorical way of speaking about the nature of heaven, which ignores some of the difficulties involved. It was universally accepted that the central act of heaven was communion with God, but how this act might occur was not easy to elucidate. Other Fathers tend simply to say that the dead shall see God, but it is Augustine who probes the issue at some length, especially in his 147th letter, the so-called *Book on Seeing God*. He takes it as scriptural and indisputable that the dead see God.[49] Yet at the same time the Scriptures affirm, in the words of 1 John 4:12 and 1 Timothy 6:16, that no one has ever seen God nor ever can see him. In this context, Augustine distinguishes between the eyes of the body, which cannot see a pure spirit, and the eyes of the spirit or the heart, which are capable of this.[50]

It was also justifiable to say that, given human finitude and the divine infinity, the vision of God was liable to be experienced in a continually expanding fashion. "Really seeing God means that desire is never satisfied," writes Gregory of Nyssa. "But it is always necessary that, to the extent possible, one burn with the desire to see still more. Thus no limit cuts off growth in the ascent to God, since there may be found no limit to the good, nor is the increase of desire for the good terminated by satisfaction."[51]

The other great act of heaven was the communion of love that the redeemed would enjoy among themselves in the presence of God. For this we turn again to Augustine and the conclusion of his *Handbook on Faith, Hope and Love*. Love, he writes, is characteristic of both the earthly and the heavenly life.

> Now [we love] God by faith, then [in heaven] by sight, and now [we love] our neighbor himself by faith. For as mortals we do not know the hearts of mortals, but then God will bring to light things hidden in darkness, and he will disclose the purposes of the heart, and everyone will receive his praise from God. For that which is brought to light by God, lest it be hidden, will be praised and loved by one's neighbor in his neighbor. And passion is diminished while love increases, until this latter becomes so great that it cannot be greater, for greater love has no one, than that one lay down his life for his friends. But who can understand how great the love is there, where there will be no passion for it to overcome by the exercise of restraint? For supreme well-being will exist when the struggle with death is no more.[52]

Finally, this mutual enjoyment of God and of one's neighbor did not cut off the blessed, as by a kind of excess of bliss, from the Church on earth. For all were in fact one Church, and all were particularly linked together in the course of prayer when, as Origen says, not only the living and the dead but also the angels were assembled.[53] The custom of praying to the blessed and seeking their help, moreover, attests to the belief that they had some continuing relationship with the living. What is perhaps the most ancient of all prayers to Mary, dating from as early as the third century, is an excellent example of this.

To you we flee for shelter and compassion, mother of God.
You alone are chaste and blessed; do not disregard our
prayers in this hour of need, but deliver us from danger.[54]

With heaven and the vision of Christ and God by the community of the blessed, these pages come to an end. Here is the
terminus of that central thrust of patristic writing that we have
referred to as a concern with and a desire for salvation. Because
true life reached its consummation here, it is easy to see why
Augustine, certainly the greatest of the Fathers, could, in an
immortal phrase, speak at the beginning of his *Confessions* of life
on earth as a driving restlessness. Whether restless with purpose
or restless without purpose, this life was not yet what it was to
be, and no thing of beauty, no human loveliness enjoyed by the
earthly eye could do more than rouse nostalgia for what was to
be. This nostalgia colors the Fathers' view of every aspect of
human life: it is why they continually look for higher or deeper
meanings in things, and it is the reason for an often surprising
disengagement from the pressing affairs of the world. They must
be read as persons who had an eye on one thing, and that one
thing we may call salvation, or Christ, or God, or eternal life.
Impatient as they are for that one thing, and so frequently self-
assured about it, we read them occasionally with frustration, but
more often with astonishment that they have so firmly laid hold
of what seems so elusive to us.

A Patristic Reading Program

The following is a short list of important and representative works by the Fathers, along with indications of where they can be found and a very brief description of each. This list is determined by, among other things, the works' availability in English translation; that has meant the unfortunate omission of one or two things that have never been translated into English. Likewise, not every English edition is mentioned, as that would lengthen the bibliography unnecessarily. The order is chronological, rather than thematic or according to theological tradition. If the reader has a little time to spend with one of these every day, and can look over the introduction and notes that appear in most translations (particularly ACW and LCC), he or she will experience the Fathers in a way that is otherwise simply impossible.

Where a work appears in a series, only the volume number of the series is given. For the abbreviations used, see pp. 238f.

The first five works belong to the corpus of the Apostolic Fathers (as do several other works)—so called because it was felt that they actually knew the apostles personally or were extremely close in time to the apostolic tradition. For a recent commented translation of all the Apostolic Fathers cf. Robert M. Grant, ed., *The Apostolic Fathers: A Translation and Commentary*, in six volumes (New York/Camden 1964–1968).

Didache, or *The Teaching of the Twelve Apostles*. This short anonymous work, whose publication for the first time in 1883 created a sensation, is possibly the earliest of all non-scriptural

Christian writings. It contains a kind of moral catechism, a brief outline of some liturgical practices (baptism and maybe the Eucharist as well, although the latter is not certain) and a tantalizingly elusive description of a hierarchical structure that may date to the middle of the first century. Trans. in: ACW 6; FC 1; LCC 1; LCL, Apostolic Fathers 1.

First Epistle of Clement. This exhortatory letter was written about the year 96 by a certain Clement, whose precise function we do not know but who represented the Church at Rome, to the Church at Corinth, whose members were divided by a schism. It demonstrates the concern of one community for another and gives a glimpse into the thinking of the Roman Church at an early date. Trans. in: ACW 1; ANF 1; FC 1; LCC 1; LCL, Apostolic Fathers 1.

Ignatius, *Epistles.* These seven letters, written toward the beginning of the second decade of the second century by the bishop of Antioch on his way to martyrdom in Rome, are jewels of Christian literature. Short and intense, they are marked by a profound desire on Ignatius' part to die for Christ (note especially the letter to the Romans) and by his consuming zeal for unity in the Church. Trans. in: ACW 1; ANF 1; FC 1; LCC 1; LCL, Apostolic Fathers 1.

Epistle to Diognetus. Written by an unknown author, possibly in the third decade of the second century, this may well have been addressed to the Emperor Hadrian under the pseudonym of Diognetus. It is probably the earliest work that we possess in defense of Christianity. Chapters 5 and 6, on the Church's relation to the world about it, are particularly famous. Trans. in: ACW 6; ANF 1; FC 1; LCC 1; LCL, Apostolic Fathers 2.

The Martyrdom of Polycarp. This first-hand and somewhat elaborated report of the death of the bishop of Smyrna, written shortly after he died about the year 156, is a description both of the ideal pastor and of the martyr who is so closely conformed to Christ as to imitate his death at almost every point. It is in many respects the archetypal martyrdom narrative. Trans. in ACW 6; ANF 1; FC 1; LCC 1; LCL, Apostolic Fathers 2; Herbert Musurillo, ed. and trans., *The Acts of the Christian Martyrs* (Oxford 1972).

The Odes of Solomon. These forty-two baptismal hymns are of an extremely exalted and mystical character. They were composed sometime in the second century, probably in Syria or Palestine, and it has been argued since their discovery in 1905 that they are tinged with Jewish and gnostic elements. Scholars tend now to emphasize their uniquely Christian aspects. Trans. in: J. H. Bernard, ed., and Rendel Harris, trans., *The Odes of Solomon* = *Texts and Studies* 8.3 (Cambridge, Eng. 1912).

Justin Martyr, *First Apology.* This famous apology presents the position of the Church vis-à-vis paganism and Judaism in the middle of the second century and exposes Justin's idea of a kind of "anonymous Christianity." Its final chapters contain an important description of baptism and the Eucharist. Trans. in: ANF 1; FC 6; LCC 1; LF.

Melito of Sardis, *On the Pasch.* Probably delivered between the years 160 and 170, this Easter homily is rich in typology and compelling in style, despite its anti-Jewish character. Trans. in: A. Hamman, ed., and Thomas Halton, trans., *The Paschal Liturgy: Ancient Liturgies and Patristic Texts* (Staten Island 1969); Stuart George Hall, ed. and trans., *Melito of Sardis: On Pascha, and Fragments* (Oxford 1979).

Irenaeus, *Proof of the Apostolic Preaching.* Irenaeus' work *Against Heresies* is more significant than this and available in more translations, but this is shorter and less complicated, and many of the author's most important ideas appear here in abbreviated form. It was written toward the end of the second century and is a compendium of what the early Church preached. Trans. in: ACW 16.

Tertullian, *Apology.* Perhaps the most important of Tertullian's works, this very comprehensive defense of Christian thought and practice includes, in chapter 39, a beautiful if idealized description of the early Christian community. Trans. in: ANF 3; FC 10; LCL; LF.

Tertullian, *On Baptism.* This is the only treatise on a sacrament to have come down to us from the Church's first three centuries. The first half of it is taken up with a theology of baptism and the second half with particular questions. Trans. in: ANF 3; LF.

Hippolytus, *The Apostolic Tradition*. This short treatise provides an extensive picture of early Christian life, especially from the liturgical point of view. It was written about the year 215 in Rome and purports to record a tradition going back even earlier. Trans. in: Gregory Dix, ed. and trans., *The Treatise on the Apostolic Tradition of St. Hippolytus of Rome, Bishop and Martyr*, reissued by Henry Chadwick (London 1968).

Didascalia Apostolorum. This anonymous work, composed in Syria sometime during the first half of the third century, is similar to *The Apostolic Tradition* of Hippolytus in giving extensive information about an early Christian community, but it is considerably more detailed. Trans. in: R. Hugh Connolly, ed. and trans., *Didascalia Apostolorum: The Syriac Version Translated and Accompanied by the Verona Latin Fragments* (Oxford 1929).

Origen, *On First Principles*. Although an early work of his, this displays Origen's sweeping genius more than any other of his writings. The first systematic theological treatise produced by a Christian, it has unfortunately come down to us in a Latin translation with "improvements" by Rufinus, and we cannot be certain how much of the real Origen has been preserved. Trans. in: G.W. Butterworth, ed. and trans., *Origen: On First Principles* (New York 1966).

Origen, *On Prayer*. Of the several tracts on prayer written by the Fathers, this is perhaps the greatest. In three main sections, the first is devoted to prayer in general, the second to an interpretation of the Lord's Prayer, and the third treats of certain particulars in praying. Trans. in: ACW 19; LCC 2; Rowan A. Greer, ed. and trans., *Origen: An Exhortation to Martyrdom ... Homily XXVII on Numbers* (New York 1979).

Origen, *Exhortation to Martyrdom*. For a description cf. pp. 133ff. of the present book. Trans. in: ACW 19; LCC 2; Greer, *op. cit.*

Origen, *Against Celsus*. This monumental defense of Christianity is particularly important because it is in the form of a response to the highly cultivated pagan author Celsus, whose provocative objections to Christianity, many of them still relevant, are included by Origen and answered one by one—which occasionally also contributes to tedium. Trans. in: ANF 4; Henry

Chadwick, ed. and trans., *Origen: Contra Celsum* (Cambridge, Eng. 1953; reprinted 1980).

Origen, *Commentary* and *Homilies on the Song of Songs*. Here the Origen who exercised the deepest influence on the subsequent development of Christian mysticism is at his best. Of the *Commentary* Jerome wrote: "While Origen surpassed all writers in his other books, in his *Song of Songs* he surpassed himself." Trans. in: ACW 26.

Cyprian, *Epistles*. These eighty-one letters, including a number for which Cyprian is the recipient, were written between the years 250 and 258. They are significant for the light that they shed on the Church both in time of persecution and in time of grave internal stress, as they give details of a dispute between Rome and Carthage on the subject of the rebaptism of heretics. Trans in: ACW 43–44 (incomplete); ANF 5; FC 51; LF.

Cyprian, *On the Unity of the Catholic Church*. This work has been until only recently the subject of some controversy by reason of two different redactions of chapters 4 and 5, each apparently from the pen of Cyprian himself and each having a slightly varying view of the role of Peter and the bishops. Written in the year 251, and provoked by a schism in either Rome or Carthage, it is primarily a defense of unity in the Church, as the title indicates. Trans. in: ACW 25; ANF 5; FC 36; LCC 5; LF.

Eusebius of Caesarea, *Ecclesiastical History*. This is the great indispensible source for the history of the Church from the time of Christ until the end of the period of persecutions at the beginning of the fourth century. Eusebius not only records many things that cannot be found elsewhere, but he is also rather accurate. Trans. in: FC 19 and 29; LCL (2 vols.); NPNF, 2nd Ser., 1; G.A. Williamson, trans., *Eusebius: The History of the Church* (New York 1965).

Athanasius, *On the Incarnation of the Word of God*. Athanasius seems to have written this in the 320's, and until the early Middle Ages it was the first extensive attempt to explain why the Word of God took on human form. In the context of its Christology it contains a brilliant description of the creation and fall and a polemic against paganism and Judaism. Trans. in: LCC 3; NPNF, 2nd Ser., 4; A Religious of C.S.M.V. S.Th., trans., *The Incarnation of the Word of God* (New York 1946).

Athanasius, *The Life of Saint Anthony*. For a description cf. chapter 8 of the present book. Trans. in: ACW 10; FC 15; NPNF, 2nd Ser., 4; Robert C. Gregg, ed. and trans., *Athanasius: The Life of Antony and the Letter to Marcellinus* (New York 1980).

Cyril of Jerusalem, *Catechetical Lectures*. These twenty-four lectures or homilies, nineteen delivered before Easter to those about to be baptized and the final five (known as the Mystagogical Catecheses) delivered to the newly baptized during Easter week, are very valuable for their teachings on the Creed and the sacraments. They date from about the year 350. Of all such lectures that have come down to us, these are the most famous and perhaps the most beautiful. Trans. in: FC 61 and 64; LF; NPNF, 2nd Ser., 7.

Gregory Nazianzen, *Theological Orations*. These five homilies (numbering 27–31 in the list of Gregory's orations) merited for their author the title of "The Theologian." Given at Constantinople in the summer of 380, they represent the high point of Gregory's speculative genius and deal with the nature of theology, the existence and nature of God, the divinity of the Son and that of the Spirit. Trans. in: LCC 3; NPNF, 2nd Ser., 7.

Gregory of Nyssa, *The Great Catechetical Oration*. Although not so vast as Origen's *On First Principles*, this is the first subsequent attempt at a systematization of theology. It is brilliant and original. Trans. in: LCC 3; NPNF, 2nd Ser., 5.

Gregory of Nyssa, *The Life of Moses*. This is a moral-mystical work that uses the life of Moses, interpreted both literally and spiritually, as a model for Christian life in general. The overriding theme is that of continual progress in perfection. Trans. in: Abraham J. Malherbe and Everett Ferguson, ed. and trans., *Gregory of Nyssa: The Life of Moses* (New York 1978).

John Chrysostom, *On the Priesthood*. Although Chrysostom is best known for his preaching, this is his most famous single work. Probably written in the 380's, it is an elevated dissertation on the glories and duties of the priesthood (or episcopate). Chrysostom asserts that he wrote it to explain why he fled from the possibility of ordination. Trans. in: NPNF 9; Graham Neville, trans., *St. John Chrysostom: Six Books on the Priesthood* (Crestwood, N.Y. 1977).

Ambrose, *On the Duties of the Clergy*. Modeled on Cicero's *De officiis*, this treatise is one of Ambrose's most influential and manifests his ideals for the clergy, his Roman soberness and his sense of order. Trans. in: NPNF, 2nd Ser., 10.

Ambrose, *On Virgins*. This work is perhaps the best example of Ambrose's thought on virginity, of which he was a great proponent. Trans. in: NPNF, 2nd Ser., 10.

Sulpicius Severus, *The Life of Saint Martin*. Written at the end of the fourth century, this biography of a monk-bishop is full of miracles and supernatural events. It is perhaps the most important hagiography to have been produced in the West, and it made its hero, Martin, a saint to be reckoned with for centuries after. Trans. in: NPNF, 2nd Ser., 11.

Jerome, *Epistles*. Jerome's letters are the most important part of his writings, although of the many that he wrote and received only slightly more than 150 have survived. They include biblical exegesis, ascetical instruction, eulogies and social commentaries; and nothing else gives such an insight into this psychologically complex personality. Trans. in: ACW (epistles 1–22); LCL (selected epistles); NPNF, 2nd Ser., 6 (an extensive selection).

Jerome, *Against Jovinian*. In this treatise, written in the year 393, Jerome discourses on marriage and virginity, fasting and several other points in opposition to a certain Jovinian, whose opinions on these were at variance with Jerome's. This is interesting as a kind of ascetic manifesto in the Latin Church, and it provides some typical examples of the invective for which Jerome was renowned. Trans. in: NPNF, 2nd Ser., 6.

Augustine, *Confessions*. This greatest of all Christian autobiographies is the story of an interior journey to conversion, written in the form of a prolonged prayer addressed to the Father. The depth of Augustine's insight into himself and his power of expression gives the work its truly universal quality. The final three books are philosophical-theological reflections on time and eternity, matter and form and creation. Trans. in: FC 21; LCC 7; LCL; LF; NPNF 1; and in numerous other editions.

Augustine, *On Christian Doctrine*. Intended as a kind of manual for the preacher on the interpretation of Scripture, this treatise proposes to place all knowledge at the service of divine truth. The first book, which deals with Augustine's famous distinction between use and enjoyment, is especially important. Trans. in: FC 2; NPNF 2; D.W. Robinson, trans., *Saint Augustine: On Christian Doctrine* (Indianapolis 1958).

Augustine, *The City of God*. This vast theology of history was instigated by Alaric's sack of Rome in the year 410. Through twenty-two books Augustine follows the fortunes of the human and divine cities— the one inextricably tied up with the other, to be separated only at the end of time—and he culminates his work with a sublime vision of heaven. Trans. in: FC 8, 14 and 24; NPNF 2; Marcus Dods, trans., *St. Augustine: The City of God* (New York 1950); Henry Bettenson, trans., *Augustine: City of God* (Harmondsworth, Eng. 1972).

Vincent of Lerins, *Commonitory*. The aim of this short work, written sometime in the first half of the fifth century by a French monk, was to help the reader in distinguishing between orthodoxy and heterodoxy. Vincent asserts in a renowned formula that that which has been held "everywhere, always and by everyone" is the true faith, and he links this with the possibility of an organic development of doctrine. Originally in two books, unfortunately only one has survived. Trans. in: FC 7; LCC 9; NPNF, 2nd Ser., 11.

Benedict, *Rule*. This is the most famous and influential of Western monastic rules and is attributed to Benedict, although the details of its authorship remain mysterious. Trans. in: Timothy Fry, ed., *RB 1980: The Rule of St. Benedict in Latin and English with Notes* (Collegeville, Minn. 1981); and in numerous other editions.

Gregory the Great, *Pastoral Care*. This comprehensive guide for bishops, especially with regard to preaching, was written at the end of the sixth century and set the standard for the episcopacy and for all diocesan clergy into well beyond the Middle Ages. Trans. in: ACW 11; NPNF, 2nd Ser., 12.

Maximus the Confessor, *Four Centuries on Charity*. These four groups of one hundred apophthegms apiece, all on charity, are among the finest examples of the writings of a seventh-century Byzantine monk who has only recently been rediscovered and highly acclaimed for the profundity of his mystical teaching. Trans. in: ACW 21.

John Damascene, *On the Orthodox Faith.* This last great theological work from the last of the Fathers, written about the year
730, is actually the final section of a large three-part treatise entitled *The Fount of Knowledge.* It synthesizes virtually everything
that Greek Christianity had produced until that time. Trans. in:
FC 37; NPNF, 2nd Ser., 9.

Select Bibliography

Editions of the Fathers in the Original Languages (The abbreviations by which the editions are known follow each entry.)

Corpus Christianorum. Series Latina. Turnhout, 1953ff. CCSL

Corpus Scriptorum Christianorum Orientalium. Louvain, 1903ff. Texts in the original language accompanied by a modern language or Latin translation. CSCO

Corpus Scriptorum Ecclesiasticorum Latinorum. Vienna, 1866ff. CSEL

Die griechischen christlichen Schriftsteller der ersten drei Jahrhunderte. Leipzig, 1897ff. GCS

Loeb Classical Library. London/Cambridge, Mass., 1912ff. This series contains relatively few patristic texts, which are in the original language with an English translation on the facing page. LCL

Patrologia Graeca. Edited by J.-P. Migne. Paris, 1857ff. Texts in the original Greek with a Latin translation on the facing page. PG

Patrologia Latina. Edited by J.-P. Migne. Paris, 1841ff. Supplementary volumes: Paris, 1958ff. PL and PLS

Sources chrétiennes. Paris, 1942ff. Texts ordinarily in the original language with a French translation on the facing page. SC

English Translations of the Fathers, in Series (The abbreviations by which the series are known follow each entry.)

Ancient Christian Writers. Westminster, Md./New York, 1946ff. ACW

The Ante-Nicene Fathers. New York, 1926. ANF

The Fathers of the Church. Washington, 1947ff. FC

Library of Christian Classics. Philadelphia, 1953ff. Vols. 1–8, part of Vol. 9 and all of Vol. 12 deal with our period. LCC

Library of the Fathers of the Holy Catholic Church. Oxford, 1838ff. LF

A Select Library of Nicene and Post-Nicene Fathers of the Christian Church. Buffalo/New York, 1886ff. This contains works by Augustine and John Chrysostom exclusively. NPNF

A Select Library of Nicene and Post-Nicene Fathers of the Christian Church. Second Series. New York, 1890ff. NPNF, 2nd Ser.

English Translations in Selection

Bettenson, Henry, ed. and trans. *The Early Christian Fathers: A Selection from the Writings of the Fathers from St. Clement of Rome to St. Athanasius.* London, 1969.

Bettenson, Henry, ed., and trans. *The Later Christian Fathers: A Selection from the Writings of the Fathers from St. Cyril of Jerusalem to St. Leo the Great.* Oxford, 1972.

Fremantle, Anne, ed. *A Treasury of Early Christianity.* New York, 1953.

Musurillo, Herbert A., ed. and trans. *The Fathers of the Primitive Church.* New York, 1966.

Wiles, Maurice, and Santer, Mark, eds. *Documents in Early Christian Thought.* Cambridge, Eng., 1975.

Bibliographical Tools

Schneemelcher, Wilhelm, ed. *Bibliographia Patristica: Internationale Patristische Bibliographie.* Berlin/New York, 1959ff. An annual publication that attempts to give a complete patristic bibliography for each year, beginning with 1956.

Sieben, Hermann Josef. *Voces: Eine Bibliographie zu Wörten und Begriffen aus der Patristik (1918–1978).* Berlin/New York, 1980. A bibliography for the years indicated, arranged alphabetically under Greek and Latin words or phrases.

Bibliography Arranged according to Chapters (The following list, which is not exhaustive, does not include articles or books concentrating on a single Father. An asterisk denotes a collection of texts with commentary.)

I. Beginning To Read the Fathers (Included here are general works on the Fathers and the patristic period, which usually stress the doctrinal aspect, but not histories of the early Church.)

Altaner, Berthold. *Patrology.* Trans. by Hilda Graef. New York, 1960.
*Barr, Robert. *Main Currents in Early Christian Thought.* Glen Rock, N.J., 1966.
Brown, Peter. *The World of Late Antiquity, A.D. 150–750.* New York, 1971.
Campenhausen, Hans von. *The Fathers of the Greek Church.* Trans. by Stanley Godman. New York, 1959.
Campenhausen, Hans von. *Men Who Shaped the Western Church.* Trans. by Manfred Hoffmann. New York, 1964.
Cross, F. L. *The Early Christian Fathers.* London, 1960.
*Daley, Brian J. *The World of the Fathers = Message of the Fathers of the Church* 1. Wilmington, to appear.
Daniélou, Jean. *The Development of Christian Doctrine before the Council of Nicaea.* 3 vols. Trans. by John Austin Baker and David Smith. London/Chicago/Philadelphia, 1964–1977.
Goodspeed, Edgar. *A History of Early Christian Literature.* Revised and enlarged by Robert M. Grant. Chicago, 1966.
Hamell, Patrick J. *Handbook of Patrology.* Staten Island, 1968.
Harnack, Adolph. *History of Dogma.* 7 vols. bound as 4. Trans. by Neil Buchanan. Reprinted New York, 1961. Vols. 1–4 deal with our period.
*Jurgens, William A. *The Faith of the Early Fathers.* 3 vols. Collegeville, Minn., 1970–1979.
Kelly, J.N.D. *Early Christian Doctrines.* 5th rev. edition. London, 1977.

Pelikan, Jaroslav. *The Christian Tradition. A History of the Development of Doctrine. I: The Emergence of the Catholic Tradition (100–600)*. Chicago, 1971.

Quasten, Johannes. *Patrology*. 3 vols. Utrecht/Antwerp, 1950–1960; reprinted Westminster, Md., 1983.

Rand, Edward Kennard. *Founders of the Middle Ages*. Cambridge, Mass., 1928.

Rusch, William G. *The Later Latin Fathers*. London, 1977.

Wiles, Maurice. *The Christian Fathers*. New York, 1982.

II. Scripture

Lubac, Henri de. *Exégèse médiévale: Les quatre sens de l'Ecriture*. 4 vols. Aubier, 1959–1964. Vols. 1–2 deal with our period.

Margerie, Bertrand de. *Introduction à l'histoire de l'exégèse*. 3 vols. Paris, 1980–1983.

Smalley, Beryl. *The Study of the Bible in the Middle Ages*. 3rd rev. edition. Oxford, 1983. Pp. 1–36 deal with our period.

*Trigg, Joseph W. *Biblical Interpretation* = *Message of the Fathers of the Church* 9. Wilmington, to appear.

III. God

*Burns, J. Patout, and Fagin, Gerald M. *The Holy Spirit* = *Message of the Fathers of the Church* 3. Wilmington, 1984.

Norris, Richard A., Jr. *God and World in Early Christian Theology: A Study in Justin Martyr, Irenaeus, Tertullian, and Origen*. New York, 1965.

Prestige, G.L. *God in Patristic Thought*. London, 1936.

*Rusch, William G., ed. and trans. *The Trinitarian Controversy*. Philadelphia, 1980.

IV. The Human Condition

*Balas, David. *Grace and the Human Condition* = *Message of the Fathers of the Church* 15. Wilmington, to appear.

*Burns, J. Patout, ed. and trans. *Theological Anthropology*. Philadelphia, 1981.
*Cummings, John T. *Sin and Forgiveness* = *Message of the Fathers of the Church 12*. Wilmington, to appear.
Wallace-Hadrill, D.S. *The Greek Patristic View of Nature*. New York, 1968, pp. 40–79 are relevant.
*Walsh, P. G., and Walsh, James. *Divine Providence and Human Suffering* = *Message of the Fathers of the Church 17*. Wilmington, to appear.

V. Christ (Liturgy is listed separately under this heading.)

*Carmody, James M., and Clarke, Thomas E. *Word and Redeemer: Christology in the Fathers*. Glen Rock, N.J., 1966.
*Ettlinger, Gerald H. *Christ: Lord and Savior* = *Message of the Fathers of the Church 2*. Wilmington, to appear.
Grillmeier, Alois. *Christ in Christian Tradition. I: From the Apostolic Age to Chalcedon*. 2nd rev. edition. Trans. by John Bowden. Atlanta, 1975.
*Norris, Richard A., Jr., ed. and trans. *The Christological Controversy*. Philadelphia, 1980.
Prestige, G.L. *Fathers and Heretics: Six Studies in Dogmatic Faith with Prologue and Epilogue*. London, 1948.
Sellers, R.V. *Two Ancient Christologies: A Study in the Christological Thought of the Schools of Alexandria and Antioch in the Early History of Christian Doctrine*. London, 1940.
Smulders, P. *The Fathers on Christology: The Development of Christological Dogma from the Bible to the Great Councils*. Trans. by Lucien Roy. De Pere, Wisc., 1968.
Turner, H.E.W. *The Patristic Doctrine of Redemption: A Study of the Development of Doctrine during the First Five Centuries*. London, 1952.

Daniélou, Jean. *The Bible and the Liturgy*. Notre Dame, Ind., 1956.
*Deiss, Lucien, ed. *Early Sources of the Liturgy*. Trans. by Benet Weatherhead. Staten Island, 1967.
Dix, Gregory. *The Shape of the Liturgy*. London, 1945. Pp. 1–545 deal with our period.

*Halton, Thomas, and Carroll, Thomas K. *The Making of the Liturgical Year* = *Message of the Fathers of the Church* 21. Wilmington, to appear.
*Hamman, A., ed. *Baptism: Ancient Liturgies and Patristic Texts.* Trans. by Thomas Halton. Staten Island, 1967.
*Hamman, A., ed. *The Mass: Ancient Liturgies and Patristic Texts.* Trans. by Thomas Halton. Staten Island, 1967.
*Hamman, A., ed. *The Paschal Liturgy: Ancient Liturgies and Patristic Texts.* Trans. by Thomas Halton. Staten Island, 1969.
Jungmann, Josef A. *The Early Liturgy to the Time of Gregory the Great.* Trans. by Francis A. Brunner. Notre Dame, Ind. 1959.
Jungmann, Joseph A. *The Place of Christ in Liturgical Prayer.* 2nd rev. edition. Trans. by A. Peeler. Staten Island, 1965. Pp. 1–212 deal with our period.
Mitchell, Leonel L. *Baptismal Anointing.* London, 1966.
*O'Connell, Patrick. *Baptism and Confirmation* = *Message of the Fathers of the Church* 6. Wilmington, to appear.
Quasten, Johannes. *Music and Worship in Pagan and Christian Antiquity.* Trans. by Boniface Ramsey. Washington, 1983.
*Sheerin, Daniel J. *Eucharist* = *Message of the Fathers of the Church* 7. Wilmington, to appear.
*Whitaker, E.C. *Documents of the Baptismal Liturgy.* London, 1977.

VI. Church and Ministry

*Bastian, Ralph J. *Priesthood and Ministry.* Glen Rock, N.J., 1969.
Campenhausen, Hans von. *Ecclesiastical Authority and Spiritual Power in the Church of the First Three Centuries.* Trans. by J.A. Baker. Stanford, 1969.
*Eno, Robert B. *Teaching Authority in the Early Church* = *Message of the Fathers of the Church* 14. Wilmington, 1984.
*Halton, Thomas. *The Church* = *Message of the Fathers of the Church* 4. Wilmington, to appear.
*Lienhard, Joseph T. *Ministry* = *Message of the Fathers of the Church* 8. Wilmington, 1984.
Murray, Robert. *Symbols of Church and Kingdom: A Study in Early Syriac Tradition.* Cambridge, Eng., 1977.

Plumpe, Joseph C. *Mater Ecclesia: An Inquiry into the Concept of the Church as Mother in Early Christianity* = Studies in Christian Antiquity 5. Washington, 1943.

Rahner, Hugo. *Symbole der Kirche: Die Ekklesiologie der Väter.* Salzburg, 1964.

Streeter, Burnett Hillman. *The Primitive Church, Studied in Special Reference to the Origins of the Christian Ministry.* London, 1929.

VII. Martyrdom and Virginity

Baumeister, Theofried. *Die Anfänge der Theologie des Martyriums* = Münsterische Beiträge zur Theologie 45. Münster, 1980.

Camelot, Thomas. *Virgines Christi: La virginité aux premiers siècles de l'Eglise.* Paris, 1944.

*Clark, Elizabeth A. *Women in the Early Church* = Message of the Fathers of the Church 13. Wilmington, 1983.

Delehaye, Hippolyte. *Les origines du culte des martyrs.* 2nd edition. Brussels, 1933.

Frend, W.H.C. *Martyrdom and Persecution in the Early Church: A Study of a Conflict from the Maccabees to Donatus.* Garden City, N.Y., 1967.

Gryson, Roger. *Les origines du célibat ecclésiastique du premier au septième siècle.* Gembloux, 1970.

Kötting, Bernhard. *Der Zölibat in der alten Kirche.* Münster, 1970.

*Musurillo, Herbert, ed. and trans. *The Acts of the Christian Martyrs.* Oxford, 1972.

Rader, Rosemary. *Breaking Boundaries: Male/Female Friendship in Early Christian Communities.* New York, 1983.

VIII. Monasticism

Bousset, Wilhelm. *Apophthegmata: Studien zur Geschichte des ältesten Mönchtums.* Tübingen, 1923.

Chitty, Derwas J. *The Desert a City.* Oxford, 1966.

*Koch, Hal. *Quellen zur Geschichte der Askese und des Mönchtums in der alten Kirche.* Tübingen, 1931.

Malone, Edward E. *The Monk and the Martyr: The Monk as the Successor of the Martyr* = *Studies in Christian Antiquity* 12. Washington, 1950.

Rousseau, Philip. *Ascetics, Authority and the Church in the Age of Jerome and Cassian.* Oxford, 1978.

Vööbus, Arthur. *History of Asceticism in the Syrian Orient: A Contribution to the History of Culture in the Near East.* 2 vols. Louvain, 1958-1960.

*Waddell, Helen. *The Desert Fathers.* Ann Arbor, 1957.

IX. Prayer

Bradshaw, Paul F. *Daily Prayer in the Early Church.* London, 1981.

Brown, Peter. *The Cult of the Saints: Its Rise and Function in Latin Christianity.* Chicago, 1981.

*Cunningham, Agnes. *Prayer* = *Message of the Fathers of the Church* 16. Wilmington, to appear.

*Hamman, A., ed. *Early Christian Prayers.* Trans. by Walter Mitchell. Chicago/London, 1961.

Kötting, Bernhard. *Peregrinatio Religiosa: Wallfahrt und Pilgerwesen in Antike und alter Kirche* = *Forschungen zur Volkskunde* 33-35. Münster, 1950.

Louth, Andrew. *The Origins of the Christian Mystical Tradition: From Plato to Denys.* Oxford, 1981.

X. Poverty and Wealth

*Avila, Charles. *Ownership: Early Christian Teaching.* Maryknoll, N.Y./London, 1983.

*Hamman, A., ed. *Riches et pauvres dans l'Eglise ancienne.* Paris, 1962.

Hengel, Martin. *Property and Riches in the Early Church.* Trans. by John Bowden. London, 1973.

*Phan, Peter C. *Social Thought* = *Message of the Fathers of the Church* 20. Wilmington, 1984.

*Sierra Bravo, Restituto, ed. *Doctrina social y económica de los Padres de la Iglesia: Colleción general de documentos y textos.* Madrid, 1967.

XI. The Christian in the World

Bevan, Edwyn. *Holy Images: An Inquiry into Idolatry and Image-Worship in Ancient Paganism and in Christianity.* London, 1940.

Chadwick, Henry. *Early Christian Thought and the Classical Tradition: Studies in Justin, Clement and Origen.* New York, 1966.

Cochrane, Charles Norris. *Christianity and Classical Culture.* Oxford, 1949.

*Coleman-Norton, P.R. *Roman State and Christian Church: A Collection of Legal Documents to A.D. 535.* 3 vols. London, 1966.

*Cunningham, Agnes, ed. and trans. *The Early Church and the State.* Philadelphia, 1982.

Festugière, A.-J. *Les moines d'orient. I: Culture ou sainteté.* Paris, 1961.

Jaeger, Werner. *Early Christianity and Greek Paideia.* Oxford, 1961.

Laistner, M.L.W. *Christianity and Pagan Culture in the Later Roman Empire.* Ithaca, N.Y., 1967.

Mattingly, Harold. *Christianity in the Roman Empire.* New York, 1967.

Momigliano, Arnaldo, ed. *The Conflict between Paganism and Christianity in the Fourth Century.* Oxford, 1963.

Rahner, Hugo. *Greek Myths and Christian Mystery.* Trans. by Brian Battershaw. New York, 1963.

XII. Death and Resurrection

*Dewart, Joanne E. McWilliam. *Death and Resurrection* = *Message of the Fathers of the Church* 22. Wilmington, to appear.

Kirsch, J.P. *The Doctrine of the Communion of Saints in the Ancient Church: A Study in the History of Dogma.* Trans. by John R. McKee. Edinburgh/London, 1910.

Pelikan, Jaroslav. *The Shape of Death: Life, Death and Immortality in the Early Fathers.* Nashville, 1961.

Rush, Alfred C. *Death and Burial in Christian Antiquity* = *Studies in Christian Antiquity* 1. Washington, 1941.

A Patristic Chronology

Fathers and Patristic Writings	Religious Events	General History
The Didache, c. 70?		Titus captures Jerusalem after the revolt of Judea, 70. Eruption of Vesuvius and destruction of Pompeii, 79.
Clement of Rome, *First Letter,* c. 96.	Death of John, c. 100.	
Ignatius of Antioch, *Letters,* c. 112. *Letter of Barnabas, Letter to Diognetus,* c. 125? Hermas, *The Shepherd,* c. 120– c. 154.	Gnosticism flourishes in various forms throughout the second century and into the third.	Jewish revolt under Bar-Cochba, 132–135.
The Martyrdom of Polycarp, c. 157. Justin Martyr, d. c. 163–167.	Montanism flourishes from the middle of the second to the beginning of the third century.	
Tatian, Athenagoras, Melito, fl. c. 160–180. Origen, b. c. 185. Clement of Alexandria, fl. c. 190–202.	Sabellianism flourishes at the end of the second and beginning of the third centuries.	

Fathers and Patristic Writings	Religious Events	General History
Irenaeus, *Against Heresies*, c. 190.	Quartodeciman controversy over the dating of Easter, c. 190.	
Tertullian, fl. c. 197–220.		
Minucius Felix, *Octavius*, c. 200.		
Passion of Perpetua and *Felicity*, c. 215.		Persia begins to be an important power hostile to Rome in the second quarter of the third century.
Hippolytus, *Apostolic Tradition*, c. 215.		
Didascalia Apostolorum, before 250.		
Cyprian, bishop of Carthage 249–258.	Controversy over Christians who lapsed in the Decian persecution, at Carthage and Rome, 251.	1000th anniversary of the founding of Rome celebrated under Philip the Arab, 248.
Origen, d. c. 254.	Controversy between Carthage and Rome over the rebaptism of heretics, 254–257.	
	Manicheanism flourishes from the middle of the third century with varying success for several centuries.	

Fathers and Patristic Writings	Religious Events	General History
		Valerian defeated and captured by the Persians, 260.
	Council of Antioch condemns Paul of Samosata, 268.	
		Establishment of the tetrarchy, with Diocletian and Maximian as Augusti and Constantius and Galerius as Caesars, 293.
	Diocletian persecution, end of the third and beginning of the fourth century.	
Methodius of Olympus, fl. c. 300.		
Arnobius of Sicca, *Against the Pagans*, c. 305.		
Lactantius, fl. c. 300–c. 320.	Donatist schism begins in Carthage, 312, and flourishes in North Africa for a century. "Edict of Milan" grants universal toleration, 313. Constantine shows favor to	Constantine wins the Battle of the Milvian Bridge ("In this sign you shall conquer"), 312.

Fathers and Patristic Writings	Religious Events	General History
	Christianity in different ways over the course of his reign. Council of Arles addresses Donatism, 314. Egyptian monasticism takes its rise in the first half of the fourth century. Beginning of the Arian controversy, c. 318.	
Eusebius of Caesarea, *Ecclesiastical History*, c. 325.	Council of Nicea addresses Arianism and establishes the term *homoousios*, 325.	
Athanasius, bishop of Alexandria, 328–373.	Numerous councils struggle with the Arian problem over the course of about fifty years following Nicea.	Founding of Constantinople, 330. Constantine, d. 337.
Cyril of Jerusalem, fl. c. 350. Augustine, b. 354.		

Fathers and Patristic Writings	Religious Events	General History
Anthony of Egypt, d. 356.		
	Restoration of paganism under Julian the Apostate, 361–363.	
Ephrem, d. 373. Basil, bishop of Caesarea, 370–379.	Apollinarianism is briefly successful in the second half of the fourth century.	
Gregory Nazianzen, bishop of Constantinople, 379–381	Council of Constantinople affirms the divinity of the Spirit and largely curtails the influence of Arianism, 381.	Valens killed and Romans defeated by barbarians at Adrianople, 378.
Ambrose, bishop of Milan, c. 374–397.		
Augustine converted, 386.		
Gregory of Nyssa, d. c. 394.	Execution of Priscillian and others for heresy at Trier, 385.	
Martin of Tours, d. 397.		The Roman Empire definitively split into East and West with the death of Theodosius, 395.
Theodore, bishop of Mopsuestia, 392–428.	Paganism gradually suppressed by the emperors from the end of the fourth through much of the fifth century.	
John Chrysostom, bishop of Constantinople, 398–404, d. 407.		
Augustine, bishop of Hippo, 395–430.		

Fathers and Patristic Writings	Religious Events	General History
	Controversy over the theology and person of Origen in the East, end of the fourth century.	
	Council of Carthage successfully condemns Donatism, 411.	Alaric captures and sacks Rome, 410.
	Beginnings of Pelagianism, c. 411.	
Jerome, d. c. 420.		
Cyril, bishop of Alexandria, 412–444.	Nestorian controversy, 428–431.	Vandals invade Africa 429.
Paulinus of Nola, d. c. 431.	Council of Ephesus condemns Nestorius, 431.	
Cassian, d. c. 432.		
Leo, bishop of Rome, 440–461.	Rise of monophysitism, 440's.	
	Council of Chalcedon condemns monophysitism, 451	
	Monophysitism makes gains throughout the East for centuries following Chalcedon.	

Fathers and Patristic Writings	Religious Events	General History
		Odoacer deposes Romulus, the last emperor in the West, 476.
	Acacian Schism between Constantinople and Rome, 484–519.	
Caesarius, bishop of Arles, 503–542.		Justinian becomes emperor, 527. The Code of Justinian published, 534.
Benedict, d. c. 546.	Second Council of Constantinople condemns "Nestorian" writers and deals with Christological issues, 553. Mohammed, b. c. 570.	Justinian, d. 565.
Gregory the Great, bishop of Rome, 590–604.		Persians conquer Jerusalem and seize the cross, 614.
Isidore, bishop of Seville, c. 600–c. 636.	The Hegira, 622. Mohammed, d. 632. Monothelitism flourishes during much of the seventh century.	Heraclius defeats the Persians, 627–628, and restores the cross to Jerusalem, 630.

Fathers and Patristic Writings	Religious Events	General History
		Islamic armies conquer much of the Middle East and North Africa soon after Mohammed's death.
Maximus, the Confessor, d. 662.	Third Council of Constantinople condemns monothelitism, 681.	
		Islamic armies conquer Spain, 714.
Bede, d. 735. John Damascene, d. c. 750.	Rise of iconoclasm during the reign of Leo III, 717–741.	Charles Martel repulses the Islamic advance near Poitiers, 732.

Notes

I. Beginning To Read the Fathers

1.Cf. *Ep.* 22.7.
2.Cf. *De princ.* 1.6.1.
3.*Ep.* 54.1–2.
4.Cf. *Hist. eccl.* 5.22.
5.Cf. *De deitate Filii* (PG 46.557).
6.Cf. esp. *De doct. christ.* 4.11.26–13.29.
7.*Ep. ad Leandrum* 2. On the question of "longwindedness" cf. H.–I. Marrou, *Saint Augustin et la fin de la culture antique* (Paris 1938) pp. 74–76.
8.Cf. *De unitate cath. eccl.* 5–8.
9.*Eph.* 9.1.
10.Cf. *De Sp. Sancto* 27.66.
11.Cf. *Commonitorium* 23.54–59.
12.*Ep.* 28.1.
13."The benefit that the theologian can derive from them [the Fathers] far surpasses anything that he can get from any other text or argument: from them one gains an education in the *sensus catholicus,* much as one learns his native language from intimacy with the greatest writers of its history." Yves Congar, "Tradition in Theology," in *The Great Ideas Today, 1974* (Chicago 1974) p. 18.
14.On this possibility cf., e.g., D. Tracy, *Blessed Rage for Order* (New York 1978) pp. 6–10; *idem, The Analogical Imagination* (New York 1981) pp. 398–399, n. 7.
15.*Or.* 27.3.
16.Cf. *ibid.* 7.

II. Scripture

1. A classic example of such a position is Edward Hatch, *The Influence of Greek Ideas on Christianity* (New York 1957), first published in 1890.
2. Cf. 1 *Apol.* 59–60.
3. Cf. *De doct. christ.* 2.28.43.
4. Cf. *Retract.* 2.4.2; *De civ. Dei* 8.11.
5. *Apol.* 19.2–4.
6. *In Esaiam,* prol.
7. Cf. *Comm. in Cant. Cant.,* prol. 3 (GCS Orig. 8.75–79).
8. *De doct. christ.* 2.42.63.
9. Cf. *In Diatessaron* 1.19.
10. *De princ.* 1, praef. 8.
11. *Tract. de Ps.* 95.2.
12. Cf. *Adv. nationes* 5.33.
13. Cf. *ibid.* 5. 41.
14. Cf. H.A. Wolfson, *The Philosophy of the Church Fathers. I. Faith, Trinity, Incarnation,* 3rd ed., rev. (Cambridge, Mass. 1970) pp. 24–29.
15. Cf. Irenaeus, *Adv. haer.* 1.25.1.
16. Cf. Augustine, *C. Faustum, passim.*
17. *Conf.* 6.4.6.
18. Cf. H.–I. Marrou, *Saint Augustin et la fin de la culture antique* (Paris 1938) pp. 484–494.
19. *C. Celsum* 3.45.
20. Cf. *De doct. christ.* 2.6.7–8.
21. Cf. *In Ioann. Evang.* 122.8.
22. Cf. *De princ.* 4.3.1.
23. Cf. *De civ. Dei* 13.21.
24. Cf. *Tract. de Exodo, in vigilia Paschae.*
25. Cf. *De princ.* 4.2.4
26. Cf. *Exp. Evang. sec. Luc.,* prol. 2.
27. Cf. *De util. cred.* 3.5.
28. *Conlat.* 14.8.
29. Cf. *Serm.* 89.6.
30. *De Gen. ad litt.* 11.1.2.
31. Cf. *De princ.* 4.3.5.
32. Cf. J.N.D. Kelly, *Early Christian Doctrines,* 2nd ed. (New York 1971) p. 76.
33. *In Psalmos,* praef., ed. L. Mariès, in *Recherches de Science Religieuse* 9 (1919) 88.
34. *Serm.* Caillau-Saint-Yves 2.19.5 (PL Suppl. 2.438).

35.*Quis dives* 5.

36.Cf. *ibid.* 11ff.

37.Cf. *De divitiis* 10.2 (PL Suppl. 1.1394).

38.Cf. *ibid.* 18.2–6 (*ibid.*1408–1410).

39.*Ibid.* 18.10 (*ibid.* 1411). Even the great allegorizer Origen is aware of the problem mentioned here. Commenting on Luke 2:34 ("Behold, this child is set for the fall and the rising of many in Israel"), he complains against those who spiritualize away the severity of the verse: "And is it right, when something like this appears in the Gospel, to resort to allegories and new understandings . . . ?" *In Luc.* 16.6.

40.*In Genesim* 16.1–2 (SC 244.204).

41.*In Esaiam* II.3.7.

42.Cf. *De princ.* 4.2–3.

43.Cf. *De doct. christ.* 3.15.23.

44.Cf. *Conlat.* 8.3.

45.*In Ioann.* 13.26.

46.*De cat. rud.* 3.6.

47.*Origen*, trans. by W. Mitchell (New York 1955) p. 161.

48.Cf. *De civ. Dei* 17.15.

49.*De statuis* 1.1.

50.*Tract. in Marc.* 1.13–31.

51.Cf. *Comm. in Cant. Cant.* 3.16 (GCS Orig. 8.235–241).

52.*De incarn. Verbi* 57.

III. God

1.*Adv. Marcionem* 1.2.2–3.

2.Cf. the critique in V. White, *God and the Unconscious* (London 1952).

3.*Adv. Prax.* 1.1.

4.1 *Apol.* 13.

5.*Cat. mag.* 3.

6.Cf. Theophilus, *Ad Autol.* 2.10.

7.On this cf. V. Corwin, *St. Ignatius and Christianity in Antioch* (New Haven 1960) pp. 123–124.

8.*Magn.* 8.2.

9.*Eph.*15.1–2; 19.1.

10.Cf. *Excerpta ex Theodoto* 29: "Silence, the mother of all things that have been produced from the abyss."

11.Cf. Irenaeus, *Adv. haer.* 1.11.4; 1.21.3.

12.1 *Apol.* 61.

13.2 *Apol.* 6.
14.Cf. *Or.* 27.2.
15.Cf. *Or.* 28.9.
16.Cf. *Or.* 28.11–12.
17.Cf. *Or.* 28.22–31.
18.*Adv. haer.* 2.28.6.
19.*Exp. Symboli* 4.
20.*Serm.* 53.11.12.
21.Cf. *Or.* 28.17.
22.*Cat.* 16.24.
23.*C. gentes* 46.
24.*De incarn. Verbi* 11.
25.Cf. Origen, *De orat.* 22.4.
26.1 *Apol.* 46.
27.*Adv. haer.* 4.6.6.
28.*Ibid.*
29.*Protrep.* 1.
30.*C. gentes* 42.
31.Cf. *De princ.* 1.3.5.
32.*De Sp. Sancto* 9.23.
33.*Trad. apost.* 21.
34.*Adv. haer.* 3.24.1.
35.*Or.* 31.26.
36.Cf. Basil, *De Sp. Sancto* 10.24–26; Gregory Nazianzen, *Or.* 31.4 and 28.
37.*Quod tres dii non sint* (PG 45.133 B-C).
38.Cf. Ambrose, *De Sp. Sancto* 1.11.20; Augustine, *De Trin.* 15.17.29.
39.For the contemporary ramifications of this issue (known as the *Filioque* controversy from the Latin word indicating that the Spirit proceeds from the Father *and the Son*) cf. L. Vischer, ed., *Spirit of God, Spirit of Christ: Ecumenical Reflections on the Filioque Controversy* (London and Geneva 1981).
40.*De princ.* 1.3.7.
41.*Cat.* 16.24.
42.Cf. Gregory Nazianzen, *Or.* 29.10–15.
43.Cf. *De Trin.* 5.2.3.
44.*Ibid*, 5.8.9.
45.Cf. *ibid.* 5.5.6.
46.Cf. *De pud.* 2; *De spect.* 30.
47.Cf. *De lapsis* 21–26.
48.Cf. *Op. imperf. c. Iul.* 1.48.

49.*Serm.* 6.
50.Cf. Origen, *De orat.* 23.3.
51.*C. advers. legis et proph.* 1.20.40–41.

IV. The Human Condition

1.*Demonstratio* 14, trans. by J.P. Smith in ACW 16.56.
2.*Adv. haer.* 4.38.3.
3.Cf. *Demonstratio* 12; 16.
4.*Protrep.* 11.
5.*C. gentes* 2.
6.*In Rom.* 5.18–19.
7.*C. gentes* 3.
8.Cf. *De incarn. Verbi* 4.
9.Cf. *C. gentes* 8.
10.*Hom.* 10 (SC 44.366).
11.Cf. *Selecta in Gen.*, on Gen. 3.21.
12.Cf. Ambrose, *De paradiso* 13.63 and 65.
13.Cf. *De civ. Dei* 13.21.
14.*De nupt. et concup.* 1.6.7.
15.Cf. *De civ. Dei* 14.24.
16.Cf. *ibid.* 13.13.
17.*De hom. opif.* 2.
18.*In Psalm. inscrip.* 2.6.
19.Cf. *Peri Pascha* 48.
20.*Symposium* 3.7.
21.Cf. *De civ. Dei* 14.13.
22.Cf. *De orat.* 29.18.
23.Cf. *Hymnes sur le paradis* 3.4 (SC 137.54–55).
24.*De exces. frat.* 2.6.
25.*Serm.* 177.2.
26.*In Num.* 27.4.
27.Augustine, *Serm.* 60.2.2.
28.*Idem, De civ. Dei* 13.10.
29.*Idem, Serm.* 80.2.
30.*Idem, Serm.* Denis 13.8.
31.Cf. *Strom.* 7.12.74.
32.*Ibid.* 7.12.80.
33.Cf. *ibid.* 7.12.72.
34.*In Cant. Cant.* 6.
35.Cf. *V. Moysis* 1.10; 2.239.
36.Athanasius, *V. Antonii* 20.

37.*De peccat. meritis* 2.6.7.

38.*Ibid.* 2.26.17.

39.Cf. *De princ.* 3.2.1–2.

40.Cf. *Pastor, mand.* 6.2.1–10.

41.Cf. *De princ.* 3.2.4.

42.*V. Antonii* 21.

43.Ambrose, *De Nabuthae* 1.2.

44.*Peri Pascha* 51.

45.Cf. *De civ. Dei* 22.24.

46.Cf., e.g., *Conf.* 4.8.13–9.14.

47.Cf., e.g., 1 *Clem.* 20; Gregory of Nyssa, *De orat. dom.* 1 (PG 44.1124–1125).

48.Cf. *Reg. fus. tract.* 2. W.J. Burghardt, *The Image of God in Man according to Cyril of Alexandria* = *Studies in Christian Antiquity* 14 (Washington 1957) has been particularly useful for much of what follows.

49.*De princ.* 3.6.1.

50.Burghardt, p. 4.

51.Cf. *Div. hereseon liber* 137.2ff.

52.Cf. *De dogm. solutione* 3.

53.Cf. *Or. ad Graecos* 15.

54.Cf. Augustine, *De div. quaest.* 51.3.

55.*Hexaem.* 6.8.44.

56.1 *Apol.* 46.

57.*De incarn. Verbi* 3.

58.Athanasius, *Serm. maior de fide.*

59.*De virg.* 12.

60.Cf Cassian, *Conlat.* 13, *passim.*

61.*Frag. in Gen.*, on Gen. 1.26.

62.*De statuis* 7.2.

63.Cf. p. 152.

64.*De Trin.* 14.7.10 and 8.11.

65.For the problem and for examples of each position cf. Burghardt, pp. 154–156.

66.Cf. *De officiis* 1.49.250 and 254.

67.*Or.* 7.23.

V. Christ

1.*De resurr. carnis* 6.

2.Cf. *Adv. haer.* 5.16.1–3.

3.Cf. *De incarn. Verbi* 6–7.

4.*Ibid.* 8.

5.Cf. *Trall.* 10.

6.*Ep. ad episc. Diocaes.* 2 (H. Lietzmann, *Apollinarius von Laodicea und seine Schule* [Tübingen 1904/Hildesheim 1970] p. 256).

7.Theodoret of Cyrrhus, *Eranistes, dial.* 2 (PG 83.153).

8.Cf. *De carne Christi* 4.

9.With regard to Arianism in particular cf. the thesis advanced in R.C. Gregg and D.E. Groh, *Early Arianism—A View of Salvation* (Philadelphia 1981).

10.*Ep.* 101.

11.Cf. *Smyrn.* 4.2.

12.*De incarn. Verbi* 7.

13.Cf., e.g., *Adv. Nest.* 4.4.

14.*Adv. haer.* 3.16.6.

15.*Ibid.* 3.22.4.

16.*Ibid.* 2.22.4.

17.*Tract. in Marc.* 11.1–10.

18.*In Matth.* 9.7.

19.Cf. *Eph.* 18.2.

20.*Cat. mag.* 27.

21.*Ibid.* 32.

22.Cf. *De incarn. Verbi* 21–25.

23.Ps.-Hippolytus, *Hom. pasch.* 51 (SC 27.177–179).

24.*Mart. Andr.* 19.

25.1 *Apol.* 55.

26.Cf. *Serm.* 37.1–3 (CCSL 23.145–146).

27.Cf. *Cat. myst.* 2.5–6.

28.*Serm.* Pap.-Ker. 2.7, trans. by P.W. Harkins in ACW 31.150.

29.*Ibid.* 11 (*ibid.* 152).

30.*Cat. myst.* 4.3.

31.*C. Fabianum* 28.18–19.

32.*Demonstratio* 34, trans. by J.P. Smith in ACW 16.69–70.

33.Ps.-Hippolytus, *Hom. pasch.* 55 (SC 27.183).

34.*Serm.* 53.3 (CCSL 23.215).

35.Cf. Ps.-Epiphanius, *Hom.* 2 (PG 43.461–463).

36.*Hymn* 38.13 (SC 128.302).

37.Cf. *Ep. Barn.* 9, 11–12.

38.*Ep.* 38.3.

39.Cf. *De doct. christ.* 1.14.13.

40.*Serm.* 27.6.6.

41.*De inst. virg.* 5.34.

42.*De fide* 5.4.54.

43.Cf. *Or.* 29.19–20.

44.*Div. hereseon lib.* 32.7–8.

45.Cf. *Or.* 38.

46.*Serm.* 186.1.

47.André Tuilier, who established the critical text that appears in SC 149, argues against considerable opposition in favor of attributing it to Gregory rather than to a much later Byzantine dramatist.

48.Cf. *Adv. haer.* 5.19.1.

49.*Homily on the Nativity* 161–166, trans. by S. Brock, in *The Harp of the Spirit* (*Studies Supplementary to Sobornost* 4 [1975]) p. 68.

50.Cf. *Eph.* 19.1.

51.Cf. *V. Moysis* 2.21.

52.CF. Ambrose, *De virginibus* 2.2.6–15.

53.*Ep. ad Diog.* 9.6.

54.*Dial. c. Tryph.* 100.

55.Cf. *In Ioann.* 1.2.125ff.

56.Cf. *Or.* 30.20–21.

57.*Carm.* 6 (PL 13.378).

58.Cf. *Exhort. ad mart.* 46.

59.Cf. *Or.* 2.98.

60.*De myst.* 2.7.

61.Augustine, *De doct. christ.* 1.14.13.

62.*Eph.* 20.2.

63.Cf. Clement of Alexandria, *Paed.* 1.9.83.

64.Cf. *De incarn. Verbi* 15.

65.*Enarr. in Ps.* 126.3.

66.Cf., e.g., *C. Celsum* 6.77.

67.*The Place of Christ in Liturgical Prayer*, 2nd ed., rev., trans. by A. Peeler (New York 1965) pp. 127ff. On the point at issue cf. also J. Quasten, "The Liturgical Mysticism of Theodore of Mopsuestia," in *Theological Studies* 15 (1954) 431–439.

68.*In Luc.* 15.2.

69.Cf. Ambrose, *De virginibus* 1.9.44–51.

70.*Carm.* 16.282.

71.Cf. *Ep.* 125.20.

VI. Church and Ministry

1.*Ep. ad Diog.* 6.1–7.

2.Cf. *ibid.* 7–9.

3.*Apol.* 16.

4.2 *Apol.* 7.

5.*Pastor,* vis. 2.4.1.

6.2 *Clem.* 14.1–2.

7.*Comm. in Cant. Cant.* 2.8 (GCS Orig. 8.157).

8.1 *Apol.* 23.

9.Cf. *ibid.* 44; 59–60.

10.*De bono mortis* 11.51.

11.Cf. *De mysteriis* 8.44–46.

12.*De unitate cath. eccl.* 5.

13.*Ibid.* 6.

14.*C. Faustum* 12.16.

15.*De unitate cath. eccl.* 6.

16.Cf. *ibid.* 5–9.

17.Cf. pp. 9–10

18.Cf. Rufinus, *Exp. Symboli* 2.

19.*De unitate cath. eccl.* 14.

20.*Apol.* 39.

21.Cf. *De unitate cath. eccl.* 18.

22.*In Ep. Ioann.* 1.8.

23.*De unitate cath. eccl.* 23.

24.*Magn.* 7.1–2.

25.*Philad.* 7.2.

26.1 *Cor.* 46.7.

27.*Enarr. in Ps.* 61.4.

28.*Serm.* 272.

29.Cf. *Serm.* 57.7.

30.*Ep.* 69.5.

31.Cf. *In Ioann.* 26.17.

32.*Ibid.* 26.18.

33.*De bapt.* 3.10.15.

34.*De unitate cath. eccl.* 5.

35.*Serm.* Stav. 4.1, trans. by P.W. Harkins in ACW 31.66.

36.Cf. *Trad. apost.* 21.

37.Cf. *Gynecology* 2.11[31].18[87].

38.*Ep.* 243.4.

39.*Ibid.* 8.

40.*Serm.* 49.3 (CCSL 23.193–194).

41.Cf. *C. Faustum* 12.15.

42.Cf. *ibid.*

43.*Dial. adv. Lucif.* 22.

44.Cf., e.g., Chrysostom, *Serm.* Stav. 3/PK 4.16, in ACW 31.61.

45.Cf. *Serm.* 91.7.

46.*De virginibus* 1.6.31.

47.Cf. *Didache* 11–13.

48.*Didasc. apost.* 2.25.7.

49.*Smyrn.* 8.1–2.

50.*Didasc. apost.* 2.25.7.

51.*Serm.* 230.5.

52.*Serm.* Frangipani 2.4.

53.*De sacerd.* 4–5.

54.Cf., e.g., *In Ezech.* 1.9.29.

55.Cf. *Reg. past.* 1.7.

56.*Serm.* 17.2.

57.*Serm.* 147.

58.Cf. *In Exod.* 13.3.

59.Cf. *Tract. in Ps.* 147 (CCSL 78.338).

60.Cf. *Serm.* 78.2.

61.*Trad. apost.* 3.

62.*Didasc. apost.* 2.20.11.

63.Cf. *De sacerd.* 3.16–17.

64.*Serm.* 78.3, 6.

65.Cf. pp. 109–110.

66.Cyprian, *De unitate cath. eccl.* 5.

67.Augustine, *Serm.* Guelph. 32.3.

68.*In Ep. ad Titum* 1.5.

69.*Magn.* 6.1.

70.*Didasc. apost.* 2.28.4.

71.Cf. *Trad. apost.* 7.

72.*Phil.* 6.1.

73.*Trad apost.* 8.

74.*Didasc. apost.* 2.44.4.

75.Cf. 1 *Apol.* 67.

76.Cf. *De septem ord. eccl.* (ed. A.W. Kalff, diss. Würzburg 1935, p. 39).

77.*Magn.* 6.1.

78.Cf. *De eccl. hier.* 5.2.6.

79.Cf. B.H. Streeter, *The Primitive Church, Studied with Special Reference to the Origins of the Christian Ministry* (London 1929) pp. 249–250.

80.*Chron. palat.* 19 (PL 94.1170).

81.Cf. p. 78.

82.Cf. Paulinus, *V. Ambrosii* 3.6–9.

83.Cf. *Or.* 2, *passim*.

84.Cf. Possidius, *V. Augustini* 4.

85.Cf. Palladius, *Hist. Laus.* 11.
86.Ap. Jerome, *Ep.* 51.1.
87.*Ep.* 67.4.
88.Cf., e.g., Ambrose, *De officiis* 2.26.129ff.
89.Cf. *Res gestae* 27.3.12–15.
90.Cf. *Ep.* 22.28.

VII. Martyrdom and Virginity

1.*Didasc. apost.* 5.1.2.
2.*Trad. apost.* 9.
3.Cf. Tertullian, *De anima* 55.
4.*De morte Peregrini* 12–13, trans. by A.M. Harmon, in LCL Lucian 5.15–17.
5.*De unitate cath. eccl.* 14.
6.*Serm.* Morin 11.13.
7.*Adv. haer.* 4.33.9.
8.*Apol. 50.*
9.Cf. *De incarn. Verbi* 27.
10*Mart. Pol.* 2.1.
11*Ibid.* 4.
12.*Strom.* 4.10.
13.Canon 60.
14.Cf. *Ep.* 81.
15.*Passio SS. Scillitanorum* (Musurillo, *The Acts of the Christian Martyrs*, p. 88).
16.Cf. *Mart. Pol.* 7.1–3.
17.Cf. *ibid.* 12.1.
18.Eusebius, *Hist. eccl.* 5.1.35.
19.*Passio Perpet. et Felic.* 6.1.
20.Trans. by W. Mitchell, in A. Hamman, ed., *Early Christian Prayers* (Chicago 1960) pp. 184–185.
21.*Mart. Pol.* 2.2–3.
22.*Ibid.* 1.1.
23.*Ibid.* 14.
24.*Ibid.* 15.2.
25.Cf. *Didasc. apost.* 5.1.2.
26.Cf. Eusebius, *Hist. eccl.* 5.1.23.
27.*Ibid.* 5.1.56.
28.*Passio Perpet. et Felic.* 4.2.
29.Cf. *Peristeph.* 5.125–128.

30.Cf. *Cat.* 16.20.

31.Cf. *ibid.* 21.

32.*Rom.* 4.1.

33.V. Corwin, *St. Ignatius and Christianity in Antioch* (New Haven 1960) p. 23.

34.Cf. *Rom., passim.*

35.*Scorpiace* 8.2–4.

36.Cf. *De bapt.* 16.

37.*Exhort. mart.* 30.

38.*Ibid.* 50.

39.*Ep.* 14.2.

40.Cf. *Mart. Pol.* 14.

41.*Ad mart.* 2.

42.*Exhort. mart.* 12; 14.

43.Cf., e.g., E.E. Malone, *The Monk and the Martyr: The Monk as the Successor of the Martyr* = *Studies in Christian Antiquity* 12 (Washington 1950).

44.*De persecutione christianorum* (CCSL 78.556).

45.Cf. Athanasius, *V. Antonii* 46.

46.Cf. Eusebius, *Hist. eccl.* 6.2.5.

47.*Exhort. mart.* 42.

48.*Ibid.* 18.

49.Cf. *ibid.* 42.

50.Cf. *ibid.* 13.

51.Cf. *ibid.* 36.

52.*Ibid.* 28.

53.*Ep.* 2 (PL 20.179–180).

54.*V. Honorati* 38.4 (SC 235.174).

55.*The letter to blessed Cyril . . . by the brethren who came from Palestine,* trans. by L.R. Wickham, in Cyril of Alexandria, *Select Letters* (Oxford 1983) p. 133.

56.*Symposium* 7.3.

57.*De virginibus* 1.3.10.

58.*De. virg.* 46.47.

59.*De. virg.* 8.

60.Cf. *Strom.* 3.

61.Cf. *Ad uxorem* 2.9.

62.Cf. *Exhort. cast.* 9.

63.*Carm. in laudem virg.* 223–277 (PG 27.539–543).

64.Cf., e.g., 1 *Clem.* 38.2.

65.Cf. *C. Jovinianum* 1.47.

66.*De Gen. ad litt.* 9.5.9.

67.Cf. *C. Jovinianum* 1.13.
68.Cf. *De. virg.* 4.
69.*De virginibus* 1.6.24ff.
70.*Symposium* 8.1.
71.*De virg.* 1–2.
72.*Ibid.* 5.
73.Cf. *ibid.* 11.
74.*De virginibus* 1.3.11.
75.*Supplicatio* 33.
76.*De virg. vel.* 16.
77.Cf. *Symposium* 7.1ff.
78.*De virg.* 27.27.
79.*Symposium* 1.5.
80.*De virg.* 54.55.
81.Cf. *De virginibus* 1.6.31; cf. p. 108.
82.Cf. *De virg.* 20.
83.*De hab. virg.* 5.
84.*Ep.* 22.17.
85.Cf. *De inst. virg.* 17.104.
86.Cf. *Ep.* 22.18–19.
87.Cf. *De virg.* 12.
88.*Ibid.* 13.
89.*Ibid.*
90.*De hab. virg.* 22.
91.Cf. *De virg.* 6.27.
92.*De hab. virg.* 22.
93.*Exhort. virg.* 4.19.
94.*Serm.* 143.
95.*Mart. Pol.* 2.3; cf. pp. 128–129.
96.Cf. *De virginibus* 3.7.32ff, and for an opposing position cf.
Augustine, *De civ. Dei* 1.19.
97.*Carm. in laudem virg.* 365–367 (PG 37.549–550).
98.Cf. *De virg.* 7.
99.Cf. *ibid.* 20.
100.*De virg.* 51.52.
101.*Hist. Laus.* 47.
102.*Ibid.* 28.
103.Cf. *De virg.* 18.
104.Cf. *Symposium* 1.2–4.
105.*Apol. ad Constantium* 33.

VIII. Monasticism

1. Cf. *V. Antonii* 2–3.
2. Cf. *ibid.*, prol. and 94.
3. Cf. pp. 62–63.
4. *In Num.* 27.5.
5. Cf. p. 91.
6. *V. prima gr. Pachomii* 140.
7. *V. Antonii* 50.
8. Cf. p. 70.
9. Cf. *Hist. monach. in Aegypto* 9.5–11.
10. Cf. *ibid.* 21.15–16.
11. Cf. Sulpicius Severus, *Dial.* 1.13.
12. *Ep.* 14.10.
13. *Hom.* 5 (SC 44.132).
14. *Conlat.* 18.5.
15. *Ep.* 120.1.
16. Cf. *V. Antonii* 91.
17. Cf. *De coenob. inst.* 4.13.
18. Cf. Paulinus of Milan, *V. Ambrosii* 9.38.
19. Cf. Possidius, *V. Augustini* 5.
20. Cf. Paulinus of Nola, *Carm.* 21.488ff.
21. Cf. *V. Antonii* 47.
22. Cf. *ibid.* 4.
23. Cf. Palladius, *Hist. Laus.* 18.1–2.
24. Cf. *V. Antonii* 8–10; *Hist. monach. in Aegypto* 1.37–43.
25. Cf., e.g., *V. Antonii* 23; *Hist. monach. in Aegypto* 13.1–2.
26. Cf. Palladius, *Hist. Laus.* 25.4.
27. *V. Antonii* 16–43.
28. Cf. *Reg. brev. tract.* 75.
29. Cf., e.g., Augustine, *De civ. Dei* 9.5.
30. *V. Antonii* 14.
31. Cf. *ibid.* 67.
32. Cf. *ibid.* 93.
33. Cf. Palladius, *Hist. Laus.* 37.13–16.
34. Cf. *V. Antonii* 3.
35. Cf. Palladius, *Hist. Laus.* 11.4.
36. *V. Antonii* 73.
37. Cf. *ibid.* 74–80.
38. Cf., e.g., *V. prima gr. Pachomii* 82.

39.Cf. *Apophthegmata patrum,* De abbate Daniele 7–8 (PG 65.156–160).

40.*Ibid.,* De abbate Ammun 2 (*ibid.* 128).

41.Cf. p. 26.

42.On the concept of eternity and infinity in this context cf. H. Waddell, *The Desert Fathers* (Ann Arbor 1966; first publ. 1936) pp. 23–25.

43.Cf. *V. Antonii* 60; 65–66.

44.Cf. *ibid.* 48; 61–64; 70–71; 84.

45.Cf. *V. Martini* 7; 12; 13.

46.Cf. *V. Antonii* 59; 92–93.

47.Cf. *ibid.* 14.

48.Cf. *ibid.* 34.

49.Cf. *ibid.* 7.

50.Cf. *Dial.* 2.8.

51.*De vitis patrum* 5 *(Verba seniorum).*4.22 (PL 73.867).

52.*Apophthegmata patrum,* De abbate Hierace 2 (PG 65.232).

53.*Ibid.,* De abbate Ioseph in Panepho 6 (*ibid.* 229).

IX. Prayer

1.Cf. *Strom.* 7.7.35 and 40.

2.Cf. *ibid.* 7.7.35.

3.*Ibid.* 7.7.49.

4.Cf. *ibid.* 7.7.44.

5.*Trad. apost.* 41.

6.Cf. *De ieiunio* 10.

7.Cf. *De orat.* 25.

8.Cf. *De dom. orat.* 34.

9.*Ibid.* 35–36.

10.*De orat.* 12.2.

11.*Tract. de Ps.* 1 (CCSL 78. 5–6).

12.*Ad baptizandos* 1, trans. by A. Mingana, in *Woodbrooke Studies* 6 (1933) 3.

13.*Reg. fus. tract.* 37.

14.*Hist. Laus.* 20.1.

15.Cf. *ibid.* 20.3.

16.*De vitis patrum* 5 *(Verba seniorum).*12.9 (PL 73.942).

17.Hilary of Arles, *V. Honorati* 38.2 (SC 235.172–174).

18.*Enarr. in Ps.* 37.14.

19.*Serm.* 80.7.

20.Cf. *Ep.* 130.9.18.
21.Cf. *De orat.* 31.2.
22.*De. orat.* 17.
23.Cf. *ibid.* 14.
24.Cf. *ibid.* 17.
25.Cf. *ibid.* 23; idem, *De corona* 3.
26.Cf. Tertullian, *De orat.* 23.
27.Cf. Origen, *De orat.* 31.3.
28.*De orat.* 16.
29.Cf. *De orat.* 31.2.
30.Cf. *ibid.* 32.
31.Cf. *De Sp. Sancto* 27.66.
32.*De div. quaest. ad Simplic.* 2.4.
33.Cf. *De orat.* 24.
34.*De orat.* 31.4.
35.Cf. *ibid.*
36.Cf. *ibid.*
37.*Trad. apost.* 41.
38.*De orat.* 31.5.
39.Cf. *ibid.* 31.5–7.
40.Cf. *Itinerarium Egeriae* 4.
41.*Ep.* 46.12.
42.*Ep.* 2.
43.Cf., e.g., 2 *Clem.* 16.4.
44.Cf. Hippolytus, *Trad. apost.* 42.
45.Cf. *ibid.* 41.
46.Cf. *ibid.;* Tertullian, *De orat.* 13.
47.Cf. Justin, 1 *Apol.* 65–67; Hippolytus, *Trad. apost.* 4.
48.Cf. *Hom. in Cant. Cant.* 1.7.
49.Cf. *Conf.* 9.10.24.
50.*V. Moysis* 2.162–163.
51.*Reg. fus. tract.* 7.
52.*De vitis patrum* 5 (*Verba seniorum*).17.18 (PL 73.976).
53.*Serm.* 3.2.
54.Cf. *Sermones* 103–104.
55.Cf. pp. 113–114.

X. Poverty and Wealth

1.Cf. *C. Celsum* 3.44 and 55.
2.Cf. *Pastor, sim.* 1.

3.*Ibid., sim.* 2.5–9.

4.*Serm.* 39.4.6.

5.Augustine, *Serm.* 60.8.8.

6.*Ep.* 32.21.

7.*Exp. Evang. sec. Luc.* 8.13.

8.*Ibid.* 8.5.

9.*Quis dives* 13.

10.Cf. p. 35.

11.*Quis dives* 11.

12.*Cat.* 8.6–7.

13.Cf. C.J. Hefele, *A History of the Councils of the Church,* trans. and ed. by H.N. Oxenham (Edinburgh 1876) 2.327.

14.Cf. *Ep.* 157.23.

15.*Adv. haer.* 4.30.1.

16.*Ep.* 120.1.

17.*De contemptu mundi et saec. philos.* (PL 50.716).

18.*De. Nabuthae* 13.56.

19.*Serm.* 13.

20.Cf. *Serm.* 2.2 on Ps. 14.

21.Cf. *De Tobia* 8.29–30; 10.36–37.

22.*Apol.* 39.

23.Cf. *De lapsis* 6; 10–12.

24.*Serm.* 31.4.

25.Cf. *V. Malchi* 1.

26.*Serm.* 12.4 *in Ep. I ad Tim.*

27.*De Nabuthae* 1.2.

28.*Tract.* I.5.3.11.

29.*Enarr. in Ps.* 83.17.

30.*Serm.* 311.13.12–14.13.

31.Cf. *Enarr. in Ps.* 66.3.

31.Cf. *De interpel. Iob et David* 4.6.17.

33.*Enarr. in Ps.* 147.12.

34.*2 Clem.* 16.4.

35.*Serm.* 41.3.

36.*Serm* 22A.4 (CCSL 23.89).

37.*Serm.* 60.11.11.

38.Cf. *Comm. in Matth.* 10.42.

39.Cf., e.g., Ambrose, *Exameron* 6.8.52.

40.Cf. p. 149.

41.Cf. *Conlat.* 21.14.

XI. The Christian in the World

1.*Mart. Pol.* 9.2–3.

2.*Apol.* 35.

3.*Ibid.* 30.

4.This question is a highly controverted one. Cf. most recently, e.g., J.-M. Hornus, *It Is Not Lawful for Me To Fight: Early Christian Attitudes toward War, Violence and the State*, trans. by A. Kreider and O. Coburn (Scottsdale, Pa. 1980); L.J. Swift, *The Early Fathers on War and Military Service = Message of the Fathers of the Church* 19 (Wilmington 1983).

5.Cf. 1 Cor. 60:4—61:3.

6.Cf. pp. 25, 65–66.

7.Cf., e.g., Justin, 2 *Apol.* 5, where the demons are said themselves to have been begotten by fallen angels who, along with the demons, were taken for gods by the ancient poets and mythologists.

8.Cf., e.g., Minucius Felix, *Octavius* 20-21. This opinion is known as euhemerism, after Euhemerus, a fourth-century B.C. Greek mythographer.

9.*Quod idola dii non sint* 7.

10.Cf. *De civ. Dei* 10.19.

11.Cf. 1 *Apol.* 54–55; *Dial. c. Tryph.* 69–70.

12.Cf. 1 *Apol.* 62; 66.

13.Cf. p. 27.

14.*Adv. nationes* 5.32.

15.*Ibid.* 5.33.

16.Cf. *Apol.* 15.

17.*Ad Autol.* 1.10.

18.*Ibid.*

19.Ps.-Hippolytus, *Hom. pasch.* 12 (SC 27.139–141).

20.*Adv. nationes* 4.6.

21.*Ibid.* 4.7.

22.*Quod idola dii non sint* 8.

23.Cf. *Ad Autol.* 2.8.

24.*De spectac.* 8.

25.Cf. *De idolol.* 4–12.

26.Cf. *ibid.* 13.

27.Cf. *ibid.* 16; 18.

28.*De spectac.* 12.

29.*Enarr. in Ps.* 80.2.

30.Cf. *De idolol.* 17.

31.Cf. *De corona* 11.

32.Cf. *Ad uxorem* 2.4–6.

33.*De spectac.* 8.

34.Cf. 1 *Apol.* 6; 2 *Apol.* 8.

35.Cf. *Mart. Pol.* 3.2; 9.2.

36.*Protrep.* 2.23.

37.*Scorpiace* 5.

38.*De idolol.* 1.

39.*Ibid.*

40.Cf., e.g., Tertullian, *Apol.* 25.

41.*Ibid.* 40.

42.*Ibid.*

43.*Adv. paganos, praef.*

44.*Relatio* 10 (PL 16.969).

45.*Ad Scap.* 2.

46.The gods could also be baptized, so to speak, for there were elements of their cult that had a certain universal appeal and that could be incorporated into Christian usage. Thus Clement of Alexandria can write of Christ as a new Orpheus, harmonizing the universe (cf. *Protrep.* 1), and Maximus of Turin can compare Christ to Odysseus, whose being strapped to the mast of his ship prefigures Jesus on the cross (cf. *Serm.* 37.1–2 [CCSL 23.145]). Early Christian art in particular has a large role to give to the gods: they frequently appear either as types of Christ (as in Clement and Maximus) or as having become subject to him. As an instance of the latter cf. the sarcophagus of Junius Bassus, dating from the 350's, where, in the upper central panel of the front, Christ is shown seated above the god Caelus, who holds in his uplifted hands the arc of the heavens upon which the Lord is enthroned. On this subject of the use of pagan themes in early Christian art and literature cf. H. Rahner, *Greek Myths and Christian Mystery*, trans. by B. Battershaw (New York 1963).

47.Cf. *Conf.* 3.5.9.

48.*Conlat.* 14.12.

49.*Ep.* 22.30.

50.Cf., e.g., *De doct. christ.* 2.41.62; *Ep.* 55.39.

51.Cf. *Conf.* 10.35.55.

52.Cf. *Ep. ad Gregorium* 1–2 (PG 11.88–89).

53.Cf. 1 *Apol.* 44; 46.

54.Cf. *V. Moysis* 2.112–116.

55.Cf. *ibid.* 2.39–40.

56.*De praescrip. haeret.* 7.

57.Cf. p. 159.
58.On this issue cf. A.-J. Festugière, *Les moines d'orient* I: *Culture ou sainteté* (Paris 1961).
59.*Or.* 43.11.

XII. Death and Resurrection

1.J. Orellius, *Inscriptionum latinarum selectarum amplissima collectio* (Turici 1828–1956) 3.6234.
2.*Ibid.* 2.4815.
3.Cf. A. Rush, *Death and Burial in Christian Antiquity* = *Studies in Christian Antiquity* 1 (Washington 1941) pp. 8–9. Many of the inscriptions cited here appear in this work.
4.Orellius, 2.4793.
5.E. Diehl, *Inscriptiones latinae christianae veteres* (Berlin 1925–1931) 1.2218.
6.*Ibid.* 1.856.
7.Cited in *Dictionnaire d'archéologie chrétienne et de liturgie* 12.1.39.
8.*De incarn. Verbi* 27.
9.*Acta Pilati* 21, trans. in E. Hennecke and W. Schneemelcher, *New Testament Apocrypha* 1 (Philadelphia 1963) pp. 473–474.
10.*Serm.* 101.
11.*De excessu frat.* 1.14.
12.*Ibid.*
13.*Ibid.* 2.1.
14.Cf. *ibid.* 2.3.
15.Cited in *Dictionnaire d'archéologie chrétienne et de liturgie* 12.1.40.
16.*Conf.* 9.12.29.
17.*Ibid.* 9.12.33.
18.Cf. 2 *Apol.* 12.
19.*Octavius* 8.
20.*Ibid.* 11.
21.*Ibid.* 34.
22.Eusebius, *Hist. eccl.* 5.1.61.
23.*Ibid.* 5.1.63.
24.*Or. ad Graecos* 6.
25.Cf. Origen, *De orat.* 31.3; Justinian, *Ep. ad Mennam* (Mansi 9.516).
26.Cf., e.g., *De princ.* 2.3.3.

27.*De civ. Dei* 22.19.
28.Cf. Tertullian, *De anima* 55.
29.*De spect.* 30.
30.*Cat. mag.* 8.
31.*Serm.* 172.2.2.
32.Cf. Jerome, *Ep.* 124.10.
33.*De princ.* 3.5.8.
34.*Ibid.* 2.11.6.
35.*Ibid.* 1.6.1.
36.Cf., e.g., Theophilus, *Ep. pasch.* 8, ap. Jerome, *Ep.* 96.8.
37.Cf. Augustine, *De civ. Dei* 12.20.
38.Cf. *De princ.* 2.10.4–5.
39.Cf. *De civ. Dei* 21.4.
40.*Ibid.* 21.12.
41.Fragment 1.2–3, ap. Irenaeus, *Adv. haer.* 5.33.3.
42.*Serm.* 259.2.
43.*De civ. Dei* 22.30.
44.Prudentius, *Cathemerinon* 10 (*Circa exsequias defuncti*) 161–164.
45.Cf. pp. 56–60.
46.Cf. Gregory Nazianzen, *Or.* 8.6.
47.*Serm.* 236.3.
48.*Serm.* 362.28.29.
49.Cf. *Ep.* 147.12–16.
50.Cf. *ibid.* 52–54.
51.*V. Moysis* 2.239.
52.*Enchir.* 32.121.
53.Cf. *De orat.* 31.5.
54.From a papyrus in the John Rylands Library, Manchester (England), trans. by W. Mitchell, in A. Hamman, ed., *Early Christian Prayers* (Chicago 1960) p. 76.

Index of Personal Names and Anonymous Works of the Patristic Era